D0858052

THE ARBITRATION AND GRIEVANCE PROCESS

A Guide for Health Care Supervisors

Norman Metzger
Joseph M. Ferentino

Mt. Sinai Medical Center
New York, New York

AN ASPEN PUBLICATION®
Aspen Systems Corporation
Rockville, Maryland
London
1983

WX
159
M596a
1983

LIBRARY
CORNELL UNIVERSITY
MEDICAL COLLEGE
NEW YORK CITY

FEB 2 2 1983

Library of Congress Cataloging in Publication Data

Metzger, Norman, 1924- .
The arbitration and grievance process.

"An Aspen publication."
Includes index.
1. Health facilities—Personnel management.
2. Health facilities—Employees—Discipline.
3. Grievance arbitration. 4. Grievance procedures.
I. Ferentino, Joseph M. II. Title. [DNLM: 1. Employee
grievances. 2. Personnel management. 3. Personnel
administration, Hospital. WX159 M596a]
RA971.35.M457 1983 362.1′068′3 82-20654
ISBN: 0-89443-671-6

Publisher: John Marozsan
Editorial Director: Michael Brown
Managing Editor: Margot Raphael
Editorial Services: Jane Coyle
Printing and Manufacturing: Debbie Collins

Copyright © 1983 Aspen Systems Corporation

All rights reserved. This book, or parts thereof, may not be
reproduced in any form or by any means, electronic or
mechanical, including photocopy, recording, or any
information storage and retrieval system now known or
to be invented, without written permission from the
publisher, except in the case of brief quotations embodied
in critical articles or reviews. For information, address
Aspen Systems Corporation, 1600 Research Boulevard,
Rockville, Maryland 20850.

Library of Congress Catalog Card Number: 82-20654
ISBN: 0-89443-671-6

Printed in the United States of America

1 2 3 4 5

To our wives,
Marcia Metzger and Marge Ferentino

Table of Contents

Quotes

By and large, arbitration continues to work as a means of resolving genuine disputes between the parties who have decided to live together. Only the misuse of the peace-preserving machinery itself to do battle could destroy the effectiveness and unique utility of arbitration.

> Herbert L. Marx, Jr.
> "Arbitration from the Arbitrator's View,"
> *Handbook of Health Care*
> *Human Resources Management*, 1982, p. 832.

Only children and incomplete adults think that life is a continuous test of "strength"—and think one side must always prevail.

> Anthony Lewis
> Article, *The New York Times*.

Arbitrators are not bound by precedents. Their job is to give their best judgment as to the meaning of particular contract language. So the fact that one umpire decided a case in a particular way does not necessarily mean that another umpire would do so in a similar case.

> *Grievance Guide*, 6th ed., The Bureau
> of National Affairs, Inc., 1982, p. iii.

To assure order, there is a clear procedural line drawn: the company directs and the union grieves when it objects. . . . That challenge is made in the grievance procedure, not through rebellion.

> Arthur J. Goldberg as
> Steelworkers' Counsel.

Arbitrators are judges chosen by the parties to decide the matters submitted to them, finally and without appeal. As a mode of settling disputes it should receive every encouragement from the courts . . . a court will not set it aside for error either in law or fact.

> United States Supreme Court
> *Buchell v. Marsh*, 58 U.S. 540 (1855).

Foreword

The idea for this book came to us in August of 1981. We offered a proposal to the publisher to produce a book on labor arbitration in the health care industry. Sam Kagel, a prominent West Coast arbitrator, had written a book in 1961, *Anatomy of a Labor Arbitration,* in which he stated:

> Because arbitration is widely used as a terminal step in grievance procedures, literally thousands of labor and management representatives have had to learn about the process. For many of them arbitration was a new and confusing way to settle disputes. Undoubtedly, the best way to learn about a new technique is to become involved in it. But opportunities for such a slow (and perhaps costly) growth of skill and knowledge are not always available.[1]

We discussed Kagel's approach of presenting the case—an actual arbitration case—in our attempt to bring the invaluable experience of arbitration to many new practitioners in the field.

We then decided to offer many cases, each presented exactly as the award was issued—some sustaining management's position in a specific area, e.g., absenteeism, others upholding the grievant and the union. Following each case, we include an analysis with specific emphasis on the reasons why management's position was sustained in one instance or reversed in the other. Even where management's position was upheld, we suggest other approaches that would have improved the presentation. We endeavor to put readers into the arbitration room.

Over the years the authors have worked together in day-to-day labor relations, including active roles in third-step (last in-house step) hearings and actual arbitrations. This front-line experience has enabled us to present a very practical view of the process rather than simply an academic one. We endeavor to be pragmatic, not didactic. We have written this book with an abiding faith in the process; in its fairness—with all its shortcomings; with a recognition of its invaluable assistance in maintaining uninterrupted work flow; and in providing justice for all parties.

The authors owe special recognition and gratitude to two professionals who have lent their expertise to this book. Herbert L. Marx, Jr., is an outstanding arbitrator who has been involved in the hospital industry, among others, as a third-party neutral. His chapter (Chapter 5) on "Expecting the Unexpected in Arbitration" is one we are proud to include in our book. Allan H. Weitzman is an attorney specializing in labor law with the New York City firm of Proskauer Rose Goetz & Mendelsohn. He is an experienced negotiator and is among the outstanding legal counsel retained by the Mount Sinai Hospital, as well as many other clients. His chapter (Chapter 4) on "Preparing the Case for Arbitration: An Attorney's View" provides a rare insight that all readers will recognize as both professional and helpful.

Some of Chapter 1, "How To Discipline," appeared in *The Health Care Supervisor's Handbook,* second edition, by Norman Metzger, published in 1982 by Aspen Systems Corporation.

Norman Metzger
Joseph M. Ferentino
New York, July 4, 1982

NOTE

1. Samuel Kagel, *Anatomy of a Labor Arbitration* (Washington, D.C.: The Bureau of National Affairs, Inc., 1961), p. ix.

Part I

How the Process Operates

This first section of the book presents the basics of how the grievance and arbitration processes actually function. It discusses discipline, employee complaints, labor relations practice, preparing a case for arbitration (from the attorney's viewpoint), and warnings against the unexpected.

Chapter 1

How To Discipline

A number of years ago in a widely quoted case an arbitrator enunciated tests applicable for learning whether an employer had just and proper cause for disciplining an employee.[1] Since more collective bargaining agreements do not explain or define the term "just cause," which often is used in such contracts, the arbitrator listed serious questions that had been developed from other arbitrators' decisions over the years and could serve as criteria for determining "just cause."

'JUST CAUSE' CRITERIA

These questions were:

1. Did the company give to the employee forewarning or foreknowledge of the possible or probable disciplinary consequences of the employee's conduct?

Note 1: Said forewarning or foreknowledge may properly have been given orally by management or in writing through the medium of typed or printed sheets or books of shop rules and of penalties for violation thereof.

Note 2: There must have been actual oral or written communication of rules and penalties to the employee.

Note 3: A finding of lack of such communication does not in all cases require a "no" answer to Question #1. This is because certain offenses such as insubordination, coming to work intoxicated, drinking intoxicating beverages on the job, or theft of the property of the company or of fellow employees are so serious that any employee in

3

the industrial society may properly be expected to know already that such conduct is offensive and heavily punishable.

Note 4: Absent any contractual prohibition or restriction, the company has the right unilaterally to promulgate reasonable rules and give reasonable orders; and same need not have been negotiated with the union.

2. Was the company's rule or managerial order reasonably related to (a) the orderly, efficient, and safe operation of the company's business and (b) the performance that the company might properly expect of the employee?

Note: If an employee believes that said rule or order is unreasonable, he must nevertheless obey same (in which case he may file a grievance thereover) unless he sincerely feels that to obey the rule or order would seriously and immediately jeopardize his personal safety and/or integrity. Given a firm finding to the latter effect, the employee may properly be said to have had justification for his disobedience.

3. Did the company, before administering discipline to an employee, make an effort to discover whether the employee did in fact violate or disobey a rule or order of management?

Note 1: This is the employee's "day in court" principle. An employee has the right to know with reasonable precision the offense with which he is being charged and to defend his behavior.

Note 2: The company's investigation must normally be made before its disciplinary decision is made. If the company fails to do so, its failure may not normally be excused on the grounds that the employee will get his day in court through the grievance procedure after the exaction of discipline. By that time there has usually been too much hardening of position. In a very real sense the company is obligated to conduct itself like a trial court.

Note 3: There may of course be circumstances under which management must react immediately to the employee's behavior. In such cases the normally proper action is to suspend the employee pending investigation, with the understanding that (a) the final disciplinary decision will be made after the investigation and (b) if the employee is found innocent after the investigation, he will be restored to his job with full pay for time lost.

Note 4: The company's investigation should include an inquiry into possible justification for the employee's alleged rule violation.

4. Was the company's investigation conducted fairly and objectively?

Note 1: At said investigation the management official may be both "prosecutor" and "judge," but he may not also be a witness against the employee.

Note 2: It is essential for some higher, detached management official to assume and conscientiously perform the judicial role, giving the commonly accepted meaning to that term in his attitude and conduct.

Note 3: In some disputes between an employee and a management person there are no witnesses to an incident other than the two immediate participants. In such cases it is particularly important that the management "judge" question the management participant rigorously and thoroughly just as an actual third party would.

5. At the investigation did the "judge" obtain substantial evidence or proof that the employee was guilty as charged?

Note 1: It is not required that the evidence be conclusive or "beyond all reasonable doubt." But the evidence must be truly substantial and not flimsy.

Note 2: The management "judge" should actively search out witnesses and evidence, not just passively take what participants or "volunteer" witnesses tell him.

Note 3: When the testimony of opposing witnesses at the arbitration hearing is irreconcilably in conflict, an arbitrator seldom has any means for resolving the contradictions. His task is then to determine whether the management "judge" originally had reasonable grounds for believing the evidence presented to him by his own people.

6. Has the company applied its rules, orders, and penalties evenhandedly and without discrimination to all employees?

Note 1: A "no" answer to this question requires a finding of discrimination and warrants negation or modification of the discipline imposed.

Note 2: If the company has been lax in enforcing its rules and orders and decides henceforth to apply them rigorously, the company may avoid a finding of discrimination by telling all employees beforehand of its intent to enforce hereafter all rules as written.

7. Was the degree of discipline administered by the company in a particular case reasonably related to (a) the seriousness of the employee's proven offense and (b) the record of the employee in his service with the company?

Note 1: A trivial proven offense does not merit harsh discipline unless the employee has properly been found guilty of the same or other offenses a number of times in the past. (There is no rule as to what number of previous offenses constitutes a "good," a "fair," or a "bad" record. Reasonable judgment thereon must be used.)

Note 2: An employee's record of previous offenses may never be used to discover whether he was guilty of the immediate or latest one. The only proper use of his record is to help determine the severity of discipline once he has properly been found guilty of the immediate offense.

Note 3: Given the same proven offense for two or more employees, their respective records provide the only proper basis for "discriminating" among them in the administration of discipline for said offense. Thus, if employee A's record is significantly better than those of employees B, C, and D, the company may properly give A a lighter punishment than it gives the others for the same offense; and this does not constitute true discrimination.

Note 4: Suppose that the record of the arbitration hearing establishes firm "Yes" answers to all the first six questions. Suppose further that the proven offense of the accused employee was a serious one, such as drunkenness on the job; but the employee's record had been previously unblemished over a long, continuous period of employment with the company. Should the company be held arbitrary and unreasonable if it decided to discharge an employee? The answer depends of course on all the circumstances. But, as one of the country's oldest arbitration agencies, the National Railroad Adjustment Board, has pointed out repeatedly in innumerable decisions on discharge cases, leniency is the prerogative of the employer rather than of the arbitrator; and the latter is not supposed to substitute his judgment in this area for that of the company unless there is compelling evidence that the company abused its discretion. This is the rule, even though an arbitrator, if he had been the original "trial judge," might have imposed a lesser penalty. Actually the arbitrator may be said in an important sense to act as an appellate tribunal whose function is to discover whether the decision of the trial tribunal (the employer) was within the bounds of reasonableness above set forth—in general, the penalty of dismissal for a really serious first offense does not in itself warrant a finding of company unreasonableness.[2]

CRITERIA FOR SUSTAINING A DISCHARGE

Many arbitrators have enunciated criteria to sustain a discharge, such as the following by a prominent arbitrator, Milton Friedman:

1. The employer must prove that the alleged acts occurred and were of sufficient gravity to warrant termination.
2. The employer must show that the misconduct was not condoned but the employee was specifically warned of the consequences through progressive discipline, such as written warnings and suspension.
3. The evidence must demonstrate that the employee made no genuine effort to heed the warnings although the consequences of continued misconduct were known.
4. The employee cannot be singled out for disparate treatment for offenses that do not subject others to similar discipline.
5. When a long-service employee is involved, there must be sound cause to believe that the events are not transitory but form a consistent and recurrent pattern that is unlikely to change in the future.

Arbitrators, in assessing disciplinary discharge penalties, see their function as determining not only that cause for penalty exists but also whether the punishment fits the crime.

GOOD AND JUST CAUSE

Absent a definition of "just cause" in a union-management agreement, it once again is essential that labor relations practitioners refer to arbitrators' definitions of that term. The burden of providing "good and just cause" for discipline rests on administration. If cause has been proved, a penalty imposed by the administration will not be modified by an arbitrator unless it has been shown to be clearly arbitrary, capricious, discriminatory, or excessive in relation to the offense.

It is an unquestionable management right to discipline up through discharge *if* it has sufficient and appropriate reasons. Arbitrators normally support a management action if progressive discipline includes, first, a verbal reprimand and full explanation of what is necessary to remedy the situation, followed, second, by a written reprimand for a second infraction and a clear warning of the future penalty that may be imposed. A final warning and suspension may follow and, subsequently, the ultimate penalty of discharge.

The arbitrator also considers whether or not the employee was fully aware of the standards against which the behavior was measured. It is clear that administration must record actual events, offenses, and transgressions. Documentation lies at the heart of the due process system.

Jules Justin, a prominent labor arbitrator, lists some noteworthy rules of corrective discipline:

1. Discipline to be meaningful must be corrective, not punitive.

2. When you discipline one, you discipline all.

3. Corrective discipline satisfies the rule of equality of treatment by enforcing equally among all employees established rules, safety practices, and responsibility on the job.

4. It is the job of the supervisor, not the shop steward, to make the worker toe the line or increase efficiency.

5. Just cause of any other comparable standard for justifying disciplinary action under the labor contract consists of three parts:

   a. Did the employee breach the rule or commit the offense charged against him?

   b. Did the employee's act or conduct warrant corrective action or punishment?

   c. Is the penalty just and appropriate to the act or offense as corrective punishment?

6. The burden of proof rests on the supervisor, who must justify each of the three parts (listed in 5 above) that make up a standard of just cause under the labor contract.[3]

FORMS OF DISCIPLINE

The Oral Reprimand

Progressive disciplining usually starts with oral reprimands or oral warnings. This function often is handled in a counseling session. What is the purpose of the action? It should be to nip in the bud behavior that is inappropriate to the work area. The necessary ingredients for a successful counseling encounter are complete privacy, a well-planned agenda, enough time to arrive at agreement, and a positive attitude on the part of the supervisor.

In such sessions employees should receive a complete outline of the action in question. Details should not be spared, and dates and times and places should be communicated. The specific institution policy or rule in question should be enunciated. The specific documents (such as a union contract or a personnel policy manual) containing such rules should be examined. The employee should be given complete freedom to answer the charge, explain the behavior, and admit or deny the action.

It is obvious that an effective counseling session will develop from the point that the employee agrees that the action occurred and was inappropriate. If such an agreement is reached, a plan to improve performance should be discussed. It also is important at this time to acknowledge the positive aspects of the employee's behavior.

After the counseling session has been completed, anecdotal notes should be prepared by the supervisor and placed in the department file. It is not appropriate at this point to forward such notes to the personnel department for inclusion in the employee's folder.

A supervisor who wishes to effect corrective disciplining should be more interested in changing behavioral patterns and attitudes than in reprimanding the employee. Lateiner,[4] a widely recognized authority on supervisory techniques, offers some pointers to the supervisor interested in making criticism more constructive:

1. Don't reprimand a worker who is angry or excited. Wait until she has cooled down. Wait until you cool down, too.
2. Don't bawl out someone in front of other people. This is embarrassing and humiliating and is likely to do more harm than good.
3. Find out how the worker feels and thinks about the situation. If you want someone to do something differently, you first have to find out what she already knows.

4. When you criticize a person, it is much better to compare her performance to department standards than to the performance of another employee. A person is more likely to feel resentful or insecure if she is compared unfavorably to a co-worker.
5. Most important, if you reprimand constructively, you must show a person how to improve her performance. You don't want to destroy an employee's self-confidence. You want to build up confidence by guiding the worker in the direction of a satisfactory performance.

The oral reprimand or warning interview is a useful way for the supervisor to establish a sound relationship with all employees—those who require such warnings and those who do not. Employees normally respect supervisors who apply the rules of the institution fairly. Although criticism can be a disturbing element, the need for constructive criticism can be fully appreciated by employees.

If the supervisor is to discipline firmly and wisely, it is essential that the employee relations administrator or personnel director be fully supportive in instances in which institutional policy is being protected and carried out. It is equally important that the department head or director of the institution provide clear evidence that the supervisor will be backed up at crucial moments. This does not mean that there never will be a situation where the supervisor is overruled, but such incidences should not be based on political pressures, legal technicalities, or sentimentality. The responsibility of meting out discipline is difficult enough without undercutting the first-line supervisor.

It should be made clear that the oral reprimand or warning is not appropriate or effective in the face of flagrant offenses such as insubordination, theft, fighting, or carrying firearms. Such actions call for sharper responses— often termination.

Warning Notice

Overt flaunting of institutional rules and appropriate behavior patterns is dealt with by the first-line supervisor either by a formal warning notice, suspension, or discharge—if, and only after, a formal warning interview has been held. (This proscription does not apply if the transgression is a major and flagrant one such as those mentioned under exceptions to the oral reprimand.) Some examples of negative behavior that may call for a written warning notice are:

- insubordination or impertinence
- unauthorized or chronic absenteeism

- chronic lateness
- loafing or sleeping on the job
- misrepresentation of timecards or records
- drinking alcoholic beverages on the job
- dishonesty
- fighting on the job
- gambling

The warning notice should not come as a surprise to the employee. It is essentially the second step in the arsenal of weapons for reversing a poor behavioral pattern. It can be preceded by the oral reprimand but may directly follow a clear violation of institutional rules and regulations. In preparing the warning notice, the supervisor again is concerned with facts and not with subjective opinions.

The institution normally provides a form to be used for written warning notices. This form calls for a clear statement of the specific rule or policy that has been violated. The supervisor may have to refer to the union contract or personnel policy manual or written bulletin containing the specific rule.

Following this reference point, the written warning notice should describe the act in question. Once again the supervisor must be specific and complete. Dates, time, and, where appropriate, witnesses should be included.

The most important part of the warning notice is a statement to indicate that immediate satisfactory improvement must be shown and maintained unless further disciplinary action is to be taken. In many cases, this "immediate satisfactory improvement" can be outlined in detail. For example, an employee has shown a pattern of absenteeism—say three days each month for the last six months (many of the days were Mondays, making three-day weekends possible). The supervisor indicates that the employee's pattern of Monday absences is not acceptable, that attendance will be monitored over the next two, three, or four months to gauge improvement, and that if there is no improvement, the individual will be subject to suspension and possible termination.

The warning notice is presented to the employee in private; if possible, the employee should be asked to sign it, acknowledging receipt. More important than acceptance of the warning form is the employee's acknowledgment that the behavior is inappropriate and that improvement must be forthcoming. In some cases—more often than not where unions are involved—employees refuse to sign warning notice forms. This should be expected and understood, but the supervisor's responsibility does not end here. The supervisor, in order to emphasize the importance of the action and ensure the "legality" of the presentation, should ask another supervisor to witness the actual reading and offer of a copy of the warning notice to the employee. This is necessary only if the employee refuses to sign the form.

Despite all this, it is important to remember that the supervisor's cardinal responsibility in this procedure is to attempt a restructuring of the employee's behavior; the primary responsibility or objective is not to punish the individual.

One bit of advice is necessary before exploring the final two steps in the disciplinary arsenal of weapons: suspension and termination. There is no easy panacea that can be offered for behavior control. In a few cases, oral reprimands or warning notices never will be enough. In still more cases, suspensions may be counterproductive. The supervisor must keep in mind that constructive disciplining is a means of achieving the end product: a change in behavior patterns.

Suspension

The suspension is not universally accepted as an effective way to correct behavior patterns. Many employees find suspension a respite from the stress of the work area. Some even enjoy being out on strike. For an employee with a chronic absentee record, a suspension certainly is not the worst sort of punishment.

A one-day suspension can be as effective as a one-week one. The shock of the penalty usually brings employees to their senses. The length of the suspension has little effect on the probability of rehabilitation. The action can cause inordinate difficulties in scheduling and in meeting production quotas. The authors have come to the conclusion that a one- or two-day suspension is a sufficient final warning to employees before termination. The penalty should be accompanied with a written warning notice indicating prior attempts, both informal and formal, toward rehabilitation. Most important, the suspension should indicate that it constitutes the final warning.

Termination

To sustain a discharge where an arbitration procedure is available, the following minimal requirements must be met; in fact, they should be operative whether or not there is an arbitration procedure, whether or not there is a union:

- Facts must be presented, clearly indicating that the employee actually committed the offense. Opinion must be separated from hard documentation. Witnesses may be essential.
- The supervisor must be able to display a consistent approach to the offense in question; there must be no playing of favorites.
- The record should indicate a progressive disciplining ladder, except in the case of blatant and serious offenses.
- The punishment must fit the crime.

Progressive disciplining normally must precede the discharge of an employee. The procedure of progressive disciplining as outlined includes a verbal reprimand and a full explanation of what is necessary to remedy the situation. Normally a second infraction calls for a written reprimand with a clear warning of future penalties that may be imposed. A suspension may follow with a final warning, and the ultimate penalty is discharge.

There is a further consideration in cases that involve discharge: consistency. A double standard often is found in health care institutions: one standard for the medical staff and another for the other employees. The supervisor should be aware of the possibility of employee complaints to the union and to outside agencies of disparate treatment of professionals and nonprofessionals.

SUSTAINING DISCIPLINARY ACTION IN ARBITRATION

Many disciplinary actions are appealed to outside arbitration, where a neutral third party judges the appropriateness of the action. Following are some of the factors that arbitrators consider in sustaining or overruling management's action.[5]

Absenteeism

1. The length of time in which the employee had a poor attendance record must be noted.
2. The reasons for the worker's absence must be stated.
3. The nature of the employee's job must be described.
4. The attendance records of other employees must be included.
5. The fact that the employer has (or does not have) a clear disciplinary policy on absenteeism that is known to all employees and that is applied fairly and consistently must be made clear.

6. The fact that the employee was (or was not) adequately warned that disciplinary action could result if attendance failed to improve must be documented.

Insubordination

1. The supervisor's instructions must be very clear and must be understood by the employee to be an order; the supervisor must clearly state the penalty for failure to comply.
2. Merely protesting an order is not insubordination; refusal to carry it out is.
3. The use of objectional language to supervision often is cause for discipline. Where such language is commonplace in the worker's area, it may not be grounds for discharge.

Misconduct

1. Thefts and other kinds of dishonesty are regarded as causes for discharge. Such a discharge requires convincing proof of the employee's guilt.
2. Fighting on the institution's premises is a dischargeable offense except where the employee is acting in self-defense.
3. Misconduct occurring away from the institution outside of working hours is punishable only if it affects the employment relationship in some way.

Dishonesty

1. Evidence required to support a discharge for dishonesty usually is "proof beyond a reasonable doubt."
2. Falsification of job applications, if not an oversight or a lapse of memory but rather a deliberate act with intent to defraud, is grounds for disciplining.
3. Falsifying institution records regarding work done usually justifies discharge. The employee's action must be deliberate and intended to cheat the institution. This includes punching a coworker's timecard, improperly punching one's own timecard, falsifying expense accounts, or making false statements to obtain medical or health insurance.
4. Stealing institution property subjects the employee to discharge.

Gambling

1. Discharge normally is too severe a penalty for a first offense of gambling.
2. Discharge is appropriate where the employee is connected with an organized gambling racket.
3. The evidence connecting the employee with gambling must be substantial and convincing.

Intoxication and Alcoholism

Arbitrators usually sustain discharge for drinking or drunkenness in these situations:

1. frequent absenteeism as a result of drinking
2. drinking on the job combined with other misconduct
3. drinking on the job that results in inability to perform the work, but not generally for a first offense
4. chronic alcoholism with no signs of rehabilitation

A decision to discharge for chronic alcoholism is especially supportable in arbitration if the employer can show that the employee was offered admission to a valid rehabilitation program, whether company run or otherwise, and that the individual either refused to go or attended and dropped out, or failed.

Sleeping and Loafing

1. Discharge for sleeping on the job, with the possible exclusion of a first offense, is sustained as long as there is an institution rule or established practice calling for such termination.
2. Discharge may be sustained in the absence of a specific rule if the sleeping involves any danger to the safety of employees, patients, or equipment.
3. The employer has a heavy burden of proving that the employee was, in fact, sleeping.

Incompetence

1. The charge of incompetence must be properly investigated or substantiated.

2. The employee must be given adequate warning and an opportunity to improve the performance.
3. Other employees with equally poor performance records must be treated in the same manner.

REASONS FOR DISCIPLINE PROBLEMS

Too often institutions develop rules and policies that run counter to the prevailing customs operative over the years in the workplace. The American Management Association offers some critical reasons why disciplinary problems develop:[6]

1. The rules and regulations may be viewed by employees as meaningless. It is important to recognize that there is a great deal of difference between an employee's being told about a rule and learning the "why" behind it.
2. Violations of the rules occur when employees do not fear punishment for their violations. The employer needs to prove by actions that violators will be disciplined.
3. There are employees who violate rules because they feel underpaid or believe management discriminates against them. Inherent in this problem is management's failure to make clear exactly what the organization's discipline policy is, why it exists, and what the consequences are when it is violated.
4. Some violations are truly unintentional and reflect a lapse in memory or caution. This category includes most of the discipline and safety problems.

SUCCESSFUL POLICIES

The Bureau of National Affairs conducted a study of many successful policies that revealed the following pattern:[7]

1. Company rules are carefully explained to employees. This is especially important in the case of new workers. Indoctrination courses, employee handbooks, bulletin board notices, and many other forms of bringing rules to workers' attention are used.
2. Accusations against employees are carefully considered to see whether they are supported by facts. Witnesses are interviewed, their statements are recorded, and careful investigation is made to see that both sides of the story are available and are presented fairly. Circumstan-

tial evidence is kept to a minimum in judging the facts. Personality factors and unfounded assumptions are eliminated.

3. A regular warning procedure is established and applied. Sometimes all warnings are in writing, with the original handed to the employee and a copy filed in the worker's record in the personnel office. Sometimes first warnings are delivered orally, but a written record of that action is filed. Warnings are given for all except the most serious offenses; those that management has made clear call for immediate discharge.

4. Some companies bring the union into the discipline case early in the procedure. They provide copies of warning notices and advance notice of other disciplinary actions that management intends to take. Sometimes the action is held up until the union has time to make its own investigation.

5. The employee's motive and reasons for the violation of rules are investigated before disciplinary action is taken. Then the penalty is adjusted to the facts: whether the employee's action was in good faith, partially justified, or totally unjustified.

6. The employee's past record is taken into consideration before disciplinary action is taken. A good work record and long seniority are factors in the employee's favor, particularly where a minor offense is involved or where it is a first offense. Previous offenses are not used against the employee unless the individual was reprimanded at the time they occurred or warned that they would be used in any future disciplinary action.

7. Companies make sure that all management agents, particularly first-line supervisors, know the employers' disciplinary policies and procedures, and observe them carefully. This is particularly important in the case of verbal warnings or informal reprimands.

8. Discipline short of discharge is used wherever possible.

DISCIPLINING FOR OPTIMUM RESULTS

Much of the debate over appropriate discipline concerns the spirit, extent, or degree of enforcement that brings optimum results. Pfiffner and Fels[8] put this critical question in proper focus:

> Should discipline be strict and severe or tolerant and easy-going? The answer will not be found by locating the optimum point between strict and easy, but rather in the fundamental nature of the social organization which the supervisor must understand as

part of his disciplining duties. If the basic mores of an organization are developed in a manner that commands the respect and conformance of its members, disciplining should offer no special problem. The rank-and-file member will observe the mores either automatically or because of the pressures exerted to do so by other members of the group. That is, he probably will if he has a feeling of belonging and thus recognizing that to belong requires a contribution in accordance with his means and talents. Thus, in essence the supervisor's attempts to discipline must see discipline as a means not of immediately stopping an undesirable behavior only, but of reaching a goal of desirable citizenship.

NOTES

1. *Enterprise Wire Company* (Blue Island, Ill.) and *Enterprise Independent Union,* 46 L.A. 359 (1966).

2. Marvin Hill, Jr., and Anthony V. Sinicropi, *Remedies in Arbitration* (Washington, D.C.: The Bureau of National Affairs, Inc., 1981), pp. 283–286.

3. Jules J. Justin, *How to Manage with the Union,* Book 1 (New York: Industrial Work Shop Seminars, Inc., 1969), pp. 294–295, 301–302.

4. Alfred R. Lateiner, *Modern Techniques of Supervision* (Stamford, Conn.: Lateiner Publishing, 1968), originally published in Lateiner, *The Technique of Supervision* (New London, Conn.: National Foreman's Institute, 1954), pp. 28–39.

5. *Grievance Guide,* 6th ed. (Washington, D.C.: The Bureau of National Affairs, Inc., 1982), passim.

6. *Discipline in the Work Place Today, Supervisory Sense* (New York: AMACOM, Division of American Management Associations, 1980), pp. 10–11.

7. *Grievance Guide,* pp. 4–5.

8. John M. Pfiffner and Marshall Fels, *The Supervision of Personnel,* 3d ed. (Englewood Cliffs, N.J.: Prentice-Hall, Inc., 1964), pp. 111–112.

Chapter 2

The Grievance Procedure: Resolving Employee Complaints

In a 1980 book an author titled a chapter "Resolving Employee Complaints." He explained the rationale:

> On reading the title of this chapter the first thought that will come to some readers is 'What about employees' grievances?' It is with specific purpose that the word grievance does not appear in the title. This is because no real distinction can be made between a complaint and a grievance. In essence, complaints and grievances are the same.[1]

SOURCES OF GRIEVANCES

The authors of this book find that their own experience leads them to believe that many "grievances" are informational in nature, resulting from a lack of communication or a breakdown in communication. The employee misreads the rule, the clause, or the policy. Others result from a discontent with the rule, the clause, or the policy—they are gripes. Whether they are gripes, complaints, or bona fide grievances (as defined in the Collective Bargaining Agreement or in the Personnel Policy Manual), they must be addressed.

One large corporation, many years ago, insisted that its personnel forms not contain the word "pregnancy" when an employee requested a leave of absence for child-bearing purposes. It insisted on using the word "gravid," which dictionaries define as "pregnant." That word did not change the employee's condition. Pregnant or gravid, the employee was with child. Grievance procedure or no grievance procedure, institutions have employees with problems that must be resolved.

There are hospital administrators, especially in nonunion environments, who are opposed to formal grievance procedures. They contend that grievance procedures produce grievances. Here again is the ostrich approach to employee relations. Employees must have an avenue of appeal from first-line supervisors' decisions. A large majority of grievances result from a decision made, and/or communicated, by the first-line supervisor. Therefore, if a theory of due process is to prevail, it becomes necessary to permit an employee who contests an immediate supervisor's decision to have an avenue of recourse beyond that ruling.

Arbitrators say they will consider, as an integral part of their decision, whether or not the institution conducted a fair and objective investigation. Such a procedure is inherent in a formal grievance mechanism. One arbitrator writes, "The significance of the grievance procedure leading up to the arbitration hearing is often grossly underestimated. The major purpose of the grievance procedure is to resolve disputes bilaterally before they get to arbitration."[2]

Some institutions prefer an informal, rather than a formal, grievance procedure. This approach rarely is effective. A lower level employee will find it difficult to express frustrations, fears, and needs to a person in a much higher position who appears to be isolated from the everyday problems of the rank-and-file worker. Most high-level executives find the grievance procedure activity to be an imposition on their busy schedules. The process itself is forbidding.

The employee must make an appointment; must pass through a receptionist who often is protective of the executive's time; and must enter an office that can be large, formal, and unfamiliar. The grievant then must face an executive with whom the employee might never have talked in a year and might not in the year ahead. At this point, the grievant is expected to talk and argue freely. This is just not feasible. Or as Michael J. Quill, the late and often pungent union leader, used to put it sarcastically: "It just don't seem sane."

The central purpose of the grievance procedure is to dispose of the grievance fairly and equitably and, where possible, reach an agreement. To do this, facts must be obtained and evaluated objectively; fact finding is at the heart of the grievance procedure. Such a process requires objectivity beyond the emotional issues involved. Based on their own experience, the authors conclude that effective grievance handling, resulting in fair and equitable resolution of employee disputes, requires:

- energetic pursuit of all the facts
- omission from the hearing procedures of preconceived ideas about the validity of the grievance

- a desire to dispose of the grievance by protecting the rights of both the institution and the employee
- a willingness to admit that management is wrong, if that is the case.

THE SUPERVISOR AND THE GRIEVANCE PROCEDURE

The most important employer-employee relationship is the one between employee and the immediate supervisor. The supervisor must know all of the employees in the department and be genuinely interested in them in order to recognize their needs and problems. This can eliminate many complaints before they reach the grievance stage as well as serve as a means of increasing productivity and efficiency.

It is the supervisor's responsibility to know the details of the collective bargaining contract as well as personnel policies and how to apply them. The supervisor usually is the day-to-day interpreter of institutional policy, rules and regulations, and the administrator of the contract. Although it is clear that many employees' grievances cannot be considered as bona fide, inasmuch as they are not covered by personnel policy or the union contract, it is important that they should be heard.

Taking a legalistic approach to the procedure and summarily dismissing a grievance as only a "gripe" will be counterproductive, hard feelings will ensue, and many matters that are properly subjects of the grievance procedure and otherwise might not be grieved will be used to exert pressure on management. A supervisor's listening to a complaint, even though it is a petty gripe, can be enough in itself; the mere pouring out of the problem (catharsis) may well be enough to satisfy the employee that someone is interested.

The supervisor should listen attentively and get the complete facts and look for the underlying attitudes and feelings. The aggrieved employee should be permitted the time and the privacy to seek explanations and satisfaction. Very often complaints reflect dissatisfaction in areas other than those expressed. The hidden agenda may be far more important than the obvious subject of the grievance. Therefore, it is essential for a supervisor to find out what is really bothering the employee.

A most helpful suggestion is to rephrase the employee's statements in the supervisor's own words. This serves several purposes:

- the employee can correct any misunderstanding the supervisor may have
- the employee has the opportunity to bring the focus of the complaint into sharper perspective

- the supervisor and the employee will be certain to understand the situation thoroughly
- the employee is assured that the supervisor is on the same wavelength and is empathetic enough to try to understand the problem from the worker's point of view.

Another responsibility of supervision is to minimize grievances. It is obvious that there is no way to eliminate grievances completely. However, a supervisor who is alert to the common causes of complaints and dissatisfactions within a department, and who attempts to correct minor irritations promptly before they explode into major problems, can help eliminate unnecessary grievances. The effective supervisor knows the contract and company personnel policies thoroughly and does not knowingly violate the provisions of either document. This, of course, requires that institutions set up training programs directed at reviewing such policies.

Many grievances involve nonfulfillment of commitments made by supervisors. Before promises are made to employees, supervisors should check whether it is possible to make good on them; indeed, promises that are made should not be forgotten. Another group of grievances develops from supervisors' actions regarding poor performance of employees in their departments. This occurs when employees have received positive performance reviews earlier.

Employees must know how they are getting along so the supervisor should not wait for the formal performance review to keep them informed of progress or problems. An employee who does not measure up should be told and counselled regarding the need to meet standards. The supervisor should find out why there is a problem and provide direction and coaching.

Another key area of dissatisfaction arises from perceived or actual favoritism in working conditions or employee benefits. Consistency in words and actions can minimize employee complaints. Where deviation is justified, supervisors must clearly communicate the reasons to the employees, explaining changes in or deviations from policy, procedure, or established practice.

DEFINITION OF A GRIEVANCE

One limited definition of a grievance in prevalent use describes the grievance procedure as involving a difference of opinion between management and an employee or the union, specifically relating to the meaning and application of the terms of the collective bargaining agreement. This would reduce and limit the arbitrator's role to one of a judicial rather than a legislative nature. The arbitrator's objective then would be to interpret the already bargained position of the parties.

Grievance handling can be viewed from two vantage points: the legalistic and the clinical. The legalistic approach emphasizes form and mechanics; therefore, the definition of a grievance in the contract or in the personnel policy is limited or narrow. This directs management to accept or dismiss grievances on the basis of whether or not they are within the contract. The clinical approach attempts to get to the heart of the problem. Many experts recommend an intensive search for the fundamental determinants of a grievance rather than accepting its surface rationale at face value. This method bespeaks an empathetic probe into the actual circumstances and causes of the grievance. Actually, the latter approach can augment the former and, indeed, the two are not mutually exclusive.

A grievance exists when there is employee discontent or dissatisfaction, whether valid or not, that arises out of anything connected with the institution that such an individual thinks, believes, and even feels is unfair, unjust, or inequitable. It is essential that management accept the fact that the objective of the grievance procedure is to bring employee complaints to the surface and to settle them peacefully.

The grievance procedure is an integral part of the management communication network. If the mechanism developed to handle grievances is too cumbersome and works to discourage submission rather than to encourage it, then many unidentified and, of course, unsettled complaints will fester in their unresolved state and develop into crises far out of proportion to—indeed, much greater than—the original problem. Therefore, it serves little purpose to restrict the definition of grievances that may be submitted through the in-house steps established for handling employee complaints.

PRINCIPLES OF GRIEVANCE ARBITRATION

The basic principles of grievance adjustment have been enunciated in many ways by many experts, but rarely is there disagreement as to the core ingredients:

1. Inherent in successful grievance adjustment is a commitment to adjusting the employee's complaint promptly and on its merits.
2. Since the majority of grievances derive from a decision by a first-line supervisor, there must be a direct avenue of appeal beyond that ruling; ergo, a second or third step in that procedure.

3. A grievance procedure that has as its terminal step a review inside the institution is not as effective as one that provides for outside review (arbitration) by an impartial third party.
4. There should be a strong desire to resolve dissatisfaction and conflicts before they become real problems.
5. Supervisors should empathize with their employees, try to understand their problems, and be able and willing to listen in a nonjudgmental fashion.
6. Supervisors should balance their personal commitment to the interest of the institution with a sense of fair play on behalf of the employees. Supervisors represent the employees to the administration and the administration to the employees.
7. Employees deserve a complete and empathetic hearing of all grievances.
8. The most important job in the handling of grievances is getting the facts. Therefore, supervisors must listen attentively, encourage full discussion, and defer judgment.
9. Supervisors must look for the hidden agenda, look beyond the selected incident, and judge the grievance in context.
10. Hasty decisions often backfire. On the other hand, the employee deserves a speedy reply.
11. The supervisor should try to separate fact from opinion or impressions while investigating a grievance, consult others when appropriate, and, most important, check with the personnel office.
12. The supervisor, after coming to a decision, should communicate it to the employee promptly, giving the reason for the ruling and informing the person of the right to appeal an adverse outcome.
13. Decisions must be made and then sold to the employee. The decision is less effective if the individual does not understand the rationale.
14. Common sense is an essential ingredient in arriving at a decision.
15. Written records are most important. They serve as a review for the supervisor to ensure consistency.

MANAGEMENT'S RESPONSIBILITY

Management's responsibility in the administration and adjudication of grievances includes the following:

1. hearing and discussing the grievance facts with the employee
2. investigating the facts during and after the hearing
3. formulating a decision based on the facts
4. answering the grievance

In addition, management has the responsibility for taking action to eliminate present problems and prevent future ones, based upon careful research developing from information gathered during grievance hearings. As suggested earlier, what appears to be the rationale for the grievance may turn out to be only surface manifestation of more complex determinants.

It is important to go beyond a simplistic acceptance of the reason for the grievance as presented and, instead, to embark on an objective investigation to determine the actual causes. If the grievance administrators discharge their handling responsibilities properly, they must institute such an investigation before making a decision.

KEYS TO SUCCESSFUL GRIEVANCE HANDLING

Here are some ways to improve human relations when handling grievances. Supervisors should:

1. Be available. They should know their people are individuals and should fit their methods to them. Supervisors can cool off the hothead with patience; sense when something is troubling the quiet worker who keeps anger bottled up until it explodes; calm sensitive employees who may think they are being slighted. Supervisors can't solve the problems of strangers and, unless they are approachable, they will have strangers working for them.
2. Be relaxed. When employees bring in gripes, real or fancied, supervisors should let them sound off. If they know that their supervisors are listening and will give them a fair hearing, the complaints won't look so big.
3. Get the facts. Supervisors must get the story, ask questions and straighten out any inconsistencies, and be objective and sympathetic.
4. Investigate carefully. It is important never to accept hearsay. Supervisors must find out for themselves the answers to such questions as who, what, when, where, and why. They must check how the union contract or institutional personnel policy covers the alleged offense and review the files for precedents.
5. Be tactful. Many employees will start to tell a supervisor about unfair treatment only to realize, halfway through the story, that they don't have a real complaint. If supervisors help such employees "save face," they make a friend. A worker never should leave the grievance interview humiliated and embarrassed.

6. Act with deliberation. Snap judgment leads to impulsive action so supervisors must take time to get all the facts. What caused the grievance? Where did it happen? Has the contract been violated? Has an institutional policy been violated? Has the employee been treated unfairly? Has there been favoritism, unintentional or deliberate? Was this grievance related to others?

7. Get the answer. It may be impossible to address the grievance immediately, but employees must not be given the runaround. If supervisors can't get the facts needed to settle the case, they should say so. An employee who knows the supervisors are working on the problem is likely to be more reasonable.

8. Consider the consequences of the decision. It is essential to know the effect the settlement will have, not only on the individual but on the group.

9. Admit mistakes. All supervisors are human and make mistakes, so if decisions occasionally are reversed by superiors, admit the error. Supervisors must not bear a grudge against the employee who was proved right at their expense.

10. Sell the decision. When an employee's grievance is denied, it is necessary to explain why. A blunt "no" causes resentment. Supervisors must not pass the buck by blaming higher management for the denial.

THE GRIEVANCE PROCEDURE

A typical grievance procedure contains four steps:

Step 1: The employee submits the grievance to the first-line supervisor. In many instances, the employee's representative (the union delegate) is involved at this step. Since the majority of grievances involve decisions or actions taken by first-line supervisors, it is essential that this be the initial step in the formal procedure.

Step 2: The employee is involved along with the union representative and a department head in this, the appeal step. The specific management representative, at this point, differs from institution to institution, but the common thread is the organizational positioning of the individual. The appeal step should be conducted by a superior to the first-line supervisor. In some institutions the personnel department handles the second step.

Step 3: The employee and the union representative, or a union official who often has a broader responsibility than the delegate, appeal to a labor relations representative of the institution. In some facilities, the third step, which is the last in-house appeal, is conducted by an associate director of the institution.

Step 4: Arbitration provides the final resolution. This is discussed in detail in Chapter 4.

In the adjustment of grievances, as in so many other aspects of labor relations, time is of the essence. That is why it is customary for each step of the procedure to carry with it a time limit, at the expiration of which the dispute goes to the next stage. Management usually wants to be protected from grievances arising out of events long past. For this reason, the right to initiate grievances under many contracts is conditioned on their being presented within a specific number of days or a reasonable time following the event or incident at issue.

Not only management, however, is concerned with the prompt handling of grievances. The union and its members justifiably want and deserve safeguards against possible oversight or neglect of grievances by administration. To prevent this, many procedures specify time limits within which management representatives, at each step, must respond. Where such provisions exist and the management representative fails to answer within the time limit, some contracts require that the grievance then be settled solely on the basis of the relief sought by the employee, and not on management's position or any compromise it might have proffered. In other contracts, the union simply is free to advance the grievance to the next highest step. However, adequate opportunity for proper investigation and review of grievances should not be sacrificed simply to permit their speedy processing.

The extent to which the employer should bear the cost of time spent by employees on grievance activity can become a controversial bargaining issue. Management, quite naturally, views this question from the cost impact resulting from lost time and the effect on direct operating expense. Unions maintain that employers should absorb pay for such activity as they would any other item of normal overhead expense. Under most contracts today, employees are paid for time lost from work in the processing of their own grievances. Similarly, it is fairly common to pay union delegates or shop stewards and a specified number of grievance committee members for time spent in processing employee claims.

In determining which grievance activity is to be paid for, contracts sometimes distinguish between time spent investigating complaints and time spent actually adjusting them. Where such distinctions are made, some institutions pay only for time spent adjusting grievances but allow time without pay for the investigation or do not permit investigation during working hours.

Limitations on the amount of grievance time to be paid for by the employer vary widely. Some contracts specify a flat number of institution-paid hours per contract year; others provide similar limits but on a daily, weekly, or monthly basis; and still others limit the number of persons to be paid in any step of the grievance.[3] (Exhibits 2-1 and 2-2 provide examples of grievance and arbitration procedures.)

CONCLUSION

Pegnetter and Levey report that the grievance procedure, which frequently ends in binding arbitration, represents a trade-off in collective bargaining for both labor and management. The union gives up the right to strike over grievance disputes during the life of the contract. In return, it gets a grievance procedure with a terminal step providing for outside arbitration that is not under the unilateral control of the management. Management gives up that unilateral right to impose its interpretation of the contract on the union and gets, in return, the union's commitment and obligation not to strike over grievances during the life of the agreement but, instead, to submit disputes to the grievance and arbitration procedure.[4]

The main elements in achieving a sound grievance procedure, according to Pegnetter and Levey, are to:

1. develop a management team approach to contract administration
2. ensure involvement in understanding the contract terms at all levels of management
3. train supervisors in proper methods in investigating and handling grievances
4. establish a program of evaluation of the grievance performance of the management team
5. organize a system for monitoring the grievance and contract administration activities under the labor agreement[5]

The U.S. Supreme Court provides a clear indication of the importance of the grievance procedure:

> The grievance machinery under a collective bargaining agreement
> is at the very heart of the system of industrial self-government.
> Arbitration is the means of solving the unforeseeable by molding

Exhibit 2-1 Example of a Contract Grievance Section

ARTICLE XXXI
GRIEVANCE PROCEDURE

1. A grievance shall be defined as a dispute or complaint arising between the parties hereto under or out of this Agreement or the interpretation, application, performance, termination, or any alleged breach thereof, and shall be processed and disposed of in the following manner:

Step 1. Within a reasonable time (except as provided in Article XXIX), an Employee having a grievance and/or his/her Union delegate or other representative shall take it up with his/her immediate supervisor. The Employer shall give its answer to the Employee and/or his/her Union delegate or other representative within five (5) working days after the presentation of the grievance in Step 1.

Step 2. If the grievance is not settled in Step 1, the grievance may, within five (5) working days after the answer in Step 1, be presented in Step 2. When grievances are presented in Step 2, they shall be reduced to writing, signed by the grievant and his/her Union representative, and presented to the grievant's department head or his/her designee. A grievance so presented in Step 2 shall be answered by the Employer in writing within five (5) working days after its presentation.

Step 3. If the grievance is not settled in Step 2, the grievance may, within five (5) working days after the answer in Step 2, be presented in Step 3. A grievance shall be presented in this step to the Personnel Director or Administrator of the Employer, or his/her designee, and he/she or his/her designee shall render a decision in writing within five (5) working days after the presentation of the grievance in this step.

Failure on the part of the Employer to answer a grievance at any step shall not be deemed acquiescence thereto, and the Union may proceed to the next step.

Anything to the contrary herein notwithstanding, a grievance concerning a discharge or suspension may be presented initially at Step 3 in the first instance, within the time limit specified in Article XXXI, Section 1.

Without waiving its statutory rights, a grievance on behalf of the Employer may be presented initially in Step 3 by notice in writing addressed to the Union at its offices.

2. All time limits herein specified shall be deemed to be exclusive of Saturdays, Sundays and holidays.

3. Any disposition of a grievance from which no appeal is taken within the time limits specified herein shall be deemed resolved and shall not thereafter be considered subject to the grievance and arbitration provisions of this Agreement.

4. A grievance which affects a substantial number or class of Employees, and which the Employer representative designated in Steps 1 and 2 lacks authority to settle, may initially be presented at Step 3 by the Union representative.

Source: Collective Bargaining Agreement between League of Voluntary Hospitals and Homes of New York and District 1199, National Union of Hospital and Health Care Employees, Retail, Wholesale and Department Store Union, AFL-CIO, 1980–1982.

Exhibit 2-2 Example of a Contract Arbitration Section

ARTICLE XXXII
ARBITRATION

1. A grievance, as defined in Article XXXI, which has not been resolved thereunder may, within fifteen (15) working days after completion of Step 3 of the grievance procedure, be referred for arbitration by the Employer or the Union to an arbitrator selected in accordance with the procedures of the American Arbitration Association. The arbitration shall be conducted under the Voluntary Labor Arbitration Rules then prevailing of the American Arbitration Association.

2. The fees and expenses of the American Arbitration Association and the arbitrator shall be borne equally by the parties.

3. The award of an arbitrator hereunder shall be final, conclusive and binding upon the Employer, the Union and the Employees.

4. The Arbitrator shall have jurisdiction only over disputes arising out of grievances, as defined in Section 1 of Article XXXI, and he/she shall have no power to add to, subtract from, or modify in any way any of the terms of this Agreement.

5. A grievance contesting a discharge may, within fifteen (15) working days after completion of Step 3 of the grievance procedure, be referred for arbitration to an arbitrator appointed by the American Arbitration Association from the Panel of twenty-six (26) arbitrators listed in Schedule B annexed hereto [not included here]. Said arbitrators shall serve on the Panel for the period of one (1) year or until the termination date of this Agreement, whichever is sooner, and shall have jurisdiction only over grievances contesting discharges. The Association shall appoint said arbitrators in strict rotation order at the time it receives a request for the appointment of an arbitrator from the Panel in a discharge case. If an arbitrator so appointed is unable to hold a hearing in a particular case for any reason within one (1) month from the date of his/her appointment the Association shall appoint the arbitrator next in rotation, and so on. Should none of the arbitrators on the Panel be available within such one (1) month period, then the Association shall promptly (a) so notify both parties and (b) proceed to process the case pursuant to Section 1 of this Article XXXII, unless the parties consent to a later hearing date before the arbitrator so appointed. The fees of the arbitrators shall be borne equally by the parties. In the event of a vacancy in the Panel, the parties shall expedite the selection of an arbitrator to fill the vacancy or vacancies. If, at the expiration of the term of the Panel of Arbitrators the parties are unable to reach agreement as to arbitrators to serve thereafter, the parties shall select such arbitrators by each submitting a list of fifty-two (52) names and in turn striking such names until twenty-six (26) names remain.

Source: Collective Bargaining Agreement between League of Voluntary Hospitals and Homes of New York and District 1199, National Union of Hospital and Health Care Employees, Retail, Wholesale and Department Store Union, AFL-CIO, 1980–1982.

a system of private law for all problems which may arise and to provide for their solution in a way which will generally accord with the variant needs and desires of the parties. . . . The grievance procedure is, in other words, part of the continuous collective bargaining process.[6]

NOTES

1. Louis V. Imundo, *The Effective Supervisor's Handbook* (New York: AMACOM, Division of American Management Associations, 1980), p. 120.

2. Herbert L. Marx, Jr., "Arbitration from the Arbitrator's View" in Norman Metzger, ed., *Handbook of Health Care Human Resources Management* (Rockville, Md.: Aspen Systems Corporation, 1981), p. 830.

3. Norman Metzger, *Personnel Administration in the Health Care Industry,* 2d ed. (Jamaica, N.Y.: S. P. Medical and Scientific Books, Division of Spectrum Publications, Inc., 1979), pp. 263–264.

4. Richard Pegnetter and Samuel Levey, "Grievance Procedures in Health Organizations," in Norman Metzger, ed., *Handbook of Health Care Human Resources Management* (Rockville, Md.: Aspen Systems Corporation, 1981), p. 771.

5. Ibid., p. 784.

6. *United Steelworkers of America v. Warrior and Gulf Navigation Co.,* 363 U.S. 574, 581 (1960).

Chapter 3

How To Practice Sound Labor Relations

POLICY AND PRACTICE

The supervisor is management's day-to-day interpreter of institution policy. This individual administers the union contract and applies the organization's rules and regulations. The working relationship between employees and employer is impacted daily by the supervisor's ability to apply, consistently and fairly, personnel policy and provisions of the union contract. The contract is negotiated personnel policy.

Much of what once was determined unilaterally by management before the union gained recognition as the bargaining agent for a specific unit must, after such recognition, be the subject of negotiations; the final results are included in a collective bargaining agreement. Once the union is certified, all matters relating to wages, hours, and working conditions, which the nonunion hospital or home decided without outside interference (so long as its policies were in compliance with state and federal laws) must be determined through the collective bargaining process. The contract that is finally signed is, in effect, a statement of mutually agreed upon personnel policies.

There often is a significant difference between what individuals say they do and what they actually do. That dissimilarity is the difference between policy and practice. People are judged by their practices, not by their intentions. A policy is a statement of intention, but that intention is only a collection of words until somebody begins to apply it in everyday actions. That is why so many organizations spend time, money, and intense training effort to make sure their supervisors understand the provisions of the union contract; know how to interpret them properly; are keenly aware that their decisions (in most cases) constitute precedent; and understand that in any dispute between management and labor that goes to an arbitrator, that third party will be more likely to base the judgment on actual practice than on the language of the contract. In fact, many a hard-won management right that has been obtained by collective bargaining has been tossed away in the various departments by careless administration or supervision that has failed to exercise it.

It is not the language of the agreement that is significant, it is what the supervisor understands that language to mean. Experts may negotiate the contract but they don't administer it. That's the job of the supervisor. If that job is performed inefficiently, inconsistently, and haphazardly, the best agreement ever written will be of little value to the organization.

Supervisory decisions establish precedent through practice. It is the supervisor who has the responsibility of making on-the-spot decisions on employee problems. These decisions frequently require coming up with instant interpretations of the agreement. Therefore, it is important for each supervisor to have a precise understanding of what each contract clause means and how it should be applied. With this knowledge, they build consistency into hospital labor relations.

THE NEED FOR CONSISTENCY

A union agreement is a guide to the various aspects of employee relations. No guide ever written can be absolutely precise. In other words, no group of experts can sit down and develop a book of instructions that gives exact directions on what to do in every conceivable situation that might arise in labor-management relations. Certainly, the union-management agreement is not the document in which to find such instructions.

Essentially, each of its provisions outlines basic principles that govern some part of the employer-employee relationship. Since contract language sometimes may be subject to several interpretations, major problems arise if policy is interpreted in varying ways by different supervisors. Therefore, it is the responsibility of senior management to provide supervisors with the training required to ensure that they make uniform interpretations of the contract and understand the need for consistency in the efficient management of human resources.

THE IMPORTANCE OF PRECEDENT

Supervisors must use judgment in making decisions in employee relations matters. They are responsible to the organization as a whole and their decisions must be consistent with precedent. Discipline is a prime example. If an employee who is guilty of breaking a rule must be penalized, supervisors must follow the old management precept: make sure that the punishment is appropriate for the offense. Moreover, it is essential that the procedures as outlined in the union contract have been observed so that decisions cannot be set aside later for technical reasons, i.e., failure to give the proper number of oral and written reprimands before suspending or terminating an employee.

However, after reviewing the employee's record, considering all of the facts involved in the case, and assuring compliance with the rules of the discipline procedure, the supervisor makes a judgment call as to the extent of the penalty imposed on the employee. Since no two people view any human relations problem in exactly the same way, there always will be differences as to the appropriate action for a specific infraction. However, if these varying opinions are not contradictory to policy in general, there will be a reasonable consistency in contract administration.

CHECKLIST FOR CONTRACT ADMINISTRATION

There are specific rules that a supervisor must observe to ensure that administration of the union contract is consistent with institutional policy. Black and Ford offer these rules to supervisors:[1]

1. *Mark the boundaries of the problems.* For instance, if you are handling a grievance, you must be able to define the employee's complaint and determine whether or not it is a true grievance under the terms of the contract. If you understand the worker's gripe, you can explain to him what you can or cannot do to resolve it. In making such an explanation, use clear, nontechnical language. The supervisor who resorts to legalistic double talk to get himself off the hook in a tight situation, or to excuse his inability to take action, undermines worker respect for his leadership.
2. *Don't be a sugar-coater.* Buttering up the union delegate or organizer, appeasing the tough customer, or disregarding organizational policy to give a good guy a break are sure methods of throwing clinkers into the machinery of sound human resource/labor relations management. Settle each grievance on an equitable basis, and don't let personalities enter into your thinking.
3. *Keep good records.* Sound records are the backbone of an effective management. When you make a decision that affects an employee, it may become a grievance, and that grievance could go to arbitration. If you are forced to defend your action from hazy memory, you may wind up behind the eight-ball. But not if you have a written record of the details of matters that might become a grievance. Your records

allow you to use your decisions as precedents in handling future cases, or they will supply your management with facts on which to base its case should the argument go beyond you in the grievance procedure to the hearing in Personnel or Labor Relations or on to arbitration.

4. *Keep communications going.* Your superior should be told of key decisions, especially if they affect unusual situations. If you make a mistake and your boss knows about it quickly, it can be corrected before it leads to trouble. Keep employees informed also. If a worker knows the reason why you have denied her grievance, and your reasons make good sense, she is much more likely to accept your decisions with understanding.

5. *Be careful in writing replies to grievances.* Confine your answers to the specific complaint and make sure you have covered it. Avoid written commitments unless you are absolutely sure you can live up to them.

6. *Live up to your responsibility.* It's your job to know the union agreement and to apply its terms. If you need advice or help to do this job, see your superior. But don't try to play labor relations by ear. That's a good way to end up with a tin one.

"Management has the right to manage; the employees have the right to grieve" is an old industrial relations maxim. It simply means that the power of decision is vested in management; management has the right to act. The supervisor, when faced with a problem that involves the direction and control of the work force, must decide what to do. However, if the employee (or the union) believes that the supervisor's action represents a violation of the agreement, or that the interpretation of the provision of the agreement on which action was based is wrong, the worker has the right to challenge the judgment by using the grievance procedure. When this happens, the supervisor must be able to justify what has been done.

Any grievance in which an employee (or union) thinks the contract has been ignored or violated, or that it has been interpreted incorrectly, may be taken to arbitration unless specifically stated otherwise in the contract. Most grievances revolve around the following issues:

1. dismissal and suspension
2. rules enforcement and the administration of discipline for infraction of these rules
3. hours of work, including the distribution of overtime
4. promotions, demotions, and transfers
5. wages

6. vacations and holidays
7. seniority and layoff
8. shift premiums

A prevalent charge against supervisors who take disciplinary action is discrimination. Supervisors will find insurmountable difficulties if they do not follow correct technical procedures or do not have records available to demonstrate the fairness of the decisions or actions being grieved.

Actually, grievances are a good barometer of employer-employee relations, and certainly supervisors' skill in handling them is important to their success in management. Labor relations has become complex and juristic. Procedures are technical and time consuming to some, and it may seem a useless effort to go through a long and complicated hearing in order to dismiss an incompetent, insubordinate, and obviously guilty employee who, in preunion times, could have been fired out of hand, with no questions asked.

However, the modern supervisor knows that if the union contract is violated, even unintentionally, an employee who has been penalized for a serious infraction of rules will be back on the payroll—completely or at least partly exonerated. No supervisors want this to happen; it appears to undercut their authority and weakens their control over the work force.

ROLE OF THE UNION REPRESENTATIVE

The union is the employee's advocate. The union representative at grievance hearings usually is the delegate who speaks for that worker or at least appears with the employee to assist with the case. The delegate is elected by fellow employees and has the job of protecting their rights and advancing the interests of the union. The delegate may have received special instruction on grievance handling. This individual is supposed to have an expert knowledge of the union contract and to be especially resourceful in taking full advantage of technical mistakes that management representatives may have made if that will protect the rights of the client— the employee. The delegate is well aware of the importance of precedent or past practice, and in the grievance hearing has the initiative, or at least is on the offensive.

Why? The old precept holds—management has the right to manage, the employee the right to grieve—and the employee with a grievance is asking the supervisor to defend a decision or action. The employee's grievance usually is based on the fact that the agreement has been administered improperly, unfairly, or inconsistently or that it actually has been violated.

When such a claim is made, the supervisor must justify the action or decision and must demonstrate that the employee (and the union) is mistaken.

GUIDE TO ADMINISTERING THE PROCEDURE

Supervisors must call on all of their management skills in handling grievances: planning, judgment, communications, and decision making. The following guide may be helpful in administering the formal grievance procedure. Supervisors should:

1. *Be certain that the complaint is admissible to the grievance procedure.* In other words, be sure that the complaint is based on an alleged violation of the contract or an argument over its interpretation.
2. *Don't be influenced by emotional arguments.* Study the facts and base the decision upon them. Remember that their job is to interpret and administer company policy, not to create it by making special rulings or decisions that are inconsistent with precedent.
3. *Make sure records are in good order.* Records give information on the grievant's past performance and should provide data such as the employee's disciplinary citations, individual attendance and punctuality records, and written performance evaluations. Facts of this kind may be useful in justifying the action and can be most persuasive in an arbitration case.
4. *Don't forget the importance of past practice.* A settled grievance becomes precedent. The supervisors' objective is to keep practice consistent with policy so they must be certain their decisions are in line with the wording of the union agreement and with hospital policy in general.
5. *Be precise in replying to a written grievance.* Make certain that the words written to deny a formal grievance are explicit. Refer to the provision(s) of the union agreement, personnel policy, or established and communicated department rules that provide the authority for the decision.
6. *Understand the importance of consistency.* Observe institutional policy and practice in grievance handling. If a special situation comes up that compels making a ruling that varies from regular practice, explain the reasons why to the employee and enter that explanation in the written record. Also make certain that the union and the employee realize that an exception in one case does not

constitute precedent. Finally, before taking such a step, it's wise to discuss it with a superior or with the personnel or labor relations departments.

7. *Establish a reputation for honesty and fairness.* Live up to promises or don't make them. Don't make idle threats. If employees trust supervisors and think they are reasonable and objective, supervisors won't be swamped with manufactured grievances. The union will know the supervisors can't be intimidated.

8. *Understand the role of the union delegate.* That individual is the spokesperson for employees. The delegate may have to pursue a grievance that has little merit, because of employee pressure. The delegate can't be expected to make supervisors' work easier. Whatever supervisors do, they must not lose their tempers when the delegate goads them or makes exaggerated or untrue statements. The delegate is in a political position and holds it just so long as fellow employees keep electing that person. Naturally, the delegate wants a reputation as a person who will stand up to management.

9. *Don't make unofficial agreements with the delegate.* Keep everything above board and avoid secret understandings with union representatives. They may not be able to deliver what they promised. The delegate might not even be elected next time.

10. *Don't be thrown off stride by phony grievances.* Occasionally, as part of its deliberate strategy, a union will stir up grievances. An experienced supervisor can tell the difference between the phony grievance and the real one. If a large number of the former kind are filed, something is wrong.

11. *Build a good foundation for the case.* The organization's success at arbitration hearings may depend on how well supervisors have handled grievances at the initial stage. So supervisors must make sure both the facts of the case and their judgment in applying the rules of the agreement will persuade an arbitrator that they acted justly.

12. *Keep up with developments in labor relations.* When the labor agreement is revised, supervisors must make sure they know the intent of each new provision. When grievances come up that seem a little unusual or beyond their experience, they should seek counsel on what to do. Observe the technical regulations of the contract.

Real skill is required in grievance handling. It takes thorough knowledge of the union agreement, an intelligent understanding of the relationship of institutional policy and practice, the ability to communicate, and, finally, the capability to provide firm and consistent leadership.

Supervisors must never forget that it is the institution's right to direct and control the working activities of employees and to apply discipline when necessary. Supervisors must remember that they represent the organization and that their decisions and actions are management's decisions and actions. They must respect the duties of the delegate and know that it is that individual's job to represent employees and the union, and that in doing that job the delegate may occasionally use a worker's grievance to gain an advantage for the union. Supervisors must treat employees fairly and not perceive worker grievances as challenges to their authority or as attempts to stir up trouble.

SUGGESTIONS FOR GRIEVANCE HANDLING

The following suggestions can be useful in handling grievances. Supervisors should:

1. *Be sure they know the importance of management's rights.* Management must negotiate with the union on all matters relating to wages, hours, and working conditions. Therefore, the rights that it secures for itself as described in the union agreement are hard-won points, some of which may have been paid for by expensive bargaining concessions. It is imperative that such rights should not be lost through supervisors' lack of will to enforce them—and die they will, if they are not enforced.
2. *Be cautious in interpreting accordion clauses.* An accordion clause is a provision in the union contract that often is couched in vague terms and open to differing interpretations, based upon broad or general wording. It is the quicksand of collective bargaining agreements. Such clauses can be anathema to supervisors ill prepared to interpret them in the way the management negotiators intended. Supervisors often must rely on judgment and common sense in applying such clauses. Where there is doubt as to meaning or intent, discretion is the better part of valor: check it out with the source. This may mean calling the personnel or labor relations departments. For supervisors to admit that they do not understand a clause is not a failing. Meal time, leaves of absence, and coffee breaks are a few examples of provisions that may be construed as accordion clauses because of their nonspecificity.
3. *Be certain they know the intent of a provision before they make a decision regarding it.* Consistent administration of the labor agreement is a management "must." Therefore, if not quite sure of the

exact meaning of a contract clause, supervisors never should just take a guess; they must check and make sure before they act.

4. *Don't logroll grievances*. Don't play an intentional delaying game or postpone decisions. That is a sure way to build up trouble. The unsettled grievance can be a time bomb and when it finally explodes, the consequences may be serious. The best approach to a grievance is to solve it by fast, fair, and decisive action.

5. *Be aware of the implications of decisions*. Supervisors' decisions may establish precedents. Therefore, it is wise to make sound decisions in labor relations even if this causes delay because they must seek advice from superiors or from personnel or labor relations.

6. *Don't make the union delegate a partner*. That's codetermination. Supervisors, and they alone, are responsible for representing management. So keep the union delegate advised of decisions after they are made, not before, and above all, don't let that person make supervisors' decisions for them.

7. *Do their homework*. There is no substitute for preparation. A well-documented presentation based on fact, not feeling, is a sure-fire winner.

WRITING A REPLY TO A GRIEVANCE

When answering a worker's grievance—even orally—supervisors put their knowledge of labor relations into the official record. They also display their skill at analyzing a problem and coming to a sensible and factual conclusion. To make the right response, an orderly process is absolutely necessary. Since writing replies to grievances, and even answering them orally, causes some supervisors difficulties, the following suggestions are useful:

1. The supervisor's written answer should include a combination of the following:
   a. A brief, well-organized summary of the key points at issue is a basic element.
   b. A summary statement that gives a specific answer to the grievance is helpful.
2. Supervisors must know the facts of the case in order to reply properly to a grievance, i.e., which ones are pertinent, which have no bearing:
   a. The past record may not be material if the employee is grieving a layoff but may be vitally important if grieving discipline for violating a departmental rule.

   b. It may not be too important to refer to past practice if a specific clause in the contract is absolutely clear. However, if the agreement is silent or somewhat vague on a matter, it is essential to check past practice.
3. Supervisors, replying to a grievance, should be certain to answer such questions as:
   a. *Who?* Is the worker's right name given? Is the job listed properly?
   b. *What?* Has the grievance been restated as presented?
   c. *Where?* Is it known for certainty where the incident took place?
   d. *When?* Have the day, month, year, and time of day of the incident been given?
   e. *How?* Are the facts straight? Are supervisors sure their decision is in line with the labor agreement and can stand up against the union's arguments? If not, check with the department head or with personnel or labor relations.
4. Supervisors should be sure to assemble the specific facts relating to the grievance. Here are questions to be answered:
   a. Can the facts be proved by the record?
   b. Can the facts be supported by reliable witnesses?
   c. Is anything being taken for granted?
5. Supervisors should check on how well the facts from witnesses can be established. Their testimony may be very important in settling grievances, especially in discipline cases. In judging the validity of testimony, supervisors should make certain:
   a. The witness is competent to state information as fact from personal knowledge of the dispute.
   b. Of the extent to which the supervisor can rely on the judgment of the witness in supplying accurate information: What pressure will bear on the person? For instance, what emotional factors will influence the testimony of a fellow employee of the grievant, another supervisor, or a hospital patient?

CHECKLIST FOR REPLY TO A GRIEVANCE

In developing responses to employee grievances, supervisors should:

1. Make sure their answers are fair and respect the rights of the employee as well as protecting the interest of the institution.
2. Make sure, before writing an answer, that they have reviewed all applicable clauses in the agreement and considered prior grievance settlements in view of the precedent they may have established.

3. Be sure they have not been misled by surface similarities between the current grievance and earlier ones that have been settled. Two grievances frequently look alike at a glance but after a close study, the facts may prove different.
4. Be sure, when checking past settlements for precedents, that they did not just seek cases that supported their own arguments and ignored all others.
5. Make certain they answered the specific points of the grievant's complaint. Some supervisors tend to write replies that avoid the essential issues.
6. Be positive that the reply is based on facts. Supervisors should not omit any just because they may weaken their argument. Include them but be sure that the weight of evidence is on the side of their decision; otherwise it is likely to be reversed at the next step of the grievance machinery or in arbitration.
7. Do the best possible to write an absolutely objective and impartial answer. If supervisors show prejudice in the reply, it hurts their case.
8. Be certain that the answer is clear and concise and that the meaning cannot be mistaken. If not sure about the clarity of the reply, read it to another supervisor to see whether that person understands exactly what is meant.
9. Try to make the answer persuasive enough to get employee acceptance. A reply to a grievance may be factually correct but written in such harsh, unyielding language that it can unnecessarily annoy or anger the grievant or the union. This may accomplish its immediate purpose but cause other grievances.
10. Try to write a reply that clarifies the employee's understanding of the situation. This then becomes a guide for the future.
11. Get advice from superiors or from personnel or labor relations if not sure how to reply to a particular grievance. It is better to be safe than sorry.

UNCOVERING THE REAL CAUSES OF GRIEVANCES

If supervisors can differentiate between the underlying causes of grievances and their surface appearances, they can set about solving what may be real labor relations problems. The way to do this is to develop a system for grievance analysis. The following methods usually produce the desired answers. Supervisors should take an objective look at the whole grievance, then break it down into its parts:

1. Study the grievance in a general way. Is it related to others that have been filed recently? Is it admissible to the grievance procedure under the terms of the contract or might it be described as an expression of a worker's discontent or frustration?
2. Analyze the specific parts of the grievance. What actual conditions— job-related or other—are the source of the worker's complaint? Are the conditions complained about the causes or merely the targets of the arrows of the employee's discontent? What is the true agenda of the grievant?
3. Study the personality of the employee. What kind of person is the individual? What motivations are there? How are the employee's relations with other workers? Is the person simply a habitual complainer? Are the reasons for grieving more complex? Does the person have political ambitions in the union and seek to show fellow workers that this person will stand up to management?
4. Consider how the grievance ties in with what is known about the worker as a person. How do supervisors get along personally with the employee? Does the grievant have home, marital, or money problems or any other off-the-job emotional problems that might affect on-the-job behavior? Is there a reason, aside from those stated in the grievance itself, why the individual might be unhappy? Any one of these factors might have an adverse affect on attitude and cause the employee to look for issues on which to file a grievance.

MANAGEMENT RIGHTS

Critical to many grievances and arbitrations is the question of management rights. To establish management's right to take specific action, the contract often is the sole document referred to by arbitrators. Both parties usually have agreed that any rights not restricted by the collective bargaining agreement reside with management.

However the question as to whether management rights clauses should be expressly included in a contract has been hotly debated over the years. Most managements feel that the right to manage the business or administer the institution is solely theirs. In any case, it should be clear that when the administration enters into a collective bargaining agreement with a union, it no longer has the sole authority to administer the facility. Limitations are delineated clearly in each contract clause.

The management rights clause is a mandatory subject of bargaining. There are three differing concepts about management's freedom of action after concluding a collective bargaining contract:

1. Management maintains full freedom to act except as its functions are limited or surrendered in the agreement (residual rights).
2. Management cannot make a unilateral change in a major condition of employment during the term of an agreement even though the contract does not deal with the subject proposed.
3. Management remains free to bargain, and then to act, on all matters not covered by the contract.

The very fact that the National Labor Relations Act[3] mandates an obligation to bargain limits the right of an institution to manage anything conceded to the union in the contract. The National Labor Relations Board has held that a broad management-rights clause in no way relieves administration of its obligation to bargain. The board has rejected the residual rights theory. Management is free to insist on a rights clause, but the board and the courts have found bad-faith bargaining if an employer makes extreme demands in this area. Although three-fourths of all collective bargaining agreements contain a management rights clause, there is no "best clause" example to present here. Institutions do need as much protection as they can get in enunciating the right to manage.

The collective bargaining agreement does, indeed, limit management's action in situations outlined in each of its clauses. Management does well to define the areas in which the union waives its rights since most arbitration awards and court decisions have indicated that any administration decision or action that affects the employment relationship should be discussed with the union representing the employees, unless clearly reserved to management. If administration wishes to retain its freedom to act in specific areas without recourse to the grievance and arbitration procedure, then a management rights clause is the proper place to define those areas.

There are two major categories of management rights clauses. One is a brief, general clause not dealing with specific rights but with the principle of management rights in general. The other is a detailed clause that clearly lists areas of authority reserved to management. The key areas of authority in such a clause are the right to:

1. manage and administer the hospital and direct the work force
2. hire, discipline, and transfer
3. introduce new or improved methods or facilities
4. promulgate rules of conduct
5. set quality standards
6. discontinue jobs
7. decide employee qualifications
8. subcontract work

An example of a brief encompassing clause follows:

> The management of the Hospital and the direction of the work forces are vested exclusively with the administration, subject only to the restrictions and regulations governing the exercise of such rights as are expressly provided in this contract.

An example of a more definitive management rights clause is:

> Except as in this Agreement otherwise provided, the Hospital retains the exclusive right to hire, direct, and schedule the working force; to plan, direct, and control operations; to discontinue, to reorganize, or to combine, any Department(s) or Branch(es) of operations with any consequent reduction or other changes in the working force; to hire and lay off employees; to promulgate rules and regulations; to introduce new or improved methods or facilities regardless of whether or not the same cause a reduction in the working force; and in all respects to carry out, in addition, the ordinary and customary functions of management. None of these rights shall be exercised in a capricious or arbitrary manner.

Most practitioners believe that the primary purpose of the clause is to retain for management the right to direct all business policies. Given that purpose, it is recommended that the clause be as broad as possible. It is difficult to enumerate all of management's rights.

Experts now agree that unless a right is expressly reserved in the labor contract, it may be in jeopardy. To lessen the jeopardy, some negotiators suggest the inclusion, in addition to the broad management rights clause, of a "savings clause." Such a clause reserves to management the residual or leftover rights it would have retained regardless of the collective bargaining agreement. It specifically directs attention to the preservation of rights, powers, or authorities that the institution had prior to the signing of a collective bargaining agreement, except as limited by the contract itself. These management rights are not to be interpreted as being all-inclusive but merely indicate the type of those that belong to and are inherent to management.

DOCUMENTATION OF MINIMAL VALUE AS EVIDENCE

The terminal step in the grievance procedure is arbitration. In presenting management's case to the arbitrator, documentation may be more persuasive than other testimony. Documentation stands with the eyewitness in its impact on sustaining management's action, but weak documentation can damage (or at least not help) administration's case. Following are examples of documentation that have minimal value as evidence at arbitration; that is, arbitrators discount or minimize such weak evidence:

1. letter to employee, no return receipt requested: (a) forwarded intradepartmentally, or (b) forwarded to employee's home.
2. letter to employee, return receipt requested, where employee does not sign receipt
3. verbal communication from supervisor to employee in informal setting, i.e., party, bar, gathering, etc.
4. private evaluation counseling session where no specific reference to infraction is written
5. hearsay information
6. general statements by supervisor to departmental employees in groups and addressed to no one specific worker
7. statements by supervisor to union representatives
8. rescinded warning notices
9. verbal warnings without witnesses and with no notes in departmental file
10. verbal warnings with notes to file but without witnesses

NOTES

1. James M. Black and Guy B. Ford, *Front-Line Management* (New York: McGraw Hill Book Company, 1963), pp. 242-244.

2. *See* J.C. Phelps, *Management's Reserved Rights: An Industry View—Management Rights in the Arbitration Process* (Washington, D.C.: BNA Book, 1956), p. 102; *see* A. Cox and J.T. Dunlop, *The Duty to Bargain During the Term of an Existing Agreement,* 63 Harv. L. Rev. 1097, 1110–1117, 1125 (1950).

3. National Labor Relations Act (Taft-Hartley) 61 Stat. 136 (1947).

Chapter 4

Preparing the Case for Arbitration: An Attorney's View

Allan H. Weitzman, Esquire

The attorneys preparing to represent a hospital in arbitration proceedings usually analyze each grievance in light of their experience in prior cases and in recognition of what arbitrators look for in deciding the merits of a case. There is no magic to the attorney's inquiries in preparation for arbitration. Therefore, supervisors can adopt the same approach in handling grievances on a day-to-day basis.

Two types of cases go to arbitration, those involving

1. discharge and discipline
2. contract interpretation

Each has its own set of standards as to why an arbitrator will uphold the hospital's position in some situations and not in others.

STANDARDS FOR DISCHARGE AND DISCIPLINE

Regardless of whether the discipline imposed is discharge, suspension, or warning, the question before the arbitrator generally is the existence or nonexistence of "just cause" for the action. The collective bargaining agreement, however, does not define "just cause." Consequently, the criteria used to determine whether "just cause" exists have been developed over the years in thousands of arbitration decisions.

Each case comes with its own particular set of facts, and in some situations the criteria discussed next may not be applicable. Before imposing discipline, supervisors should study each of these enumerated factors in the same way that the hospital's attorneys will analyze them in preparation for the hearing and the arbitrator will review them in making a determination.

1. Did the employee know that discipline could result from the conduct at issue, i.e., was the worker warned?

As an element of fairness, arbitrators will not allow employee discipline in situations where the individual did not know that the conduct could lead to a penalty. Therefore, it must be established that the employee was given notice that the actions could lead to discipline. The warning can be in the form of printed rules and procedures, an individual written communication previously placed in the employee's file, or supervisory statements confirming that the worker had been advised earlier that such conduct was prohibited (this last can be corroborated by file memoranda).

It must be noted, however, that not all disciplinary actions require a warning. Offenses such as insubordination and theft are so serious that an employee can be expected to recognize, without warning, that such conduct is punishable. Wherever possible, supervisors considering discipline in situations involving insubordination should endeavor to ensure that another representative of management witnesses the insubordinate act. It also is helpful to order the employee to perform the particular task in question and explain that a refusal to do so will result in discipline.

2. Is the discipline imposed reasonably related to the ordinary, efficient, and safe operation of the hospital?

Here, the employer has the burden of demonstrating the business necessity for imposing discipline for violation of the rule. Accordingly, if an employee is being suspended for absence or lateness, the hospital must show why that individual's attendance is required on a punctual basis and how the absence hurts the overall operation of the worker's department or area.

Another example would be in the case of a no-smoking rule. In an operating room and in other sensitive areas, the hospital could ban smoking and could discipline employees for violation of the prohibition because the rule is closely tied to health and safety. The same rule, however, may not be applied to a clerical area unless necessitated by the orderly, efficient, or safe operation of the hospital.

An additional comment is warranted in regard to safety. In situations where the employee can demonstrate that a managerial order would seriously jeopardize the individual's personal safety and/or integrity,[1] the worker may have a defense if fired for insubordination.

3. Was there an investigation before imposing discipline?

All employees are entitled to a chance to defend themselves before discipline is imposed. Therefore, each employee must be told the precise nature of the offense and be given an opportunity to justify the actions or defend the conduct. This means that the investigation should be completed before the grievance procedure begins.

Even though a full investigation is required, the investigation must not be of such duration that it will appear to the arbitrator as if there is no urgency to the situation or that the hospital condones such conduct for considerable periods of time. Likewise, when a disciplinary decision is reached, it must be announced as soon after the investigation as practical.

In some situations the hospital is justified in reacting immediately before the investigation can be completed. In these circumstances, an employee who represents an imminent threat to the hospital can be suspended, pending the investigation, with the understanding that the disciplinary decision will not be made until after the inquiry and that the worker, if found innocent, will be restored to the job with full back pay.

4. *Was the investigation fair and objective?*

Management should be careful to separate the roles of prosecutor, judge, and witness. For example, the supervisor involved in an insubordination situation should not, because of personal connection to the facts of the case, be the same management official who decides whether discipline should be imposed. Before performing the judicial function, a second management official should closely question the supervisor involved in much the same way as the hospital's attorneys question their witnesses in preparation for an arbitration hearing.

5. *Was there substantial evidence supporting the discipline at the time it was imposed?*

Facts that come to the attention of the hospital after discipline has been imposed normally are not considered by an arbitrator in deciding whether there was just cause for the penalty action. Therefore, only the evidence that was known to the person at the time of making the decision concerning discipline must be able to stand on its own in support of the ruling. Consequently, the decision maker should seek out all potential witnesses and evidence, rather than accept only the data provided by those who come forward to volunteer information.

6. *Have the hospital's rules, orders, and penalties been applied evenhandedly and without discrimination?*

When the union can demonstrate that similarly situated employees have received no discipline or even a lesser form of punishment for the same offense, arbitrators normally will modify the penalty imposed. Therefore, hospital management must ensure itself that it is acting in a consistent and uniform manner before deciding on the level of discipline, if any, to be imposed.

Of course, on the issue of discrimination, the union has the burden of proof to establish that other employees, by name, have been treated differently. Nevertheless, before management imposes discipline, the hospital should thoroughly investigate any potential candidates whose name may be used by the union. This seeks to avoid claims of discrimination by revealing the past practice governing the type of offense involved.

7. *Does the penalty fit the crime?*

In deciding on the nature of the discipline, several factors must be considered:

- the seriousness of the offense
- the employee's prior work record
- the employee's seniority

Based on these factors, the level of discipline can be assessed properly. Thus, minor offenses may warrant discharge for an employee with a long record of similar or other offenses in the past, but a long-term worker with a clean record can be dealt with less harshly.

8. *Will the hospital be able to prove its case?*

Although this criterion may sound as though it should be determined by the hospital's attorneys, it should be examined from a layman's perspective before the case goes too far. Hospital supervisors should be concerned with questions such as whether the witnesses sound believable, whether the evidence has been obtained in an improper manner, whether it is based solely on hearsay, and whether the witnesses will be in a position to testify on the hospital's behalf at the time of the hearing.

STANDARDS FOR CONTRACT INTERPRETATION CASES

The arbitrator's primary responsibility in contract interpretation cases is to determine and carry out the mutual intent of the parties. It is with this in mind that hospital supervisors should administer the provisions of the collective bargaining agreement.

In most instances, hospital negotiators have done their best to ensure that the language of the contract is clear and unambiguous. Where a supervisor is administering this type of language, the task is relatively simple. Indeed, in situations where an arbitrator is asked to interpret such language, the analysis will proceed no further than the determination that the wordage is clear and unambiguous on its face.

However, when a problem arises concerning vague and ambiguous contract terminology, the task becomes more difficult. In such situations, the arbitrator will use various contract interpretation techniques to determine the parties' mutual intent.

The emphasis here is on the word "mutual." A supervisor should not act solely on the basis of individual interpretation of the language or of personal perception of what the hospital alone intended by those words.

Other situations may arise that were not contemplated by the parties when the language was drafted. Consequently, the arbitrator will be forced to make certain assumptions regarding what the parties would have done about this type of problem had it occurred to them at the time the contract was written.

When confronted with a problem of contract interpretation, supervisors can profit by analyzing the language in the same light as it would be viewed by the hospital's attorneys in preparation for the arbitration and, ultimately, as viewed by an arbitrator. Although there are numerous contract interpretation aids, ten of the most common ones are listed next.

    1. *Interpretation in light of the custom and practice of the parties.*

When interpreting ambiguous contracts, arbitrators find that what parties do pursuant to that language is more significant than what the words may actually say. Thus, past practice is a vital tool in interpreting contract language. It is important to consider what is and what is not a past practice. The two main elements of a past practice are that it is (1) mutual and (2) of sufficient generality and duration. Isolated instances do not amount to a past practice and the failure to object to a past practice out of ignorance does not constitute mutuality. Therefore, before relying on what may otherwise seem to be a past practice, the true nature of the activity should be examined.

    2. *Interpretation in light of the law.*

When one interpretation of the contract would make the agreement valid and another would make it unlawful, the arbitrator will presume that the parties intended to draft a lawful provision.

3. *Agreement to be construed as a whole.*

Sometimes the intent of the parties cannot be determined by looking at a single word or phrase. Thus, the entire contract must be examined to make a proper interpretation in light of the overall context.

For example, if a question arises concerning the rights of a part-time employee under a specific contract provision, the entire agreement should be examined to determine what other references are made concerning such workers. This will enable a supervisor to paint an overall picture for dealing with part-time employees and thereby shed light on the proper interpretation of the clause in question.

Another illlustration of this principal concerns situations in which there are two possible interpretations of a contract provision, one of which would make meaningless a provision in a different part of the contract. Normally in such a situation the arbitrator will adopt the interpretation that retains the efficacy of the other contract clause.

4. *Avoidance of harsh, absurd, or nonsensical results.*

Where, for example, one interpretation of an ambiguous bumping clause will result in the layoff of 30-year employees while 5-year ones retain their jobs and another interpretation would preserve the employment status of the 30-year workers, the former would be rejected in order to avoid a harsh, absurd, or nonsensical result.

5. *To express one thing is to exclude another.*

Arbitrators often construe words in a series to be limiting rather than illustrative. For example, if a clause read "seniority shall govern for layoffs and transfers," an argument that seniority also governs for overtime would be rejected.

6. *Doctrine of Ejusdem Generis.*

Under this doctrine (which means "of the same general class"), where general words follow an enumeration of specific terms, the general words will be interpreted to include or cover only items of the same general nature as those enumerated. Using the same example, if a clause were to read, "Seniority shall govern in all cases of layoff, transfer, or other adjustments of personnel," the words "other adjustments of personnel" would not include overtime but probably would include promotions.

7. *Interpretation in light of bargaining history.*

When the language is clear and unambiguous, it is improper for an arbitrator to alter its meaning by looking at the record of prior negotiations. Ambiguities, however, can be explained by the minutes of the bargaining sessions or oral testimony of those who were present. For this reason, a supervisor who was not present at the negotiations may not have sufficient information to interpret an ambiguous contract clause without discussing the matter with one or more members of the bargaining committee.

It also is important to examine the exact language of the proposals and counterproposals that ultimately led to the wording being interpreted. Proposals are instructive in that they may demonstrate that one side or the other had asked for something in bargaining that did not ultimately appear in the final contract language. From this it can be argued that an arbitrator cannot include in a contract a provision that a party was not able to obtain through negotiations.

8. *Prior settlements as an aid to interpretation.*

At a large metropolitan hospital, it is possible that the interpretation question confronting a supervisor has come up before. If so, a grievance may have been filed, and its resolution will be instructive as to how the parties intended to interpret the language. Prior grievances brought by the union that were not taken to arbitration would indicate the union's assent to the hospital's position. On the other hand, grievances that have been resolved in the union's favor would make it difficult to adopt a contrary interpretation in subsequent cases.

Beyond this, there may even be arbitration decisions bearing directly on the issue at hand or shedding some light on how an arbitrator may view the problematic language.

It should be noted, however, that some grievance settlements are without prejudice or precedent and cannot be used as a basis for argument in favor of one interpretation or another. Similarly, discussions concerning the settlement of a grievance or possible compromise may not be presented to the arbitrator as evidence of a concession on behalf of the other party.

9. *Industry practice.*

If a hospital is a member of a multiemployer association for collective bargaining purposes, its bargaining agreement in many respects is identical to that of other member hospitals. Consequently, an interpretation of a particular clause at other hospitals either by practice or arbitration decision can shed light on how the same language should be interpreted here. An industry practice also would be significant to an arbitrator in attempting to interpret an ambiguous contract clause.

10. *Interpretation in light of reason and equity.*

Sometimes arbitrators interpret a contract without any consideration of the criteria above but rest their conclusion on the basis of their sense of fairness and reasonableness. On the other hand, a result may be reached that the arbitrator deems to be fair and reasonable and it is issued in the guise of one of the criteria listed above.

It is because arbitrators often impose their personal views of fairness and reasonableness in contract interpretation cases that it is difficult to provide assurance that one viewpoint on the agreement ultimately will be adopted under more objective standards. Consequently, it is crucial for supervisors to weigh their actions in light of a neutral standard of fairness and reasonableness in making individual decisions concerning contract interpretation.

NOTE

1. Hezeler, Zinc Co. 8-LA 826.831 (1947).

Chapter 5

Expecting the Unexpected in Arbitration

Herbert L. Marx, Jr.

The incident giving rise to the grievance has occurred. The grievance has been filed and carried through the various procedural steps under the collective bargaining agreement. A compromise offer has been made and rejected. The matter is headed for arbitration. An arbitrator has been carefully selected or drawn from the parties' agreed-upon list. Last-minute settlement efforts are unavailing. The time and place for the arbitration hearing are set. The case is thoroughly prepared—documents and records are at hand, witnesses briefed.

Now what?

What can reasonably be expected to occur? What surprises are in store? What can you do about them? When the day or days after hearing are complete, will you be well satisfied that the most effective presentation has been made, or will you have a cold and clammy feeling of impending disaster?

Here are 12 signposts or direction signals, drawn from an arbitrator's experience in a wide variety of cases. What management does about the signs or signals remains a matter for its judgment and action. That it should anticipate, observe, and then act on them is, however, essential to effective arbitration presentation. While some of these by their nature may be of more concern to one party than the other, most of these signs and signals are applicable both to management and union.

So, if participants thought they were ready for anything, they should take a look here first.

1. WHAT IS THE ISSUE?

The arbitrator cannot proceed with the assigned task until assured by the parties as to the precise nature and limit of the issue on the table. Thus the arbitrator usually will ask the parties to "frame the issue." In some instances, they will have saved arbitral time by agreeing in advance on the wording of the issue. Since the decision will be final and binding, the arbitrator wishes to ensure that the judgment will be imposed in as narrow a range as possible and will not be presenting findings on factors or issues the parties had not introduced and on which they had not sought rulings.

Each side gets an opportunity to say how the issue should be phrased. Inexperienced advocates will attempt to slant the question, but that won't wash with the other side, obviously. The question must state the issue simply and in a neutral fashion—argument comes later. But there can be variety. A disciplinary case provides less difficulty but is not without challenge. Should the issue be: "Was the discharge of Sarah Brown for just cause?" or "Was the discharge of Sarah Brown for cause?" or, "Did the management violate Article X, Discipline, by the discharge of Sarah Brown?" The answer depends on the wording of the collective bargaining agreement and possibly other factors. It is essential to think through which is most accurate.

Matters become a little more complex if the case deals with contract language interpretation. Each side wants to phrase the question to reflect the best light on its case. Usually it is to both parties' advantage to be as precise and limited as possible, specifying contract clauses allegedly violated, names of grievant(s), and date of occurrence.

If the parties agree they simply want a yes-or-no answer, one question is sufficient. If not, a subsidiary question must be included, asking the arbitrator to determine the proper remedy if the grieved action is not sustained in whole or in part.

What happens if the parties simply cannot agree on the formulation of an issue, despite the arbitrator's entreaty to do so? Beware. The alternative is that the arbitrator will exercise the right to: (a) frame the issue unilaterally at the outset, based on the discussion presented; (b) state the intent to frame it during or after the close of the hearing; or (c) simply declare that the issue is, "What shall be the disposition of Grievance #74?" For the parties, any of these alternatives is not as satisfactory as a mutually agreed upon statement of the issue.

> *Warning Sign:* While avoiding a question slanted toward one side or the other, it is important to persevere with the adversary in framing a mutually agreeable question.

2. SHOULD WE BE HERE AT ALL?

Since virtually all grievances are brought to arbitration by the union, this is a show-stopping question, raised, if at all, by management. For one reason or another, the effect of this question is: Yes, we've followed the grievance procedure and have agreed to sit before an arbitrator, but the arbitrator should not or may not hear the merits of the case.

It is not the purpose here to examine the substance of challenges to arbitrability, whether on a procedural basis (missed time limits, skipped grievance step, etc.) or a substantive basis (subject matter outside the contract, etc.). Rather, what happens if this issue is raised? The party challenging arbitrability must do so at the outset of the hearing and at the time of the framing of the merits issue. This leads to the formulation of a preliminary or "threshold" issue such as, "Is the grievance of Sarah Brown arbitrable?" or "Is the grievance of Sarah Brown inarbitrable because of time limits?" etc. Assuming the question is obviously not totally frivolous or dilatory, the arbitrator will hear it. But no matter whose responsibility it is to go forward first on the merits issue, it is the burden of the party who raised the arbitrability issue to move promptly on that point.

If the health care institution is going to raise an arbitrability issue, it is best that the other side knows of this ahead of time; nothing is gained by surprise because the arbitrator will ensure that the other party has full opportunity to reply.

> *Warning Sign:* If the institution is contesting arbitrability, it must do so at the outset and be prepared to go forward. If faced with an arbitrability issue from the other side, it should expect the arbitrator to permit it but may insist on a fair opportunity to respond, and—if it is a surprise—the time to prepare.

3. WHO REPRESENTS THE GRIEVANT?

This is a question for management—and occasionally for the union. The grievant arrives with a personal representative (not from the union) and requests that the case be put forward by that agent, usually a lawyer. What now?

The arbitrator will state that control of the representation is in the hands of the parties appointing the referee—management and union. The next step is up to the union. If the official union representative wishes to cede presentation of the case to the grievant's personal representative, and states that the outside counsel represents the union for this purpose, the arbitrator generally will accept this despite possible resistance from management. The theory: each party has the right to designate its representation. If the union states that presentation of the case remains in its hands, this of course will be honored by the arbitrator.

Suppose the grievant then insists that the personal representative at least be present for the proceedings? The arbitrator no doubt will consult both parties, who often will agree to that presence. What if one or both parties want the outside counsel excluded? There is no pat answer here. Each side must be prepared to defend its position. Again, the arbitrator can be expected to follow a joint request from the parties but may find it difficult to decide if only one party seeks exclusion.

What about other "strangers" to the proceedings (reporters, agency officials, etc.)? These usually can be readily excluded upon request of even one party.

> *Warning Sign:* Arbitration is a private matter, in the hands of the parties. But if the grievant asks for a personal representative to be present, the parties should consider carefully the effects (possibly in other forums) of demanding exclusion.

4. WHO GETS TO LISTEN?

Before testimony begins (and sometimes before opening statements), one party or the other requests sequestration of witnesses, often a dramatic move provoking emotional response. What actually is meant is exclusion—that is, witnesses for one party should not be in the room to hear testimony of others for the same side on the theory that their later statements may be influenced or shaped by what they have heard. The arbitrator invariably will grant such requests, even if objected to by the other party. By permitting exclusion, no right to evoke testimony is hampered and the exclusion will ensure to the arbitrator that a witness is uninfluenced by what others may have said.

More complex is a request for exclusion of the other parties' witnesses. For example, management wants union witnesses out of the room while it presents its own witnesses. If both parties agree, the arbitrator will grant the request. However, if one party (in this instance, the union) resists, then the arbitrator may not go along, reasoning that there is no purpose served to prevent witnesses from hearing adverse testimony.

However, there should be no exclusion of the grievant, who is entitled to hear the entire case. Likewise, at least one management principle usually remains to advise the institution's representative (attorney); this exclusion can be handled by having this principal testify first.

> *Warning Sign:* Sequestration or exclusion is not unreasonable.
> If requested of its own witnesses, management shows added

confidence in the probity of their testimony by not resisting such a request. On the other hand, if management asks exclusion of the other party's witnesses, this may provide an assist in proving lack of credibility—or, if the witnesses' testimony is later found to be totally consistent, the union's presentation will be somewhat strengthened.

5. 'OBJECTION! OBJECTION! OBJECTION!'

It is well known that arbitration proceedings need not follow specific rules of evidence—federal court or otherwise. But one procedure almost universally followed is to permit "objection" to questions that opposing counsel believes are irrelevant, leading, repetitious, based on false premise, bad form, or many et ceteras. Not for discussion here is the basis on which arbitrators sustain or overrule such objections. Rather, the purpose here is to review the manner in which such objections are made or responded to.

In making an objection, it is sufficient to use the single word "Objection" immediately after the question is posed. The arbitrator then will prevent the answer from being made (or ignore it, if it is made) and will ask the basis of the objection. This must be stated succinctly to the arbitrator, not to opposing counsel. The arbitrator usually will ask the poser of the question for comment, then rule—with or without an explanation, as the individual sees fit. At this point, it is advisable to let it lie. Win or lose, the point probably has been made. Further discussion will not, be assured, change the ruling. Objection to an answer rather than to a question gets far less consideration from the arbitrator. The answer always can be dealt with in cross-examination.

> *Warning Sign:* The arbitrator is not the same as an untutored jury and can recognize improper testimony when it is presented. By all means, objections should be made when it is believed it is important to do so but they are easy to overdo and thus lose their effectiveness.

6. 'YOUR WITNESS'

The union's counsel has completed questioning a witness for the employee's side. The management attorney doesn't quite believe (or actively disbelieves) some of the testimony, or is confident that the questions and answers so far have not given the arbitrator the whole story—even if the testimony was factual as far as it went. The arbitrator indicates by a nod of the head or a phrase that it's management's turn. What now?

Experienced trial lawyers who also happen to present arbitrations will find no relevatory truth in the next few comments, but for all others, this could be crucial.

Ah, cross-examination! The opportunity to destroy both the credibility and the factual basis of the adversary's case. And besides, the job is not done properly unless the cross-examination exceeds the direct examination in length, and unless each redirect question is followed by several more questions on recross-examination.

Don't believe it. In arbitration (and perhaps in all adversary proceedings as well) management's case is best made for the arbitrator by its own witnesses, its own exhibits, and its own documents. Of course, if management (and/or its attorney) believes an adversary's witness is not giving credible testimony, then cross-examination may help to bring this out but it requires great skill and care to accomplish.

What about the facts that such witness did not testify to but that management wishes the arbitrator to have? Before seeking to elicit them in cross-examination, it is important to consider first whether it would not be easier and more effective for management to bring these facts out through its own witness in later direct questioning. If the institution's case has been presented already, it is always permissible to request the opportunity for a rebuttal witness, even one who has testified previously.

An arbitrator sometimes gets the feeling, in the alternation between direct and cross, that each side is convinced it must have the "last word" from the witness. The trouble is, this succession of "last words" always gets less precise and less useful.

A good rule on cross-examination: Don't ask a question unless the answer is known in advance. Exceptions to this can be made only at grave risk to management's own case. Here's an abbreviated example of all the above. It concerns the grievant's explanation of his absence from work:

> Grievant: My dog bit someone and I had to take him by car to the vet.
> Cross-Examiner: Why didn't you let your wife take the dog?
> Grievant: Dog's too vicious. Can't drive and hold the dog.
> Cross-Examiner: Aha, so how did *you* do it?
> Grievant: My wife drove, and I held the dog.
> (Cross-examiner wipes egg from face.)
>
> *Warning Sign:* While cross-examination may be necessary to some degree, it never is as effective as testimony of a party's own witnesses.

7. LETTING THE CAT OUT OF THE BAG

Watch out. Here it comes.

The department head, in the midst of otherwise relevant testimony, says something like: "When I met with the union committee, they offered to forget the whole thing if I reinstated Jim right away without back pay." Or, the grievance chairperson says: "The personnel director offered to give Hannah the posted job if she agreed to a six-month trial period."

Suddenly, the arbitrator hears there was an unaccepted offer of compromise settlement—and he has been told it either accidentally or deliberately as indication that one side or the other isn't too sure of its position.

Bad news for the arbitration process. The grievance procedure works effectively only if both parties can talk and listen with open minds and occasionally propose a resolution that is not in complete support of either side's stance. Most experienced practitioners know, when compromise does not work, that it obviously is improper to mention it to the arbitrator, and not for the obvious reason alone of influencing the case in hand; such disclosure is bound to deter possible future compromise resolutions of other matters.

Introduction of such compromise talk, as soon as it is anticipated, should be objected to vigorously. Sometimes the arbitrator will gather what is about to be presented and will prevent the disclosure. The day is not lost, however, if that offer of compromise somehow does get into the record, by innuendo or directly. The arbitrator is fully capable of disregarding it.

> *Warning Sign:* It is important to establish a firm and lasting agreement with the other party that offers of compromise have no place in the arbitration procedure. Witnesses should be warned of this. The offended side should react quickly if the other side is the transgressor and should have faith in the arbitrator's ability to ignore the disclosure.

8. 'WHAT'S THAT GOT TO DO WITH IT?'

The matter has to do with a missed overtime opportunity and the grievance (and perhaps the formulated issue before the arbitrator) specifically mentions the overtime article. At the hearing, the issue of alleged discrimination suddenly is raised.

Can the defending party blow the whistle ("Objection!") at such a turn of events?

There are no pat answers as to how arbitrators will deal with such situations. Sometimes the collective bargaining agreement requires a grievance to specify the exact contract terms allegedly violated; if such is the case, the arbitrator usually will be guided accordingly. If there is no such language, the theoretical approach is that (to use the example cited above) the employer has not had a previous opportunity to answer a charge of discrimination since the grievance dealt only with overtime. Should not the employer have such opportunity to answer and possibly convince the union of its position before the arbitrator is called upon to rule on the charge? This may have substantial weight in the decision as to whether to entertain the new basis for the grievance.

The arbitrator generally will not permit a union to process a case substantially different from the one previously put forward in the grievance itself and through the grievance procedure. It also is generally true, however, that arbitrators will permit the parties to use contractual language broadly if doing so reasonably supports the known facts of the incident.

This also works similarly when it is management that introduces a new direction. The grievant has been discharged for absenteeism, and that is all that was cited in the discharge notice. Suddenly management introduces testimony about poor work performance. To prove the propriety of the disciplinary action itself, it is now too late to introduce new charges. The union can properly say that it has had no opportunity to consider this at an earlier stage, and a weak case cannot be fortified by adding new charges at this point.

To both of these general principles, however, there are at least two exceptions:

1. To explain its interpretation of a contract clause, a party may properly refer to other sections for support or differentiation. This does not let the issue stray from the alleged violation of the originally cited clause.
2. In disciplinary matters, reference to the employee's general record of work performance and previous discipline generally is admissible (although some agreements have language to prohibit this). This may not be done, however, to prove the case but simply to support or attack the severity of the penalty if and when the charge properly on the table has been proved to the arbitrator's satisfaction.

Warning Sign: The arbitrator is limited to the stated issue presented at the hearing. Attempts to change the nature of the case at the arbitration table usually come far too late. An arbitrator who permitted the case to start over on different grounds would be improperly ignoring the entire purpose of the grievance procedure.

9. 'WE NEVER SAW THAT BEFORE'

The parties have gone through all the steps of the grievance procedure and have had several opportunities to argue their positions with each other on a bilateral basis. Records have been brought forth and previous grievances or arbitrations have been cited in support. Now, at the arbitration hearing, the adversary produces a new document, not discussed previously in the grievance procedure, and does so either in closing argument or through a witness. What can be done? There are various answers.

Sometimes exhibits are created for the sole purpose of the arbitration, such as a table showing the employee's absenteeism in the past year or a list of the qualifications of previous holders of a disputed position. These usually are acceptable to an arbitrator, with the important proviso that the party submitting the exhibit offers a witness to describe how the material was collected, what it means, and who is able to respond to requests for additional information that may not be included. In effect, documents created for arbitration are simply a welcome substitute to extensive testimony covering the same information.

Other arbitration cases and previously settled grievances are offered frequently. The arbitrator is, of course, not bound by such decisions (unless there is specific contract language to that effect) but takes them as further argument. However, the arbitrator will ensure that the opposing party will (1) have the opportunity to review and comment on such decisions at the hearing and/or (2) may grant additional time to that side to comment in a posthearing brief (see below) and/or (3) may grant that party the right to present other contradictory decisions.

Two warnings about the submission of other arbitration awards in support of a case:

1. Presenting simply a summary or excerpt of the awards will not be useful to the arbitrator. Both the arbitrator and the adversary can rightly expect that management will submit the entire awards so they can determine whether it *is* the same white horse with brown spots *and* a bushy tail. Management may, and should, of course, indicate to the arbitrator which portions it believes are particularly supportive of its position.
2. Management should read the entire awards to itself before offering them. It is remarkable how often they may contain reasoning or dicta that support the adversary's view.

Occasionally one party or the other will bring in a document that clearly is material to the case, that existed prior to the action grieved, and that was not disclosed previously to the other party. This is bad news to a smooth and reasonable arbitration hearing and should be avoided if at all possible. Arbitrators' reactions will vary, depending as always on the circumstances and the gravity of the document. An objection to its introduction may be sustained, or the parties might be directed to confer with each other to see whether the new information changes the views of the side that has not seen the document. The "surprised" party will certainly be given the time necessary to defend, possibly including a recessed hearing.

In the totally ideal situation (rarely found), none of these points will be a problem because the parties in their mature and mutually trustful relationship will have disclosed ahead of time to each other the material they plan to introduce to the arbitrator.

> *Warning Sign:* If management is surprised by new or undisclosed information, it should insist, as a minimum, on time to rebut the material or perhaps reconsider its position in light of the information. If management brings in a surprise, it can expect a similar reaction from its adversary.

10. 'MY WITNESS IS OUT OF TOWN'

The hearing nears its end when opposing counsel says to the arbitrator: "I have another witness, but she couldn't be here today, although I tried hard to arrange it. I request that we have another hearing day to hear this witness." Management opposes a delay in the completion of the hearing, noting that today's hearing was scheduled some weeks ago.

The arbitrator is responsible to the parties not only to hear the case but to do so with concern for the time and expense involved. The arbitrator will be loath to exclude testimony unless it can be shown that there is no convincingly reasonable explanation for the witness's absence. The parties may be asked if they are willing to hear in summary what the witness would have said if present; this requires consent of both sides. The arbitrator may inquire whether someone else is available who can give substantially the same testimony, or if the witness's material would be merely cumulative to that previously given. It behooves the parties at least to attempt such a resolution.

If all this fails, however, it must be remembered that the arbitrator is bound to hear all the testimony and evidence to protect the integrity of the decision. Thus, absent any other solution, a further hearing may well be ordered (but only on an early and certain date).

> *Warning Sign:* The arbitrator seeks both to avoid delay and also to ensure hearing each party's complete case. If the parties cannot agree on a method to resolve the problem of the missing witness, then the chances are strong that an additional hearing day will be scheduled.

11. THE IMPORTANT SECONDARY QUESTION

If the arbitrator finds that the discipline was properly administered and fully warranted, or that there was no agreement violation in a dispute over contract language, then the arbitrator need not be concerned with remedy. But if this is not the case, a remedy must be fashioned. The arbitrator is always deeply concerned to know the parties' views on what that solution should be. Especially in questions of remedy involving contract interpretation, there often are wide variations.

As part of the closing presentation, it should not be assumed that the other side is showing weakness if it offers guidance to the arbitrator concerning remedy, depending on the findings on the issue. Likewise, a party will be remiss if it fails to do so. The arbitrator takes it as a certainty that each side believes its position on the merits issue is totally correct. This will not change just because a party discusses the possibility that the arbitrator may not agree with that side fully or at all. As a matter of logic, the arbitrator—when remedy is required—will come closer to satisfying both sides if made aware of each side's views.

> *Warning Sign:* If the arbitrator has a "remedy" question—which it may or may not be necessary to reach—management should present its views. It will not be taken as any indication of the institution's lack of confidence in its main presentation.

12. 'ANYTHING ELSE?'

The testimony is at last completed and the arbitrator looks to both parties, asking "Anything else?" In some instances, the parties by regular practice file posthearing briefs, so no problem remains except to set a date for their receipt. In some instances, oral summary is the practice, and this too goes forward to close out an eventful day.

However, there can be an instance such as when liability is running—an employee is discharged and out of work, or the question is a rate of pay for certain work that goes on from day to day. An early decision is advantageous to both parties, either to erase the overhanging liability (by sustaining the discharge or confirming the present rate of pay) or paying and terminating the liability (by reinstating the discharge or paying a different pay rate). At this point, however, the adversary asks to file a brief and needs a month to prepare it. Management is ready for oral summary and has no interest in a brief.

Just as the arbitrator must hear all the testimony and receive all the evidence, so must each party also be provided with an opportunity to make its best argument. It follows that the arbitrator has little or no basis for refusing to receive a posthearing brief (unless the contract prohibits it), although possibly urging a reasonable time for its submission. In this instance, management is left with the opportunity to go ahead and present an oral summary without a brief of its own or to file a brief simply because its adversary is doing so.

> *Warning Sign:* Only the parties themselves can determine by mutual agreement what limits to put on the type and length of their presentations. Where no such agreement exists, the arbitrator is almost always required to grant the right to both parties to make their full presentations as they see fit.

*   *   *   *   *

These detours in the course of a simple exposition of the facts before the arbitrator are part of the pattern of the adversary procedure known as arbitration. The list is not exhaustive. Planning ahead can keep management out of some of these digressions or assist it in grappling with them if they occur.

If, in the next case, all of these happen, management will have had a bad day at the arbitration table. If half of them occur, its skill has been well tested. If none of them happen, it has a great relationship with its adversary—and maybe could have settled the matter in the grievance procedure before it ever got to the arbitrator.

In addition to those even dozen points just discussed, another list can be helpful as a guide: the Ten Commandments for the Arbitration of Disciplinary Grievances shown in Exhibit 5-1.

Exhibit 5-1 Guideposts in Labor Arbitration

TEN COMMANDMENTS
FOR THE
ARBITRATION OF DISCIPLINARY GRIEVANCES
by
Herbert L. Marx, Jr.

I. THOU SHALT HONOR THY LABOR AGREEMENT IN ALL THINGS, FOR THOU HAST NO OTHER AGREEMENT BEFORE THIS.

II. THOU SHALT NOT DISCIPLINE IN ANGER OR CONFUSION, BUT RATHER IN CALM REFLECTION AND MATURE JUDGMENT.

III. THOU SHALT ALWAYS REVIEW THE EMPLOYEE'S RECORD, FOR THE WISDOM OF THE PAST IS FOREVER, OR UNTIL THE TIME LIMIT ON USING PAST ACTIONS RUNS OUT.

IV. THOU SHALT NOT GRIEVE FRIVOLOUSLY, LEST THY TREASURY BE EMPTIED AND THY GRIEVANT END UP WORSE THAN WHEN HE STARTED.

V. THOU SHALT INVESTIGATE AND DOUBLE-CHECK AND IN THIS THOU SHALT NOT TRUST THY GRANDMOTHER, YEA, EVEN NOT THY MOTHER.

VI. THOU SHALT GRIEVE WITHIN FOURSCORE YEARS AND TEN OR WITHIN THE TIME LIMIT, WHICHEVER MAY COME SOONER, LEST THINE EFFORTS BE IN VAIN.

VII. THOU SHALT NOT BEAR FALSE WITNESS AGAINST THINE ADVERSARY; NEITHER SHALL THY WITNESS ANSWER QUESTIONS HE IS NOT ASKED, NOR SHALL HE VOLUNTEER.

VIII. THOU SHALT BE MODERATE AND FAIR IN ALL THINGS, EVEN UNTO COMPROMISE, BUT THOU SHALT KEEP A FIRM STRING ON THINE OFFER IF THINE ADVERSARY DOES NOT ACCEPT.

IX. THOU SHALT NOT ABUSE THINE ADVERSARY'S WITNESS, FOR IN HIM MAY LIE THY FUTURE COMFORT AND SALVATION.

X. THOU SHALT KNOW THAT THINE ARBITRATOR IS THE POWER AND THE GLORY AND THE WISDOM AND THE MAJESTY, AND SO THOU SHALT NOT EXPECT THAT EVERY TIME HE SHALL FASHION YOU A SILK PURSE OUT OF YOUR SOW'S EAR.

Part II

14 Arbitration Cases

This section presents a series of 14 arbitration cases intended to provide invaluable real-life experience. Each case is presented first as the award actually was issued. In many of the arbitration awards that include the background of cases, we have exercised editorial privilege to alter grammar and/or structure, to the extent possible, but never the facts. These decisions were written by arbitrators. To maintain anonymity, the arbitrators are not identified, nor are any of the participants; instead, initials are used. The seven areas are:

1. absenteeism
2. insubordination
3. dishonesty
4. patient abuse
5. alcoholism
6. theft
7. quality of performance

Two cases are presented in each category, one sustaining management's position, the other reversing it. Each case is followed by an analysis of the event, management's action, the union's position, and the arbitrator's rationale. Each analysis puts specific emphasis on the reasons why management's position was sustained or reversed. Alternatives are proposed, where appropriate, that might have improved management's case.

Readers now are transported into the arbitration room.

Chapter 6

Arbitration Cases: Absenteeism

CASE 1: DISCHARGE DURING SICK-OUT

The Issues Presented

1. Did the hospital have cause for the discharge of grievant, A.M., which took place on January 22 [1980]?
2. If not, what shall be the remedy?

Facts, Contentions, and Discussion

Grievant has a date of employment of November 24, 1972, and was a Printer A-1 in the Print Shop. The Hospital discharged him because it contends that he missed work without justification on January 21, [1980], that he was on final warning because of a notice dated August 10, and that he had a very bad personnel record—one of the worst per its witness M. S.—which justified imposition of the penalty of discharge.

The Union contends that grievant's work history shows the opposite; he worked in the Print Shop from 1972 to 1980 with two warning notices, the last of which was in August 1978. It continues that he was terminated for acting in concert with others in being absent from work as part of an organized and planned work stoppage; but he submitted a doctor's note which management did not question and was the only employee in the department who was terminated; this was unfair because his peers acted the same way and were not punished.

The arbitrator has reviewed all of the detailed evidence, including submitted documents, and the arguments, in arriving at his decision in this case.

In summary, the evidence, direct and circumstantial, demonstrates that on January 21 grievant's department and others in the Hospital were the subject of a selective sick-out which was a concerted action on the part of the employees involved, and that grievant participated in it. Grievant's contention that he was sick that day is unconvincing; his testimony as to the chronology of his visit to the doctor is internally inconsistent; the doctor's note does not state that he was seen by the doctor on that date; grievant was confronted the next day by his supervisor, Print Shop Manager A.D., and informed that he was facing a suspension pending a termination hearing for being absent as part of a sick-out; according to grievant, he assumed the notice was a discharge notice; he had a doctor's note with him at the time but did not present it to his supervisor.

In addition, he testified to returning twice to the office of the medical clinic and yet did not at any time obtain a doctor's note setting forth when he was seen, his diagnosis, treatment and prognosis, something which he could easily have done. The doctor's note that grievant did produce was dated January 25th and received by the Hospital several days later. And the Hospital's investigation did not substantiate that grievant had seen a doctor on January 21st.

Following discussion with the Union, a third-step decision by the Hospital, dated July 25, rescinded similar final warning notices issued on January 22nd to five other Print Shop employees, who had no prior disciplinary records, for the same activities. Thus, the Hospital relies upon grievant's past record as the basis for treating his employment offense differently from those of the others in his department.

Article XXIX, Section 1, of the contract provides:

> No employee shall engage in any strike, sit-down, sit-in, slow-down, cessation or stoppage or interruption of work, boycott, or other interference with the operations of the Employer.

It seems apparent that the actions of grievant and the other participants on January 21st were in contravention of that contract provision; but the Hospital did not discharge anyone but grievant; it contends that he was the only employee on final warning.

The Hospital points to grievant's many alleged violations of its policy, contending that many were serious and pointing out that they included latenesses and unexcused absences. While the alleged dishonesty regarding the doctor's note was considered in connection with the Hospital's determination of penalty, that note was not stated by the Hospital at the time as one of the bases for the disciplinary action taken.

The January 22nd warning notice refers to absence on January 21st in concert with others as part of a planned and organized work stoppage in the Printing Department, in direct violation of the terms of the collective bargaining agreement; it states that the excuse of sickness offered for grievant's absence is unacceptable. The last statement is not the same as saying that grievant was discharged for tendering a false doctor's note.

The notice goes on to state that grievant's action had serious life-threatening consequences toward patients at the Hospital and represents conduct which cannot be tolerated; that grievant had been counseled in the past for excessive and continued lateness and unauthorized absence from his department; it concludes that he was suspended pending a termination hearing. Such a hearing did not occur; at the Union's request, an expedited third-step hearing was held on January 24th.

The final warning of August 10th was related to unauthorized absence from the job in grievant's failure to report to the employee health department when he said he would. It was accompanied by a one-day suspension which was cancelled by agreement with the Union. There is no language in the warning notice, such as one might expect in a final warning, to the effect that any repetition of the conduct involved would lead to further disciplinary action up to and including discharge; it is denominated a "final warning" only by an "X" in a box which is so marked.

That warning predated the incident and issue by some seventeen months; grievant was a seven-year employee when discharged; he apparently was not warned or disciplined further in the interval between the August 1978 final warning and his discharge.

The next previous warning notice is dated January 13, 1977, and has to do with unauthorized absence from the job and failure to report after calling in on three different dates. It also states that grievant had been late 90 times over an unspecified period; but there is no showing that he was disciplined for such a large number of latenesses. This warning notice states that A.D. [the Print Shop Manager] would review grievant's record in two months and if there was no improvement would issue a final notice with suspension and then discharge. Thus this warning notice does qualify as final warning; it too is checked off as one.

The next previous warning notice is dated October 20, 1975, a first warning for alleged lateness on the average of two to three times per week. It relates the problem, refers to verbal warnings for the prior two years, but does not contain language warning grievant of the consequences of failure to improve his conduct.

The Hospital prepared a further warning notice dated February 6, 1980, some sixteen days after the incident at issue. Hospital witness Assistant Director for Support Services M.S. contended that it was understood by the Union that this further information would be furnished because the document could not be prepared in time for the expedited hearing; the Union contends that there was no such understanding; it objects to consideration of the document.

It does appear that the Hospital was able to prepare the original warning notice dated January 22nd; the following one appears to have been written up to strengthen the discharge case against grievant. This is so even though M.S. testified that all incidents were discussed at the third-step grievance hearing. For example, the notice includes a reference to alleged large numbers of latenesses in 1977, 1978 and 1979 (88, 82 and 84 times, respectively); it is difficult to understand why if that were the case, grievant was not more seriously disciplined at the time those infractions occurred.

The notice recites that on many occasions grievant was "counselled, warned and admonished" for improper behavior affecting job performance and follows with eleven instances of such alleged statements to grievant. It concludes by stating that grievant's employment record indicates a total unwillingness to respond to warnings and counsellings and has provoked his termination effective January 21st. But the original January 22nd warning notice states as the major reason for the termination grievant's participation in an unauthorized work stoppage.

Testimony of A.D. as to the eleven alleged oral warnings shows an incident of alleged insubordination in which grievant called A.D. a sneak for checking up on changes on his timecard and A.D. ordered him out of his office; the timecard is dated August 12, 1978; as to that and the other oral instances, although grievant was told what he was doing wrong, they appear to have been more in the nature of counsellings than warnings as that term is commonly understood in labor relations; only one or two involved telling grievant of specified further discipline if he did not correct his conduct; one of those instances, having to do with calling in late and not appearing at all, appears to have been merged in the warning notice of January 13, 1977.

Thus it appears that while grievant had a record of being involved in a number of infractions of Hospital work rules, the Hospital, particularly per M.S., placed greater importance upon these incidents after the January 21st incident than it did at the times they occurred. The much later preparation of the warning notice which includes the oral warnings also leads to the inference that the Hospital was attempting to buttress its position in discharging grievant while not discharging others in his department.

While reference to an employee's prior record is proper in most cases in assessing the appropriateness of a penalty for an infraction, and while grievant's past record as substantiated here is relevant, its use must be subject to a rule of reason under which management may not assess an employee with responsibility for past incidents which it did not assert at the times in question.

Discipline must be fairly administered to employees; it was not in two respects here: the adding on of the alleged oral warnings after the event which precipitated the discharge and the Hospital's lack of even-handed treatment of A.M. as compared to the other employees in his department. As a further example of the first point, A.D. testified as to one of the oral incidents, involving grievant's leaving his work area without authorization, that A.M. called him a liar but that he was not disciplined for it.

Still, grievant's unconvincing attempts to convince management that he was sick that day evidence a lack of the honesty an employee owes his employer; it may be considered as part of his overall employment record in determining the appropriate penalty for the violation at issue. This was a serious incident; A.M. certainly has on this record a less than ideal record of past employment, particularly when compared with the clear employment records of the other employees in his department who were involved in the sick-out.

Grievant's actions merit strong disciplinary action, but not action of the severity of discharge. A.D. acknowledged at the arbitration hearing that normal procedure would be for a suspension to intervene between warning notice and discharge; the one assessed against A.M. in 1978 was rescinded.

A.M. testified that he got a job at a bank through an indirect referral from A.D.; he started there February 13th, worked one month and then found changed hours not satisfactory and left; he returned [to the bank] in July and has worked there continuously since. Grievant's last salary at the Hospital was $252.16 a week; he started at the bank at $240 but with different hours; since he returned [to the bank] he has been earning $200. He also testified that in that job, he must pay for medical benefits. He did not receive unemployment insurance while not working.

In considering all of the factors set forth above and arriving at a fair balancing of them, the arbitrator determines that the Hospital did not have cause for the discharge because [discharge] is excessive on the facts of the case, that A.M. is entitled to be reinstated to his former position with all job rights and benefits, and that a proper make-whole remedy would be for the Hospital to pay him eight weeks' wages at the rate he was receiving at the time of his discharge. That will be the entire monetary remedy; with it goes accumulation of seniority for that eight-week period.

AWARD

1. The Hospital did not have cause to discharge grievant, A.M., as it did on January 22nd because that penalty is excessive on the facts of the case.

2. The Hospital shall immediately reinstate grievant to his former position with all job rights and benefits and shall make him whole by promptly paying him a sum comprising eight weeks' pay at his pay rate in effect at the time of discharge, $252.16 per week. That shall be the total monetary remedy; for the same eight-week period, grievant shall be considered to have accumulated seniority. The balance of the period during which grievant was absent from his job shall be considered a disciplinary suspension.

Analysis of the Case

One of the traps in which managements often are snared is called, for want of a better term, "catch-up." This type of disciplinary action is a planned buttressing by management of its otherwise weak position, based upon years—and often a horrendous record—of improper employee actions. The weight of the total employee disciplinary record is not insignificant. Earlier chapters emphasize the role of documentation and underscore the effects of corrective discipline and progressive disciplining on arbitrators' decisions. Some of the critical underpinnings for an effective disciplinary program bear repeating.

The primary concern in disciplining employees is to salvage them, not to scrap them. Although punishment is part of disciplinary action, it is not the primary part. Arbitrators are interested in the progressive nature of disciplining. Progressive disciplining involves oral reprimands (including counseling), written warnings, suspensions, and termination, which is defensible where the behavior infraction is serious or is *preceded by the aforementioned steps*.

Arbitrators consistently have found against employee warning notices that cite as reason for discipline past behavior that has not been dealt with by management at the time of the occurrence. Arbitrators have reasoned that employees not appropriately counseled or disciplined for unacceptable performance are not necessarily aware that their record is unacceptable and thus are prone to continue in that pattern. This is at the core of the disciplinary system.

A.M.'s terminal warning notice inappropriately written more than two weeks after his discharge on January 21 included references to 254 latenesses over a three-year period (1977-1979), and "many occasions" on which he was counseled for unsatisfactory behavior. For these offenses, A.M. received no written warnings. Rather, management chose to include these previous infractions in a second terminal warning notice two weeks after issuing its original warning. This "catch-up" or "second-thought" action on the part of management is both suspect and unsupportable.

Discipline not fairly and equitably administered is unfair and discriminatory. A.M. was the only one of six employees involved in the job action to be disciplined. This evolved when the hospital decided on January 25 to rescind the final warning notices issued to the five other participants but not the one to A.M. The hospital rationalized its action on the basis of A.M.'s poor past record as compared to the clean records of the others.

However, when one employee is disciplined, all must be disciplined. Corrective discipline satisfies the rule of equality of treatment by enforcing equally among all employees established rules and responsibility on the job. This critical basis for a sound disciplinary program is pointed out in earlier chapters.

Arbitrators are impressed with the concept of equality of treatment. If all employees had been handled equitably, the final warning notices to the remaining five employees would not have been removed from their files. Rather, this would have been their discipline for this serious infraction, making a harsher discipline for A.M. appear more credible. It is important to note that "equitable and consistent application of discipline" does not necessarily mean that all employees involved in a rules infraction or violation need receive exactly the same discipline. It does mean that all employees with similar employment records (years of service, disciplinary records, commendations, evaluations, etc.) and with similar levels of culpability must be treated equally.

A majority of collective bargaining agreements contain clauses requiring employees calling in sick to present proof of illness upon the employer's request. The hospital had such a clause in its contract. However, in demanding such proof in an effort to determine A.M.'s activities on January 21, the hospital made several mistakes:

1. The job action incident occurred on January 21. On January 25 the hospital received a doctor's note dated January 25. The note did not state specifically that A.M. had been seen by a doctor on January 21. Further investigation was indicated, yet none ensued. The employee may have been to the doctor for a routine examination on the date in question or he may have been legitimately ill when he visited the doctor but not ill on the date he called in sick.

2. A doctor's note tendered under false pretenses is a fraudulent document because it purports that the employee was ill and unable to work when in fact he was not. This is an act of dishonesty by the employee and should be so treated by the employer. The arbitrator in his award stated ". . . while the alleged dishonesty regarding the doctor's note was considered in connection with the Hospital's determination of penalty, that note was not stated by the Hospital at the

time as one of the bases for the disciplinary action taken.'' The arbitrator also quotes the January 22 terminal warning notice in which the hospital states that '' . . . the excuse of sickness offered for grievant's absence is unacceptable.'' Per the arbitrator, this is not the same as saying that the grievant was discharged for offering a false doctor's note. Once determining that the note was not valid, management should have administered discipline for this fraudulent act standing by itself. It should be noted that such an act is serious enough to warrant suspension or termination.

3. A.M. was the only employee out of six offenders required to produce proof of illness. As discussed above, this inconsistent treatment is both unfair and discriminatory.

The arbitrator makes several references to the hospital's failure, in written warnings preceding the terminal notice to A.M., to make clear the consequences of continued unacceptable behavior. The employer must show that the misconduct was not condoned and that the employee was specifically warned of the consequences. In addition, the arbitrator highlights several instances in the past in which management threatened A.M. with specific further discipline for continuing his pattern of unacceptable behavior and then did not follow through.

Management testified at the arbitration that standard operating procedures in administering discipline to employees was to suspend after issuing a final warning but before termination. (It is interesting to note that such sequencing of discipline did not in fact occur in the case of A.M.) This practice may not be appropriate in all cases.

The administration of discipline must spring from the facts of the case. Whether or not management suspends an employee prior to termination, or whether or not it issues a final warning notice before termination, depends upon the totality of the evidence. What is the past record of the employee? What do the facts indicate? What action was taken in similar cases? What effect will management's action have in the interest of salvaging the employee? What will be the effect of the action on the rest of the employees?

CASE 2: ABSENTEEISM AND LATENESS

Pursuant to the rules and procedures of the American Arbitration Association and the Collective Bargaining Agreement (hereinafter ''Agreement'') between the Hospital and the Union, the undersigned was designated as Arbitrator to hear and render a final and binding Award concerning the following issue:

Was the discharge of M.R. by the Hospital on January 13 for cause?

If not, what shall the remedy be?

On written notice to both parties, hearing was held on August 27 at the offices of the American Arbitration Association. The parties were afforded full opportunity to develop respective positions by examination and cross-examination of witnesses, by presentation of evidence, and by argument.

Background

M.R. (hereinafter "grievant") has been in the employ of the Hospital for eighteen (18) years; in the Building Services Department for four years, and thereafter as a transporter in the Transportation and Information Department. In the course of employment at the Hospital, grievant has received twenty-one (21) Warning Notices and a memo relating to excessive lateness. In addition, she was suspended on four separate occasions for the same reason, excessive lateness.

Notices, dates, and bases follow:

11/20/63	Warning	(20 latenesses)
2/18/64	Final Warning	(4 latenesses)
2/01/65	Warning	(7 latenesses)
9/30/65	Warning	(10 latenesses)
2/07/69	Warning	(5 latenesses)
2/27/69	Second Warning	(4 latenesses)
1/22/70	Third Warning	(2 latenesses)
7/27/70	Third Warning	(5 latenesses)
7/30/70	Final Warning	(1 lateness)
10/16/70	Final Warning—1-Day Suspension	(4 latenesses)
6/08/71	Final Warning	(6 latenesses)
12/23/71	Final Warning—2-Days' Suspension	(6 latenesses)
5/15/72	First Warning—Unrelated to Lateness	
6/15/72	Final Warning	(15 latenesses)
11/01/72	Final Warning—3 Days' Suspension	(11 latenesses)
8/20/74	First Warning	(11 latenesses)
6/22/76	First Warning	(9 latenesses)
9/03/76	Second Warning	(8 latenesses)
8/02/77	Second Warning	(40 latenesses: 1/1–8/2)
6/06/78	Third Warning	(13 latenesses: 2/1–6/6)
12/28/78	First Warning—Unrelated to Lateness	

10/25/79	Final Warning	(13 latenesses: 6/5–10/25)
8/18/80	Memo	
10/14/80	Final Warning—2 Days'	
	Suspension	(6 latenesses: 8/18–10/14)
1/13/81	Discharge	(9 latenesses: 10/14–1/13)

Mr. M.C., Director of Traffic and Information for the Hospital, testified that a transporter moves patients around the Hospital (room to services, admitting to room, emergency to room or services) and moves specimens around the Hospital. In addition, the Traffic and Information Department is responsible for the pneumatic tube system through which many specimens and medications are moved about the Facility. Grievant was assigned to the tube room prior to October. Lateness in arriving for duty caused a delay in opening the pneumatic system, due to commence operating at 8:00 A.M. The delay in turn caused a backup in the movement of specimens and medication, disrupting procedures and interfering with the needs of patients.

Mr. A.S., Supervisor in Transportation and Information Department, had several meetings with grievant to discuss her lateness at which time he warned her about the consequences of continued lateness. He alleged that at one meeting (date unclear) he offered to change grievant's hours, which grievant refused.

Testimony and Evidence

The parties stipulated that the dates and times are accurate as charged. The Hospital contends that grievant has been given ample opportunity to improve her performance with respect to lateness and that she has taken no corrective action. Hospital cites grievant's continued pattern of lateness, nine additional incidents in the two and one-half month period following the final warning and two-day suspension in October.

Grievant alleges her lateness was caused by transportation problems. She maintains that subway transportation from her home to the Hospital is unreliable, often suffering breakdowns, delays, and overcrowding. Grievant offered several publications and news articles detailing mass transportation problems, as well as confirmation of delays from MTA on the No. 5 and No. 6 Lines on specific dates.

Grievant stated that she was never offered a change in hours. However, she contends that she requested such a change from Miss H. on January 9, but was terminated before any action was taken.

Opinion

Grievant has a long history of excessive lateness. The 21 Warning Notices and memo speak of more severe discipline to follow unless grievant improved her attendance record. Grievant was suspended for one day in one year and two days in the next year and three in the following, and subsequently two days in October eight years later, as a result of the repeated lateness.

For the last five years, the Hospital has pursued a record of discipline progressing from warnings (first, second, third, final) to the two-day suspension in October and finally to discharge on January 13 of this year. Grievant, despite warnings and her suspension, persisted in continuing a pattern of excessive lateness. In fact, grievant had approximately one hundred incidents of lateness during the last five years. After the Final Warning Notice and suspension in October, grievant was late on nine additional occasions between October 27 and January 8. These last nine incidents ranged from four (4) minutes to forty-four (44) minutes. Even disregarding three instances where grievant was tardy by four (4) minutes, there remain six (6) serious latenesses during this period.

Grievant contends that the mass transit system is at fault—overcrowding, delays, and breakdowns. There is no doubt that grievant has a substantial trip from her home in the Baychester section of the Bronx to the Hospital. In view of grievant's allegation that the trains regularly suffer overcrowding, delays, and breakdowns, grievant should have allowed for these problems in allotting travel time rather than regularly and habitually arriving late.

Grievant's pattern of excessive lateness predates alleged transit problems. Throughout most of her 18 years of employment at the Hospital, grievant has [had] an unacceptable attendance record with respect to lateness, despite repeated warnings and ample opportunity to improve.

There was conflicting testimony relating to a possible schedule change. The Hospital had no obligation to offer grievant such a change. In addition, grievant's alleged request for an adjustment in hours just prior to discharge was itself too late to alter the outcome of this matter.

Under the circumstances, Hospital had cause to discharge grievant. Unfortunately, 18 years of service cannot excuse such a continuing and flagrant record of excessive lateness.

AWARD

M.R. was discharged for cause on January 13.
Grievance denied.

Analysis of the Case

Inasmuch as termination of employment is perceived by arbitrators as tantamount to occupational execution, they are loathe to uphold discharges unless it is clear that grievant was: made aware by supervision of her deficiency(ies), counseled as to what acceptable behavior should be, given guidance/assistance in effecting behavior modifications, and disciplined in a timely and progressive fashion. Arbitrators wish to ensure that due process was, in fact, used.

Historically and consistently in arbitrators' decisions, these basic prerequisites to discharge have been required in cases of lateness/absenteeism offenses by long-term employees. This reluctance by arbitrators to uphold discharge in such cases grows in direct proportion to the increase in years of employee service.

In the case of M.R., the hospital was upheld in its decision to discharge. The arbitrator cites as most significant in reaching this judgment the following reasons:

1. The employee had a clear history of excessive lateness.
2. The employer gave more than sufficient notice of its dissatisfaction with employee's behavior and did so progressively.
3. The employer took into consideration the employee's many years of service.
4. The employer made other attempts at helping the employee with her problem, i.e., schedule and time adjustment offers that the grievant refused.

While all's well that ends well, the authors believe that the employer need not have tolerated the behavior of this employee over such an inordinately long period. In fact, the longer it waited to discharge the employee, the more it had to tolerate inappropriate behavior in order to make its ultimate action tenable. Action could have been taken to discharge the employee at the end of her eighth year of employment. The record of warnings for latenesses received by M.R. in the first eight years of her employment is as follows:

11/20/63	Warning	20 latenesses
2/18/64	Final Warning	4 latenesses
2/01/65	Warning	7 latenesses
9/30/65	Warning	10 latenesses
2/07/69	Warning	5 latenesses
2/27/69	Second Warning	4 latenesses
1/22/70	Third Warning	2 latenesses

7/27/70	Third Warning	5 latenesses
7/30/70	Final Warning	1 lateness
10/16/70	Final Warning—1-Day Suspension	4 latenesses
6/08/71	Final Warning	6 latenesses
12/23/71	Final Warning—2 Days' Suspension	6 latenesses

The record is troublesome and reflects management's desire to credit the long service of the employee but in doing so permitting the individual to amass an outrageously unacceptable work record.

Using the following proposed strategy, one of firm but fair and progressive discipline, the hospital could have discharged her on December 31, 1971, with clear evidence of having first made all attempts at corrective behavior modification:

11/20/63	Verbal Counseling (changed from a Warning)	20 latenesses
2/18/64	First Warning (changed from Final Warning)	4 latenesses
2/01/65	Second Warning (changed from Warning)	7 latenesses
9/30/65	Third Warning (changed from Warning)	10 latenesses
2/07/69	Third Warning (changed from Warning)	5 latenesses
2/27/69	Final Warning (changed from Second Warning)	4 latenesses
1/22/70	No Action (changed from Third Warning)	2 latenesses + 5 latenesses
7/27/70	Final Warning (changed from Third Warning)	= 7 latenesses
7/30/70	No Action (changed from Third Warning)	1 lateness + 4 latenesses
10/16/70	Final Warning—1-Day Suspension (same as before)	= 5 latenesses
6/08/71	Final Warning—1-Week Suspension (changed from Final Warning)	6 latenesses
12/23/71	Discharge (changed from Final Warning—2 Days' Suspension)	6 latenesses

Discipline in this fashion would have been both progressive and decisive. The employee's problem is first identified in a counseling session. Warnings are effected in strict sequential order from February 18, 1964, to September 30, 1965. Once the pattern begins again after almost three and a half years of nonoffensive behavior, discipline should be administered again but with acknowledgment of the "good time" earned. Consequently, instead of moving on to the final steps of February 7, 1969, the employee again is given a third warning. Instead of giving warnings for two latenesses and one lateness, the authors would have waited for more significant numbers to be amassed as shown. The latter approach makes it clear that continued unacceptable behavior will indeed lead to more severe discipline culminating in discharge. No doubt is left in the employee's mind.

Arbitrators require that employees understand the ramifications and possible disciplinary action if their pattern of unacceptable behavior continues. The final warning issued on February 27, 1969, which could have produced a discharge, did not result in one. It was necessary, after almost a year and a half, for a final warning, rather than discharge, to be issued on July 20, 1970. Again, some three months later the action of a suspension, short of discharge, was an indication of consideration for the employee's seven years of service as of that date. A final warning with another one-week suspension was implemented some eight months later.

To not discharge on December 23, 1971 in light of the blatant behavior established by the employee up to that point in time would have been tantamount to informing that individual and other workers that final warnings with suspensions were meaningless. It is this consistently firm but fair approach to discipline that will impact on unacceptable employee behavior.

Chapter 7

Arbitration Cases: Insubordination:

CASE 3: REFUSAL TO ATTEND CONFERENCE

Issue

1. Was the grievant, J.Q., suspended for one and one-half days for just cause?
2. If not, what shall be the remedy?

Background and Discussion

Grievant is a Registered Nurse employed at the Hospital and has been so employed since 1979. Her record up to the instant matter has been quite a good one, with her personal record showing several commendations from supervisors and others.

In early 1981 administration at the Hospital determined that it would be to the advantage of certain staff members to have them attend a workshop or conference regarding "Intradepartmental Relations in Utilization Review" and a program was scheduled for March 25 to be held at a location off the premises. Grievant worked in a department that would be assumedly benefited by attendance at this workshop or conference. Grievant's supervisor at the time was S.W., who unfortunately has since passed away.

The location of the conference sustained some injury by a flooding in February, thus putting in question the locus of the conference. The building that was to be used for the conference apparently had a large conference room holding approximately 200 people and a smaller room holding somewhat less, perhaps about 100 or so. Attendees at the conference were to be from a number of health care institutions within the area. As a result of the doubt as to the size of the conference room, preparations were made as to priorities of attendees so that in the event the larger conference room could not be utilized, which would accommodate all possible attendees, lesser numbers of attendees could be housed in a smaller conference room. Grievant testified that on several occasions she became aware by over-hearing telephone conversations by S.W. that attendance would probably be limited at the conference.

A memorandum was placed on grievant's desk on or about March 3 from her supervisor noting it was "for your information" and having handwritten thereon the following: "Please let me know how many are going." Attached to this memorandum was a flyer from the sponsoring group for the conference to be held on March 25, noting the time of the conference would be from 1:30 to 4:00 P.M. At the bottom of this flyer was a form to be detached providing for the name of the hospital, the telephone number and address of the hospital, as well as the name of the attendee and his or her title. There was also noted and underlined the following: "Seating is limited and parking is available. Early registration is requested." It appears that on the flyer form the word "early" was additionally under-lined, assumedly by grievant's supervisor.

Grievant on several occasions informed her supervisor that she would not be attending the conference. Grievant is married and has two children, one is a ten-year-old attending a parochial school to which she must be taken and picked up at approximately 2:45 P.M., also a younger child who is attending nursery school. Grievant's husband works nights and thus ordinarily picks up his and grievant's ten-year-old child at about 2:45 from her school. Sometime prior to the conference date of March 25, grievant's husband was hospitalized and remained in the hospital until March 29, having entered the hospital on or about March 12.

Prior to March 25, the credible evidence was that grievant had never been ordered or mandated to attend the conference. In fact, the evidence would appear to be that there was some question as to who could go to the conference because of the doubt as to which conference room would be used.

On March 24, which was the day before the conference and a Tuesday, grievant's supervisor just before she left at 4 P.M. spoke to grievant and commented that she had observed that grievant had not returned her registration form and said there were now enough seats for all who would attend. Grievant replied, according to her testimony, "S.W., I didn't plan to attend the meeting. You had promised initially whoever attends would take notes that are relevant to the Utilization Review Department (the department where grievant and her supervisor worked)."

Grievant also commented that March 25 was a Wednesday, which was payday, and paychecks are usually given out in the afternoon. Grievant offered to collect the checks of all who were attending the conference.

According to grievant, her supervisor replied, "I did not think of the paychecks." According to grievant, the supervisor then immediately called the Payroll Department, which indicated that the checks came from an outside servicing agency; however, if they were in early in the day, the Payroll Department would try to pay the employees at noon prior to their leaving for the conference.

According to grievant, on March 24 her supervisor never indicated that grievant would have to attend the conference or in any way ordered her to attend the conference on March 25. The following day, which was March 25, grievant spoke to her supervisor somewhere before 10 A.M. and, according to grievant, S.W. said to her, "I would like you to attend the meeting at 1 P.M." This was the first time, according to grievant, that her supervisor told her that she wanted her to attend the meeting. Grievant replied, "It is now 10 A.M. and you are now mandating that I attend the meeting at 1 P.M. I did not make any plans before leaving home to leave the building."

Grievant, according to her testimony, was referring to the fact that because of her husband's illness and hospitalization grievant had to pick up her ten-year-old daughter at about 2:45 P.M. from the child's school. Grievant used her two contractually granted 15-minute breaks in combination of 30 minutes to leave the hospital, pick up her daughter at school, and then take her daughter home, and then return obviously to work at the hospital again. According to grievant, her supervisor was well aware of grievant's needs because grievant had since March 12 or so been leaving the Hospital premises to pick up her daughter and drop her off.

Grievant was not fully aware of the exact location of the conference; however she did know, according to her testimony, that the conference location was in the opposite direction from where she had to go to pick up her daughter and return her daughter home, and then come back to the hospital.

According to grievant's testimony, sometime later at approximately 10:45 she was paged and summoned to go to her supervisor's office. According to grievant, her supervisor again said, "I would like you to attend the meeting today." Grievant replied to the effect that she had just told her supervisor that she had not made plans to leave the building and she would not be able to attend the meeting on that date. According to grievant, without any further ado her supervisor said, "You are suspended," and thereupon left the office, giving grievant no opportunity to make further discussion or explanation.

According to grievant, when her supervisor left the office, she (the grievant) was confused and did not know what to do and did not fully understand what her supervisor meant. Grievant then spoke to a colleague who suggested that she call the Union representative. Grievant did call her Union representative and was on her way to see the Union representative when she met the Personnel Director, the Associate Executive Director of the institution, and her supervisor. According to grievant, she was asked if they could discuss the matter in the office of the Associate Director of the institution.

Grievant at first asked the Associate Director if she could have a discussion with him because she claimed she wanted to let him know what had happened. Grievant asked if her workmate could accompany her; however, she was told no. Grievant said that she was not told she could have her Union representative present. Grievant says she explained that she had been mandated to attend the meeting at 1 P.M.; however, prior to that day, that is March 25, she had never been told that it was mandatory that she attend the meeting. Grievant says she told them that she had not made any arrangements to cover her obligations before leaving home that day. Grievant said at the hearing that all seemed to be aware of her problem, but she was still told she was suspended.

There is some dispute as to what actually happened at this meeting between grievant and hospital administration and the supervisor. However, I do not believe that the discrepancies are vital to a determination of this matter. I might point out that from my reading of the situation, there was a difficulty in communication between grievant and others, perhaps due to grievant's apparent difficulty in understanding all the nuances of American dialect. Grievant was born, raised, and educated in Trinidad and perhaps has occasional difficulty in fully comprehending the subtleties of the American dialect.

Grievant contacted her Union representative after she left the administration office, and the Union representative apparently thereupon took over the matter but was unable seemingly to make contact with Hospital administration. Regardless, grievant was suspended for a day and a half without pay.

As a result of the incident on March 25, a warning notice was given to grievant from her supervisor, S.W., for insubordination with the specific reasons being as follows:

> On March 25, I directed you to attend a conference outside of the Hospital during your normal work time. Details and requests regarding your attendance at this conference took place on several occasions previously. Whatever your understanding was about our previous discussions, I directed you at least twice on Wednesday, March 25, 1981, to attend the conference. You refused my directions and therefore were suspended for the remainder of that

day and the entire next day. At the time of your refusal to attend the conference you did not offer to me any valid extenuating circumstances. By not attending the conference, you missed important information you need to perform your job. Insubordination is a serious violation of Hospital's regulations; and, if this occurs again in the future, you will be faced with additional disciplinary action up to and including discharge.

A letter dated March 25 was sent by the Director of Personnel at the Hospital to the Union reading as follows:

Ms. J.Q., a Utilization Review Nurse at the Hospital and a member of the Union, was suspended today for insubordination. She refused to attend a conference during normal working hours. If you have any additional questions regarding this, please contact me.

A grievance was filed by the Union organizer, dated March 30, reading as follows:

J.Q., R.N., was suspended for one and a half days for refusing to attend a workshop and a warning notice for insubordination was placed in her personnel file.

Approximately three weeks before the workshop, a memo was distributed to all interested nurses to attend the workshop. S.W., Supervisor, stated that the Hospital asked for 18 seats; however, there were only ten openings and they would be filled on a first come, first served basis. At this time Ms. J.Q. expressed her option not to attend and that she would rather remain at the institution.

On 3/24, all interested nurses filled out the appropriate application form for the workshop. S.W. again asked Ms. J.Q. if she would attend and her answer was the same.

On 3/25, the day of the workshop, Ms. J.Q. was approached by S.W. and told that she must attend the workshop. Ms. J.Q. replied, "S.W., as was stated to you on two different occasions when asked if I wish to attend, my response was no. Why now, on the morning of the conference, am I being told that I must?" Ms. J.Q. was then informed by S.W. that she was suspended for insubordination, but not for how long. Upon leaving the institution, Ms. J.Q. attempted to explain the situation to Mr. M., Director of Personnel, who told her that the suspension stands and she should call his office in the morning.

On 3/25, [Union] Delegate C.A. informed me of the suspension.

On 3/26, I called Mr. M.'s office two times, no response. I then informed Ms. J.Q. that she should return to work on the following day, which she did.

On 3/27 a Third Step Grievance was scheduled for 3/30.

Third Step Grievance—3/30—Present: Mr. M., S.W., C.A., Ms. J.Q., and myself. Union demanded that grievant receive all lost wages, removal of warning notice, and be made whole in every way. On 4/8—grievance denied by management.

Arbitration requested.

The Hospital's position here is that grievant was given a lawful order by her supervisor and offered no valid reason why she could not obey the direction of her supervisor. As grievant did not obey the appropriate and permissible direction of her supervisor, thus grievant was guilty of insubordination and a penalty of a day-and-a-half suspension and warning notice were levied and were appropriate under all the circumstances. The Hospital argues that grievant did not fully explain her position and that her attendance was required at the conference, which was of importance.

The Union on behalf of the grievant argues to the contrary, that it is impermissible to penalize grievant for her failure to attend the conference because prior to the actual date of the conference grievant was never informed that she was mandated to attend the conference. Further, there were circumstances which militated against grievant going to the conference in that she had an obligation to pick up her daughter and further that grievant was concerned that if she left the Hospital and went to the conference, if there were a problem with her daughters or her husband, she could not be easily contacted.

The matter is properly before me for determination.

Opinion

It is difficult for me to piece out exactly what happened in this matter inasmuch as one of the major protagonists has unfortunately died, so that to a great degree I am forced to reply on the version of events as presented by the surviving participant in the dialogue between grievant and her supervisor on March 25, and prior thereto. I would note, of course, that my reliance is necessarily corroborated by other evidence.

The evidence appears to me to demonstrate that prior to March 25 it was not mandated that grievant attend the conference on March 25. For this conclusion I rely not only on the testimony of grievant herself, but the memorandum and circular sent around regarding the conference. There is further some support for this inference from even the testimony of the Hospital witnesses.

The next question to be faced is, given that no direction was made by grievant's supervisor to attend the conference until March 25, the very date of the conference itself, in fact but a few hours before the conference, is such an order or direction of such standing under all the circumstances to warrant refusal thereof to result in the penalties imposed on grievant?

Ordinarily a lawful order given by a supervisor must be obeyed by the subordinate employee. The rule, as all of us in labor relations know, is that under such circumstances an employee must obey and grieve later. However, there are certainly exceptions to this rule as there are to most rules. An impartial hearer of such a matter must apply a sense of reason to the matter, considering all the circumstances involved.

Here we have an employee who up until but a few hours prior to the conference had no knowledge that her attendance was mandated. This employee had certain obligations which tinged the incident with a sense of exigency. There is further a requirement in industrial relations that when an order is given by a superior, an employee must be advised of the consequences from a refusal to obey. Here the evidence is not very clear as to whether or not grievant was in fact told that her failure to attend the conference would result in disciplinary action. There is some inference from the Hospital witnesses' testimony that at the conference held between grievant and administration grievant was perhaps advised of the consequences of her refusal. However, this matter is somewhat clouded.

There is further the consideration that in assessing discipline, an employee's total work record and employment history should be considered. Together with this is the generally accepted principle of progressive discipline; that is, an employee if in fact guilty of misconduct should be treated in an escalating mode of discipline. It is generally considered [that] progressive discipline as an overall principle requires first something in the nature of a warning, then a suspension, and so on.

I make all these points to show that my following determination here to remit the disciplinary penalties imposed is not based on one ground alone, but based on several grounds. They are as noted above the question as to whether or not under all the circumstances it was reasonable to mandate grievant's attendance at the conference on March 25, when the evidence does not disclose that grievant up until a very short time prior to the conference was directed to attend.

In this regard I must further note that the conference was off the Hospital premises and, although not very far, was some distance away, some mile or two. There is further the concern articulated by grievant that there might be difficulty in reaching her at a time when her husband was in the hospital and her children might have had need of her. Taken together with grievant's need to pick up her child at 2:45 from school, this adds an additional fillip to grievant's defense against the charges levied on her.

Then I must consider the additional circumstances I note above, that is, the possible deficit in the employer's case by grievant not being told of the consequences of her action; and that grievant's work history was a good one; and further, the question whether the principle of progressive discipline was appropriately applied.

I believe taken all together the circumstances and evidence in this matter are such as to warrant a finding that the employer has not met its burden of showing there was just cause for the discipline of grievant. In disciplinary matters, as all are aware, the employer has the burden of demonstrating by a preponderance of the evidence in matters such as is before me here that the disciplinary penalties were warranted.

To restate it, I don't believe that the employer has met its burden. At best the evidence and circumstances supporting the parties' positions here is in equipoise. Therefore I believe I have no alternative but to find there was not just cause for the disciplining of grievant for the events of March 25.

In light of the conclusions reached hereinabove, I see no reason to discuss any other evidence or arguments submitted here by the parties; suffice it to say all relevant, competent, and material evidence and arguments submitted by the parties have been considered, although perhaps not set forth or discussed herein at length.

AWARD

The grievant, J.Q., was not suspended for one and one-half days for just cause. The remedy shall be the remission to grievant of the pay lost for the day and a half of suspension and further the removal from her personnel files of the warning notice relating to the incident of March 25.

Analysis of the Case

In his finding the arbitrator stated ". . . In disciplinary matters . . . the employer has the burden of demonstrating by a preponderance of the evidence in matters such as is before me here that the disciplinary penalties were warranted.'' In ordering the hospital to make the employee whole for pay that it had withheld as part of supervision's discipline, the arbitrator concluded that such burden had not been met. Supervisors or managers should be ever mindful of this basic principle of industrial relations and consider its importance before making disciplinary decisions, not after.

In highlighting one of the most widely quoted industrial relations rules on the subject of insubordination, i.e., employees who disagree with the lawful orders of their supervisors should nevertheless obey and then grieve later, the arbitrator notes that as with all rules, there are exceptions.

The supervisor in the case of Ms. J.Q. obviously acted precipitously: the grievant refused to attend the conference, thus she was guilty of insubordination and had to be disciplined.

But what of the poor communication and lack of definite management direction prior to March 25? Was the employee clearly aware that she had to attend the conference, given (1) the uncertainty of the status of the conference and (2) the fact that with her husband hospitalized, she had the burden of transporting her young child home from school?

Arbitrators are loathe to rule against employees in insubordination cases where mitigating circumstances prevail, especially where they involve the welfare of children or family illness. In reviewing the literature on cases involving refusal to obey orders, it is clear that the general rule ''Obey now, grieve later'' is mitigated in certain situations where it is recognized that an overriding right or interest of the employee may require such an exception. Arbitrators universally will make such an exception when an employee has reasonable grounds to believe that the order would put the individual into a hazardous situation that could be substantially injurious to the worker's health or abnormally dangerous.

That was not the point in this case. The mitigating circumstances here were the poor timing of the final order to attend the conference; the obligations of the employee, which had been recognized in the past; and the absence of a clear indication that failure to attend would result in disciplinary action. The hospital's position was that Ms. J.Q. had offered no valid reason why she could not obey the direction of her supervisor. Yet each day for two weeks prior to the conference, Ms. J.Q. was leaving the hospital premises to transport her daughter from school to home, finding the time to do so by combining her two fifteen-minute break periods. The fact that she did normally leave and return to the institution in midday and the extraordinary break-coupling accommodation certainly were visible to management.

It should be clear that the case of Ms. J.Q. may not have had to reach the arbitration stage. The third-step grievance hearing, in the hospital, could have identified the holes in this case. This is a critical point and deserves additional discussion. In the day-to-day operation of health care institutions, many management decisions are made at all levels. There are bound to be some errors in judgment. A properly conducted grievance hearing will flush out these errors, saving the institution the embarrassment of having an arbitrator reverse a management decision.

As stated previously, the grievance procedure is a useful, necessary, and productive management tool only insofar as it makes use of fact finding, objective evaluation, and equity. It is a counterproductive tool if it is used to rubber-stamp unjust management decisions. Consistency protects the people who depend on due process from erring supervisors and from unfair treatment; consistent and fair adjudication of grievances is the cornerstone of good employee-employer relations.

It is worthwhile to reiterate several points made by the arbitrator that deserve consideration when disciplining for insubordination. Supervisors and managers should:

1. make sure the facts warrant the level of discipline being imposed
2. make sure that the employee has been advised of the consequences of refusal to obey a supervisory order
3. consider the employee's total work record and employment history in assessing discipline, except in cases when the insubordination is so severe as not to warrant it

CASE 4: REFUSAL TO PERFORM JOB

This proceeding involves a claim by the Union that the Hospital discharged Ms. A.V.D. (the "grievant") without just cause in violation of the collective bargaining agreement (the "Agreement"). The controversy having been unresolved in accordance with the Agreement, the Union filed a demand for arbitration, and the undersigned was selected by the parties as Arbitrator in accordance with the procedure of the American Arbitration Association.

A hearing was held before the Arbitrator at the offices of the Association in New York City, New York, on April 21, at which the parties were afforded full opportunity to present oral and written evidence, cross-examine witnesses, provide oral argument, and otherwise support their respective positions. Following the hearing, each party submitted a memorandum. The evidence adduced and the positions and arguments set forth at the hearing and in the posthearing memoranda have been fully considered in preparation and issuance of this Opinion and its accompanying Award.

The Issue

Did the Hospital have just cause to discharge Ms. A.V.D., and
If not, what shall be the remedy?

Facts

Ms. A.V.D., the grievant, was employed by the Hospital 13 years ago.
She worked as a maintenance "C" employee, or maid, in the Building
Services Department until her discharge six months ago.

It is undisputed that by long-standing Building Services policy, nurses
clean the "bulk" or the major portion of any fecal matter in patient areas,
with Building Service employees only completing the cleaning. That policy
apparently is based on disease control considerations.

Mr. W.C., a Building Services Area Manager at the Hospital, testified
as follows: The grievant worked under his overall supervision. Six months
ago he received a telephone call from Ms. E.U., the Clinical Supervisor
for 3 North, an inpatient unit. Ms. E.U. informed Mr. W.C. that a nurse
on 3 North had asked the grievant to finish the cleaning of a bathroom in
which there had been fecal matter but that she [grievant] had refused and
left the floor to seek her supervisor.

At that point Ms. A.V.D. entered Mr. W.C.'s office and told him the
work she had been asked to do was not the responsibility of her job
position. Mr. W.C. replied that as he understood the assignment, it was
properly the grievant's work. They argued, and finally Mr. W.C. ordered
a Building Services Supervisor to accompany the grievant to 3 North and
observe the situation about which she was complaining.

Shortly thereafter the Building Services Supervisor called Mr. W.C.
and told him that while he was talking to the grievant, she threw herself
on the floor and was "moaning and thrashing about." Mr. W.C. went
directly to 3 North, where he found the grievant restrained in a wheelchair
in a hallway, being attended by three nurses and a physician. Patients
were standing in the doorways of their room observing the commotion. In
his presence, the grievant was asked several times by the doctor and
nurses about the problem she was experiencing, but the grievant's only
reply was that she wanted her "Union delegate."

The grievant was then taken to Employee Health Services, from which
she was released about a half-hour later. The cleaning job in question was
performed later that day by another maid. Mr. W.C. suspended the grievant when she returned to work after having her regular two days off. Mr.
W.C. later determined to discharge the grievant.

The Building Services Supervisor testified that on the day in question, at Mr. W.C.'s direction, he accompanied the grievant to 3 North. He observed the bathroom that the grievant had been asked to clean and determined that the remaining cleaning was the job of a maintenance employee. He instructed the grievant to do the work. She refused, and argued loudly with him in the adjoining bedroom, in which there was a patient. They went out into the hallway, with the grievant continuing to argue that the work was not part of her job.

Suddenly the grievant "threw herself on the floor," where she rolled from side to side while "moaning and groaning." Patients came out of their rooms to observe, and several nurses came to assist the grievant. The nurses put the grievant into a wheelchair; the Building Services Supervisor called Mr. W.C. and the Main Office. When he returned to the grievant, she was being attended by a physician. He heard the grievant asking for a "Union" delegate.

Ms. M.H., Staff Nurse, testified as follows: She had asked the grievant to do the cleaning at issue, after she herself had spent 45 minutes cleaning up the bulk of the fecal matter—all that was left was splattering. Later she saw the grievant in the hallway, lying flat on the floor, moaning, rolling, and flailing her arms and legs. She helped get the grievant into a wheelchair. The grievant was asked if she was experiencing pain but her only response was that she wanted a Union delegate. She took the grievant's blood pressure, which was quite high. She helped take the grievant to Employee Health Services; the only thing the grievant said on the way was that she wanted a Union delegate.

Pursuant to a stipulation by the parties, there was introduced into evidence an affidavit of Dr. C.O., a resident physician. Dr. C.O. treated the grievant when she was brought to Employee Health Services on the date in question. Dr. C.O. stated in part as follows:

4. In substance, the grievant informed me as follows: that she was very upset about a problem that she had had with her supervisor that day; that the problem arose because she had been asked to clean a bathroom; that it was her opinion that she should not have to do the work requested of her; that her supervisor had insisted she do the work; that she did not want to do it; and that she had, therefore, become very upset. The grievant also told me that "they" got her all excited and that this kind of thing gives her a headache. I recall no other complaint of pain, physical distress, or other medical symptoms by the grievant during my examination.

5. During my examination of the grievant, I found no heart or lung abnormality. Her blood pressure was, however, higher than normal range. I do not recall the blood pressure readings and, because I no longer have access to the grievant's Employee Health Service records, cannot verify the readings by resort to those records.

6. On the same day, I reviewed the grievant's medical records for the purpose of comparing the two blood pressure readings taken on that date with readings recorded on a number of previous visits to the Employee Health Service and for the purpose of identifying complaints, if any, of symptoms associated with high blood pressure. I found no such complaints, and the blood pressure readings taken that date were unchanged from those recorded on numerous previous occasions. In other words, the grievant's blood pressure on that date, although high, was normal for her.

7. Based upon my examination of the grievant and my review of her medical records, I made two diagnoses. The first was "tension cephalgia secondary to occupational (job-related) stress." I used "cephalgia" to mean headache and "secondary to" to mean as a consequence of and of lesser importance than the job-related stress. Thus, it was and is my opinion that if the grievant suffered from a headache on that date, it was a tension headache resulting from the disagreement that she had with her supervisor. The sole basis for my diagnosis of cephalgia (or headache) was the patient's subjective complaint. I observed no medical condition or symptom which would otherwise support the diagnosis.

8. My second diagnosis was "hypertension (chronic, under treatment)." I used "hypertension" to mean persistently high arterial blood pressure, and "chronic" to mean persisting over a long period of time. I described the condition as "under treatment" because the grievant's medical records indicated that medication had been prescribed for the condition and because the grievant told me that she was taking medication for the condition.

9. It was and remains my opinion that if the grievant experienced a headache on that date, the headache was not the result of or associated with her hypertension. My opinion is based on: (a) the fact that her blood pressure readings on that date were unchanged from numerous readings taken, as a matter of routine, when she visited the Employee Health Service on previous occasions for reasons unrelated to the hypertension and without any complaint of headache; (b) the absence in her records of any mention of head pain associated with high blood pressure read-

ings; (c) the fact that the hypertension was under treatment; and (d) the grievant's subjective explanation of her primary complaint as stress resulting from a disagreement with her supervisor.

10. After I completed my examination of the grievant, I told her that she was able to return to work. I also told her that her headache was the result of her disagreement with her supervisor and had nothing to do with her high blood pressure.

11. I prescribed APC tablets for the grievant. APC tablets are an analgesic, i.e., a pain-alleviating agent. The composition, potency, usage, and effects of APC tablets do not differ significantly from those of aspirin tablets sold over-the-counter in pharmacies.

*   *   *   *   *

13. I did not refer the grievant for any further medical treatment. I did suggest that she make an appointment with Mr. L.D., a social worker employed at the Hospital as an Employee Assistance Counselor. A copy of a pamphlet describing the Employee Assistance Program at the Hospital is attached as Exhibit B [not included here]. I referred the grievant to Mr. L.D. because it was my opinion that the grievant's complaint presented an administrative, rather than a medical, problem.

*   *   *   *   *

15. Based on my examination of the grievant and my review of her medical records, it is my opinion that, when I examined her on the date in question, she was suffering from no medical condition that would have caused her, during the two or three hours preceding my examination, to lose consciousness; to suffer a loss of memory; to fall on the floor; to suffer such pain that she would unknowingly or involuntarily emit screams, shouts, moans, or groans; or to thrash about on the floor, flail her arms, or engage in any other unusual, uncontrolled, or uncontrollable activity.

16. "Hyperventilation" is a medical term used to describe abnormally prolonged, rapid, and deep breathing and a state in which there is an increased amount of air entering the pulmonary alveoli, which may eventually lead to an excessive loss of carbon dioxide from the body. The symptoms of hyperventilation do not normally include screams, shouts, moans, groans, or other inarticulate sounds or noises; nor do they normally include increased activity such as flailing of arms or legs, rolling or thrashing about, or other types of increased activity. I have on numerous occasions observed individuals in a state of hyperventilation and have

never observed any of the aforementioned symptoms. Hyper-ventilation may, however, occur if an individual emits repeated loud and inarticulate noises and engages in increased and unusual activity.

By stipulation a statement was also received from Dr. J.P., of the Manhattan Internal Medicine Associates. Dr. J.P. stated as follows:

In reviewing the statement of Dr. C.O. it would be my impression that she stated the complaint of headaches and diagnosis of tension cephalgia were secondary to occupational (job-related) stress. This statement implies that the symptoms the patient offered were due to job-related stress.

Ms. A.V.D., the grievant here, testified as follows: On November 14 a nurse called her to clean a patient bathroom. She went immediately, though it was her breaktime. When she came to the bathroom she observed fecal matter "all over the walls, toilet, and floor." She went to the Head Nurse, who nevertheless told her to do the cleaning. She then went to Mr. W.C. and explained the situation to him. Mr. W.C. nevertheless also told her to do the work.

When she persisted in her objection, Mr. W.C. sent Mr. A.P., the Building Services Supervisor, with her to 3 North. Mr. A.P. looked at the bathroom and instructed her to do the cleaning. He said, "Do it for courtesy's sake." She said she would do the job, but as she went to get a bucket felt a pain in her head and fell down the corridor.

Her memory fades at that point; she remembers nurses asking her what was the matter, to which she replied that she had a "pain" in her head. A doctor in Employee Health Services to whom she was taken asked her if she had any pain other than in her head, to which she replied, "only in my head." That doctor prescribed medication for her and instructed her to go home. At no time on November 14 did she ever ask for a Union delegate. She has high blood pressure but never [had] experienced any problem similar to that which occurred on November 14.

The grievant received the following prior discipline: verbal warnings for using profanity and/or engaging in intemperate outbursts to supervisors, on September 26, November 7, April 25, and May 5 (various years); a first written warning on January 24 (six years ago) for insubordination and abusive conduct toward a supervisor; a second written warning on April 14 (five years ago) for the same offenses; and a third written warning on April 25 (five years ago) for the same offenses. Ms. A.V.D. grieved her second written warning, but the grievance was denied and not appealed.

Her first written warning, on January 24 (six years ago), had been preceded by a suspension for the same infractions, which suspension she grieved and which suspension was reduced to a written warning.

The Parties' Contentions

The Hospital argues as follows: The grievant was properly discharged for insubordination and conduct detrimental to patient care. She disobeyed direct, appropriate orders from supervisors and then threw a "temper tantrum that disturbed patients, diverted medical resources from patient care, and totally disrupted the operation of a medical unit." The fact that this conduct was engaged in by the grievant is established by the overwhelming weight of the evidence. In contrast, the grievant's purported explanation finds no support in the testimony of any other witness, or in the sworn statement of the physician who treated her. Given the grievant's past disciplinary record, her discharge was not only warranted but required.

The Union argues as follows: The grievant did not in fact refuse to perform the work assigned to her. However, when she questioned the application of the policy regarding cleaning fecal matter, she upset the supervisory staff and this, "in turn, put her in such a condition that she could no longer function but had to be taken to Employee Health." The grievant had devoted thirteen years to working for the Hospital, and deserved better from it. As to the Hospital's evidence concerning the grievant's disciplinary record, the Union was given no notice of it, and it should therefore be disregarded.

Discussion

There is no question here of the grievant being given instructions by other than a representative of her own department. While the grievant initially was asked to do cleaning by a member of the nursing staff, ultimately she was given a direct order to perform that work by her own supervisors: Building Services Supervisor A.P. and Area Manager W.C.

There may not, in fact, be any question either as to the proper application on November 14 of the policy concerning cleaning fecal matter. Not only did the Building Services Supervisor A.P. visit the work location and conclude that it was Building Services work, but the grievant testified that she ultimately dropped her objection to doing that work. In any event there was considerable evidence supporting the Hospital's position on this point.

Mr. A.P. testified that the work was properly assignable to the grievant. Mr. W.C. testified he had reached a similar conclusion on the basis of his understanding of the situation. Nurse M.H. was of the same view, and testified without contradiction that she had already spent 45 minutes cleaning the bathroom. There is also evidence that Clinical Supervisor Ms. E.U. concurred with M.H. Under the circumstances the grievant surely had an obligation to do the work and, if she wished to protest her assignment, to present a grievance with respect thereto.

The Arbitrator is persuaded by what he regards as overwhelming evidence in the record that the grievant, while arguing loudly and persistently with Building Supervisor A.P. in a patient area on November 14, deliberately threw herself on a corridor floor and rolled about moaning to manifest her displeasure with her work assignment. Moreover, the evidence establishes that the grievant's action caused a commotion, diverted medical resources, and interrupted patient activities.

In reaching these conclusions, the Arbitrator has taken note of the essentially consistent description of the grievant's behavior by all of those who witnessed the events at issue, and the medical analysis of the grievant's condition by Dr. C.O., who treated her in Employee Health Services. In this connection the grievant's denial that she had ever at the time in question asked for a Union delegate was uniformly contradicted by other witnesses and by Dr. C.O., who recalled the grievant asking for a Union delegate.

Also, Dr. C.O. stated unequivocally in her affidavit that the grievant was not suffering from any "medical condition that would have caused her, during the two or three hours preceding my examination, to lose consciousness; to suffer a loss of memory; to fall on the floor; to suffer such pain that she would unknowingly or involuntarily emit screams, shouts, moans, or groans; or to thrash about on the floor, flail her arms, or engage in any unusual, uncontrollable or uncontrolled activity." Dr. C.O.'s conclusion is buttressed by the grievant's having had no history of similar attacks, and by the fact that her blood pressure on November 14 was no different than on the prior occasions when she had been at Employee Health Services.

In addition to the foregoing, further support for the conclusion that the grievant's actions in the corridor on November 14 were in protest to her assignment is to be found in the documentary evidence that she had engaged in a pattern of disruptive and insubordinate behavior going back six years. While the Union objects to such evidence on the ground that it was not apprised of the Hospital's warnings on those occasions, the evidence itself indicates that a Union delegate was present in connection with each of the verbal warnings to the grievant, and that two of her three written warnings were formally grieved, one being appealed by the Union to Step 3, where the Hospital's adverse decision was finally "accepted" by the Union delegate.

The Arbitrator also found the grievant to be a less credible witness than those witnesses who, without exception, took issue with her factual assertions. In the Arbitrator's perception, the grievant's comprehension and responses were remarkably selective on a number of important points.

The Arbitrator finds, given the serious nature of the grievant's offense on November 14, and the unsatisfactory quality of her prior record, containing numerous warnings with respect to similar conduct, that the Hospital had just cause to discharge.

CONCLUSION

For the foregoing reasons the discharge will be upheld and the grievance denied.

Analysis of the Case

Insubordination cases present a clear record of agreement among arbitrators. They rarely upset discipline for clear refusal to carry out appropriate orders. Arbitrators time and time again rule that in order to protect a job, a worker must obey an order and then grieve if the person feels the order is inappropriate. Of course, there are exceptions where such orders would require the employee to endanger health or safety of self or of other workers. The critical point in insubordination cases is that the orders must be clear, they must be understood by the employee to be an order, and the employee must understand from the supervisor's statement what penalty would ensue for failure to comply.[1]

Insubordination does not arise where an employee merely protests an order. It is the direct refusal to carry out an order that defines insubordination. This case provides the ingredients for a supportable management action: termination for insubordination. The incident can be examined step by step:

1. The employee was given a job assignment that was consistent with established policy. She refused the assignment.
2. Management investigated before taking action. The investigation was at the scene and was conducted immediately to determine whether the job assignment was presented correctly and was in the scope of established policies and procedures. Management made no assumptions.

3. Management determined, on site, that the job assignment was appropriate, then presented a direct and clear order to the employee to complete the assignment; the employee refused once again. Management reassigned the job to another employee similarly classified; it was done by another maid. This other employee completed the assignment without protest. Two clear facts were established by this action: (1) the immediacy of the need to complete the assignment, (2) the appropriateness of the assignment springing from the acceptance of the order by a similarly classified employee.

4. Management, fully aware that the grievant might possibly use an illness as a defense, promptly requested and obtained a medical evaluation. This eliminated illness as a legitimate reason for refusal and established inappropriate, unreasonable behavior directly related to the employee's desire not to complete the assignment.

5. Management obtained first-hand evidence as to the employee's refusal and subsequent behavior from the nurse involved in the job assignment situation.

6. Management imposed discipline that considered both the severity of the action itself and the employee's work history. Regarding the employee's work history, there is clear evidence of similar repeated behavior. Progressive disciplining, over a protracted period of time, was established: (1) six years preceding the incident at issue management had reduced a suspension to a first warning when it recognized such discipline as not progressive; (2) management did not issue a formal written warning until it had tolerated four separate incidents of profanity and intemperate outbursts. The case was built on documentation, reflecting fair and corrective application.

The employee's action was visibly harmful to patient care, which added to the level of severity of her behavior and indicated the need for termination rather than a lesser level of discipline.

The union's arguments regarding policy, the employee's longevity of service, and non-notification of prior discipline were far outweighed by excellent documentation and by evidence that indicated the corrective and progressive nature of the discipline applied over the past to this employee. The burden of providing "good and just cause" for discipline was met by the management.

NOTE

1. *Grievance Guide,* 6th ed. (Washington, D.C.: The Bureau of National Affairs, Inc., 1982), p. 24.

Chapter 8

Arbitration Cases: Dishonesty

CASE 5: FALSIFICATION OF SIGN-IN SHEET

Submission

The question at issue as stipulated by the parties is as follows:

1. Whether the discharge of R.H. was for cause and,
2. If not, what shall be the remedy?

Background Facts and Circumstances

The grievant, R.H., at the time of his discharge was a Community Youth Counselor employed by the Hospital's Adolescent Clinic. The grievant worked with troubled youths on a one-to-one basis at the youths' homes and in the neighborhood area. Two times a week, on Tuesdays and Fridays 9:00 A.M. to 12:00 noon, the grievant was assigned to provide counseling to the Hospital's patients at the Sports School. The grievant had been first employed by the Adolescent Clinic in February 1977.

The circumstances leading to the grievant's discharge were set forth in detail at the arbitration hearing, summarized, and evaluated by the parties in their respective posthearing briefs. Suffice it to cite for convenience of reference the termination notice on March 12, 1980:

Rule Violated:
    Any willful act detrimental to patient care or to Medical Center operations.
Details of Violation:
    On 3/11/80 we were made aware by the principal of the Sports School, where you are assigned to provide counseling services

for select students two or three mornings per week, that you have been calling the school, excusing yourself from your work there because you were supposedly needed at the clinic. This specifically occurred at least on Tuesday, 3/4, Thursday, 3/6, and Tuesday, 3/11. On Tuesday, 3/4, and Tuesday, 3/11, when you arrived in the clinic, you signed the sign-in sheet, indicating that you were at the school between 9:00 A.M. and 12:00 noon. On Thursday, 3/6, you failed to sign in at the clinic at all. In addition, you reported on your weekly census for the week of 3/3 to 3/7 counseling visits with students that never occurred. When confronted with these facts on 3/11, you admitted to both M.K., your immediate supervisor, and myself that they were true. Such behavior is extremely detrimental to our ability to provide counseling services within the community and, in fact, endangers the funding of the counseling program. It indicates a total disregard for your coworkers, your supervisors, and to your standing as an employee of this institution.

In view of this, we have no alternative but to terminate your employment effective today, 3/12.

Note: The employer later corrected the date and changed Thursday 3/6 to Friday 3/7.

Position of the Parties

The employer's position, as set forth in its posthearing brief, is essentially as follows:

1. That the grievant was discharged "for conduct detrimental to patient care—consisting of his failure to perform his assigned direct patient care responsibilities and his subsequent attempts to fraudulently conceal his activities;"
2. That on at least two days the grievant did not appear at the local public Junior High School to which he was assigned to meet with troubled youngsters on Tuesdays and Fridays;
3. That the grievant attempted to conceal his not meeting with his patients on the days in question by falsifying critically important time and patient care records; and
4. That after the grievant "was confronted with the facts of his misconduct, he concocted a series of purported justifications and totally unsupported and sometimes contradictory excuses and defenses."

The Union, on the other hand, contends as stated in its posthearing brief as follows:

1. That the grievant who had been hired in 1977 "was an excellent, competent and committed counselor . . . had received strongly favorable performance evaluations from his superiors throughout his employment . . . was the only counselor at the Employer's Community Youth program to be granted a Social Work Residency, in conjunction with his efforts toward a master's [degree] in social work, to begin in September, 1980 . . . was a hardworking, devoted and talented counselor (as evidenced by) the many hours of work devoted outside his normal working hours and on weekends;"
2. That the accusation the grievant was not at his school assignment on mornings scheduled "even if completely indefensible, hardly constitutes sufficient cause for the extreme and severe penalty of discharge;"
3. That the grievant "in fact was working on the days cited, March 4, 6 and 11" and his "behavior was not detrimental to patient care, and any of his actions which may later have been judged administratively incorrect were clearly not willfully detrimental;"
4. That the grievant "freely admitted . . . he had scribbled 'School' in the sign-in book on March 4 and 11, failed to sign in at all on March 6, and reported School visits on his March 3–7 census;" and
5. That "the absence of the word 'fraud' or 'falsification' in the Termination Notice" evidences that the grievant was not considered by the Employer "to have engaged in 'fraud' or 'falsification' when he was discharged."

Opinion

With respect to the charge of not having been at the School to meet with his student clients on the mornings of March 4, March 7, and March 11, the grievant admits that this was so for Tuesday, March 11. However, the grievant contends that he had made home visits involving two other clients on those mornings; that he had telephoned the principal of the School early to tell him he wouldn't be at the School and the principal had said "fine;" and that later after his discharge he had obtained affidavits from those with whom he had made the home visits to verify his whereabouts on the mornings of March 4 and March 11. On Friday, March 7, the grievant contends that he was at the School as assigned that morning.

The testimony of the principal differs from that of the grievant. The principal maintains that the grievant was not at the School on Friday,

March 7, testifying that he [Grievant] "had an office on the 5th floor . . . almost always came to my office and I'd round up the students for him . . . unless he saw the students outside there was no way he could see them without seeing me first . . . I had the key to his office." The principal testified also that the grievant "might have called me direct but I don't remember . . . I wrote the letter and was positive of the dates . . . he was not there other times as well . . . I picked the students and we discussed them . . . he would meet with those we felt would benefit from counseling . . . he met with them in the beginning individually, then in groups . . . after a while he didn't come . . . got five or six calls . . . woman who said she was his secretary said he was ill . . . happened for certain twice and believe more times."

Union argument to the contrary notwithstanding, there is no basis to disbelieve principal's testimony. But there are some mitigating considerations nonetheless. Chief among these are the following:

That the principal never spoke with the grievant and asked him to be more regular in meeting with the students; that principal's recollections at the arbitration hearing were not all that consistent as to the stated cause for the grievant's absences from School, testifying at one point that a woman representing herself as the grievant's secretary called and said he was ill while elsewhere he testified that the grievant said he was needed at the Clinic; that the principal never spoke with the grievant's Supervisor (M.K.) or with P.C., the Assistant Director of the Adolescent Health Center, to check or complain about the grievant's absence from the School; that the principal didn't recall the grievant's exact days of the week he was assigned to the School; and that the principal's query as to the grievant's work at the School came about incidentally when speaking on another matter with another employee at the Clinic (S.C.), and he mentioned that he "was sorry" the grievant was "so sick and was not coming to the School."

The failure to discuss the grievant's absences from School directly with the grievant, or with the Clinic's managers, or with both, seems inconsistent with the allegations that the grievant did not meet with the students he was counseling at the School "on numerous occasions" after his initial months on the assignment.

It raises questions, too, as to the extent and seriousness of the grievant's wrongdoing and lends support to the Union's contention, in effect, that the grievant's supervisors and Hospital officials overreacted; that the grievant was inadequately forewarned as to his shortcomings and the consequences of his failure to mend his ways; and that the lack of thorough investigation and forewarning prior to discharge was in violation of the essentials of progressive discipline and due process to which the grievant was especially entitled in view of his exemplary three-year record of competent, dedicated, and hardworking service as a Counselor in the Hospital's Community Youth program.

With respect to the grievant's contention supported by affidavits that he made home visits on March 3 and March 11, counsel for the Hospital argued that "the affidavits themselves are seriously suspect" and that "based on . . . conflicting testimony coupled with the failure of the Union to produce any live witnesses, these documents should not be given any weight whatsoever."

In regard to the failure "to produce any live witnesses," it needs to be noted as the Union argued in rebuttal that Article XXVIII, Section 3, of the Collective Bargaining Agreement clearly states that where a "patient does not appear at the arbitration, the arbitrator shall not consider the failure of the patient to appear as prejudicial." Further, a review of the transcript at the Unemployment Insurance hearing shows that the grievant had named the patients he had seen on March 4 and March 11, and there is nothing in the contract that would have prevented a verification check by the Hospital at that time or even during the instant arbitration when the affidavits were placed in evidence.

It was also argued, in effect, that the grievant's reference to house visits as a justification for his absence from the School on March 4 and March 11 was an "afterthought" and suspect as a "contrived" excuse. And, in support of this contention, it was pointed out that in the disciplinary interviews with the Supervisor and P.C. which led to his discharge, the grievant did not mention being on home visits and, in fact, offered to resign. Such a conclusion, however, is speculative and conjectural at best.

The grievant admitted that he had not presented factual support in his defense and had offered to resign at the disciplinary interviews. As testified by the grievant, however, this was not because he was guilty but, rather, because in his emotional state and shock at what he believed was a grossly unfair prejudgment that he was guilty of being unfaithful, lacking in integrity, and breaching his professional responsibility he felt the best thing to do at the time was to leave the job.

This testimony is not unbelievable in the light of the grievant's prior unblemished if not impeccable record; the fact that he had never before been cautioned, let alone disciplined, for inattentiveness to, or absence from, his assigned work at the School; and that, at the time of the disciplinary interviews, one of the days he was being accused of having been absent was a day in which he had worked with his supervisor at the Clinic and had no responsibilities whatsoever at the School. However, as Hospital counsel argued, the grievant was, indeed, less than consistent in his testimony as to when and how he obtained the affidavits. But the areas of question raised in this regard are not such as to warrant the conclusion that "these documents should not be given any weight whatsoever."

The grievant is charged with having signed the sign-in sheet as being at the School when he was not there and, as argued in the Hospital's brief, deliberately falsifying critically important time and patient care records. And, in this regard, the evidence is clear that the grievant's sign-in sheets for March 4, 7, and 11, were marked as having spent the mornings at the School whereas by his own testimony he was making home visits on March 4 and 11th. Further, on the Patient Census—a client activity sheet—for the week of March 3 through March 8, the grievant recorded counseling eight students at the School whereas in fact by his own testimony he had only counseled two.

These are serious wrongdoings and it is adjudged that they warrant severe discipline even though the preponderance of evidence is not conclusive that the grievant's actions were deliberately fraudulent. The grievant's testimony that he was planning a full-day field trip for his School group on a weekend is unconvincing as an excuse for having put down "School" rather than house visits on the sign-in sheets and having recorded patients he did not see on his weekly Patient Census. In any case, the grievant's contentions in this regard are not held to be a mitigating circumstance.

But the lack of precise written guidelines, instructions, and other administrative regulatory precautions with vigilant follow-through and periodic check-up lends substance to the Union's contention in support of the grievant that standards were inexact. In this regard, it is to be noted that while Supervision stated all Counselors were expected to record their whereabouts in detail accurately and fully to account for their day's activities, the testimony and exhibits in evidence were not convincing that this was done in every instance by all Counselors.

Be that as it may, it is concluded for reasons cited above that while the grievant's wrongdoings were serious, all considered, discharge was too severe a penalty under the circumstances. Accordingly, the discharge is to be reduced to a suspension and the grievant is to be reinstated without back pay.

AWARD

I, the undersigned, to whom was submitted a certain issue between the parties hereto, having duly heard the proofs and allegations and after due consideration, do hereby award as follows:

1. That for reasons herein set forth there was cause for disciplining R.H. but discharge was too extreme a penalty under the circumstances; and
2. That the discharge be reduced to a suspension and R.H. be reinstated without back pay.

Analysis of the Case

This handbook has stressed throughout that if management expects its disciplinary decisions to be upheld through the grievance machinery (including arbitration), it must clearly demonstrate its compliance with the essentials of effective employee communication. For example, management must:

1. establish reasonable standards of performance and systems of operation
2. communicate such standards and systems clearly to all employees
3. communicate to all employees the consequences of failure to meet standards or to operate within system parameters
4. establish a system of periodic employee performance appraisal consistent and equitable to all employees
5. establish systems of constructive, fair, and progressive counseling and discipline for substandard performance, excessively poor punctuality and attendance records, and policy and rules violations
6. follow up on all counseling and discipline with the end result producing improved employee behavior—or termination

Failure to have such a system in effect was, to a large degree, the reason management's discharge decision was reduced by the arbitrator to a suspension. In the last paragraph of his opinion, the arbitrator stated (emphases added):

". . . But the lack of *precise written guidelines, instructions* and other *administrative regulatory precautions* with vigilant *follow-through* and *periodic check-up* lend substance to the Union's contention in support of the grievant that *standards were inexact*" and ". . . while Supervision stated all Counselors were expected to record their whereabouts in detail accurately and fully . . . , the testimony and exhibits in evidence were not convincing that this was done in *every instance by all Counselors.*"

Earlier in his opinion the arbitrator stated:

". . . there is no basis to disbelieve the Principal's testimony. But there are some mitigating considerations nonetheless. Chief among these are the following:

"That the principal *never spoke with the grievant* and *asked him to be more regular in meeting with the students . . .*" and ". . . *never spoke with the grievant's Supervisor* (M.K.) or with P.C., the Assistant Director of the Adolescent Health Center, *to check or complain about the grievant's absence from the School . . .*"

"*The failure to discuss the grievant's absences from School directly with the grievant, or with the Clinic's managers, or with both, seems inconsistent with the allegations . . .*" and ". . . *the grievant was inadequately forewarned as to his shortcomings and the consequences of his failure to mend his ways . . .*" and ". . . *the lack of thorough investigation and forewarning prior to discharge were in violation of the essentials of progressive discipline and due process. . . .*"

Had management better evaluated its position and identified case weaknesses before taking action, it might have suspended the employee rather than terminating him, avoiding the forced reinstatement. The lessons learned from this case are that disciplining must be progressive and equitable, and management cannot make hasty judgments regarding employee dishonesty.

Dishonesty is a serious charge and should be based upon a preponderance of evidence. As the arbitrator strongly implies, there is a great deal of difference between fraudulent action by an employee and poor judgment. Supervisors must understand this and recognize the difference.

Arbitrators will view any infraction, even of a serious nature, against a background of the employee's record. They often reverse discharges where the employee has an unblemished work record. As pointed out in previous cases and in the text of this book, discharge penalties are reduced or reversed in a high majority of arbitration cases where dishonesty is involved. It is well to repeat that a study of many successfully administered disciplinary procedures indicates this pattern:[1]

1. Company rules are carefully explained to employees.
2. Accusations against employees are carefully considered to see if they are supported by facts.
3. A regular "warning" procedure is worked out and applied.

4. The union is brought into the disciplinary case early in the procedure.
5. Before disciplinary action is taken, the employee's motive and reasons for the violation are investigated.
6. Before disciplinary action is taken, the employee's past record is taken into consideration.
7. Companies make sure that all management agents, and particularly first-line supervisors, know the companies' disciplinary policies and procedures and carefully observe them.
8. Discipline *short of discharge* is used wherever possible.

CASE 6: FALSIFICATION OF TIMECARDS

We are here concerned with the discharge, effective April 24, by the Hospital of six employees of the Medical Records Department. The very serious allegation by the Hospital is that the grievants tampered with their timecards with the result of falsifying their time records in their favor. The six grievants, F.A.F., N.C., O.G., D.V., T.W., and H.H., all deny strenuously, as does their collective bargaining representative, that they are guilty of the charge herein. On their behalf the Union requests reinstatement with full back pay.

Multiple hearings were held on these discharges. Full opportunity to adduce evidence, examine and cross-examine witnesses, and produce exhibits was afforded. Both parties were represented by labor relations counsel and a full and fair hearing was had.

The origin of the events which led to the discharges occurred in or about late November when, on a Friday, a supervisor observed that an employee who was late and had not yet appeared for work had a card in the time rack with a piece of tape on the Thursday column. She and another supervisor examined the card and then placed it back on the rack. Later that day, after the affected employee, T.T., had arrived to work, his card was examined again. The tape on the Thursday column had been removed and there was a ring-in both for Thursday and Friday with no lateness indicated on either day. That employee was immediately discharged for tampering with his timecard, with the result of a falsification in his favor. He resigned the next day, December 3.

The current cards for other employees were then scanned and it was observed that A.C., another employee in the Medical Records Department, had cards which had been altered. He was discharged, grieved, and his discharge was later upheld in arbitration. Thereafter, in January, or early February, another employee, M.P., was discharged when it was discovered that the 9:47 A.M. ring had been changed by pen to 9:17. She was permitted to resign, and the discharge accordingly was avoided.

Thus, as a result of these three incidents, Management had cause to believe that some employees were probably engaged in the jiggling of cards, namely a punch-in with either no day being entered or a day appearing in a wrong column, or by painting, that is, changing the cards by pen.

During the pendency of the A.C. arbitration hearings, the Union served a subpoena on the Hospital for production of the timecards of all employees in the Medical Records Department for all that year, evidently in an effort to establish that the Hospital lacked "just cause" for that discharge. Hospital supervision, in getting the cards together, and examining them carefully under a magnifying glass, discovered that the grievants involved in this instant matter had also assertedly engaged in the painting and jiggling process, and in one or two cases, an erasure was also observable.

Thus, as this record and its many exhibits do establish, in F.A.F.'s case, 21 timecards are material, with 46 changes. In N.C.'s case 25 cards are in evidence, with 41 changes. In O.G.'s case, 10 timecards are in evidence, with 14 changes. In D.V.'s case, five timecards are in evidence with six changes. In T.W.'s case, five timecards are in evidence with five changes, and, in H.H.'s case, five timecards are in evidence, with eight changes. Most of the changes are so-called paints, that is, ink changes or modifications; some are jiggles; a very few are erasures. There is no question that the alterations have occurred.

The Hospital contends that in each and every instance, the paintings or jiggles or erasures favored the employees. Significantly, in this connection, if an employee accumulates 15 minutes of lateness in a week, he is docked one-half hour's pay. In each and every case the alterations or modifications decreased or eliminated the lateness involved, and consequently any possible "docking of pay."

The Hospital concedes that it cannot "prove by actual observation" that any of the grievants were observed modifying their cards, but it maintains that corroboration in cases such as these is "either a product of happenstance or of perjured testimony." It relies upon the "logical and legitimate inference" that since the Supervisors had no reason to alter the cards, and have not been charged with any alteration, that the Arbitrator render his decision upon the customary evaluation of the record as a whole and the credibility of the grievants in the light of all the facts.

The Union, for its part, argues vigorously that we [the union] have six long-time employees who deny that they committed the complained-of acts. Further, it emphasizes that each timecard is checked and signed or initialed by two Supervisors; one, the immediate Supervisor, and the other, a Management employee who calculates the time involved. Since each grievant had good records, it contends that the charged infractions are not consistent with their good reputations, insisting further that the Company has the burden of proving each case "beyond a reasonable doubt."

There is no doubt that the Supervisor who initials the card and the one who calculates the time involved do not audit the card, either with the "naked eye" or with a magnifying glass, for fraud or tampering, but merely to determine whether, in fact, there is a lateness or an absence, and its quantum. It was not until the Union had subpoenaed a year's cards, and supervision had some time to examine carefully each card, that the infractions herein were observed. Further, since these grievants are not "problem employees," and Supervision was satisfied with their performance over the years, it is normally inconceivable that they would have been selected, even at random, for the kind of manipulative modification by Supervision which would result in the entrapment implied by the Union.

Significantly, as well, in terms of evaluating motives and deeds, not one of the [120] modifications on the [71] cards in evidence occurred after December 3. The date of December 3 is important because it was on that date that A.C. and T.T. were discharged and the "word" circulated within the Medical Records Department like a "shock wave" that their discharges were for altering or tampering with their timecards. No further "risk-taking," altering, or tampering, as indicated above, occurred after that date.

An examination of the 120 modifications establishes that they are for the most part very skillful and difficult to observe without very careful scrutiny either by the naked eye or with a magnifying glass. A cursory glance, normally that of a Supervisor interested only in checking for an accumulation of lateness without any indication that there had been an alteration which he or she should look for, would not result in any alarm, or discovery of modification.

There are approximately 115 employees in the Medical Records Department and these timecard alterations were "uncovered" when Supervision had the time, after they had been subpoenaed, to review each card with appreciable care.

Each of the grievants testified. Thus, F.A.F. stated that he first came with the Hospital 13 years ago and that his only infractions were latenesses in two separate years, for which he received written warnings. He denied that he had modified or altered his timecards in any way. There is no modification which took place after December 3. Grievant F.A.F. on cross-examination conceded that he knew by "rumor" that T.T. and A.C. were terminated on that date for tampering with their timecards. He agreed he had a good relationship with his Supervisors. On his behalf the Union presented a decision by the Unemployment Insurance Board granting him Unemployment Insurance.

N.C. in his testimony pointed out that he, too, had been employed for the same length of time and he, too, denied that he had modified or changed any of his timecards. His work record, he observed, was excellent, as he had never received even a written warning. He stated when he was discharged that he was told by his Supervisor, "I'm sorry, but this is Hospital policy," and that he did not respond. He, too, learned quickly about the discharge of T.T. and A.C. His timecards also reveal no changes after December 3, the date of their discharge. He maintained that the alterations on most of his cards can be observed with the naked eye, and faulted his Supervisors for not finding them at the time of their occurrence. However, he conceded on cross-examination that he had never observed the changes until his discharge. As with F.A.F. he, too, was the beneficiary of an Unemployment Insurance decision which granted Unemployment Insurance payments.

O.G. testified that he was hired 10 years ago and that he had stated immediately when he was told he was discharged that he had been "guilty of nothing." He, too, denied ever changing or altering any of his timecards and pointed out that his only discipline was a written warning four years ago for absenteeism. He agreed that all the changes in the timecards were in his favor and that none occurred after December 3.

D.V. testified that he was hired six years ago. He, too, denied that he had ever altered or modified any of his timecards and stressed that they had been approved by Supervision initially. He observed that he was "shocked" when he was discharged and emphasized that at least some of the changes on his card can be observed with the "naked eye." His Supervisors, he conceded, seemed to be favorably disposed to him, and he has had no problems in his employment. He, too, is now receiving Unemployment Insurance.

T.W. noted that he had been hired ten years ago. He stated that when his discharge notice was handed to him, he said "nothing." He has received two Service Awards and no warnings in his ten years of employment. He denied that he ever changed or modified any of his cards. On cross-examination, he, too, admitted that he "got along" with all his Supervisors; that all the changes were in his favor, that some of them were indeed observable with the naked eye, and that he had learned immediately after T.T. and A.C. were discharged that, according to the "rumors," the discharges had occurred because of their tampering with their timecards. As with the others, no changes had been observed since that date. He has not sought Unemployment Insurance, having found other work in the meantime.

H.H. testified that he came to work fifteen years ago; that he was on vacation when the discharge occurred, and that he had one warning notice during his employment, receiving, incidentally, an Award for completing a Medical Terminology course in the Spring three years ago. He denied, as well, that he had ever tampered with his timecards and conceded on cross-examination that "no Supervisor ever had it in for me." He, too, has received Unemployment Insurance and he, too, as do the others, seeks reinstatement and a make-whole order in this matter.

In resolving this matter, I have weighed the Union's argument that no one testified in this proceeding that any employee was actually observed "making the skillful changes" which resulted in the timecards' being altered. I have also carefully considered the Union's contention that the Supervisors, one of whom checked the cards merely to see if there was any lateness, and the other to calculate the hours worked, had nonetheless an obligation to find the alterations and then "talk to the employees," counsel them, and warn them. It insists that since many of the changes can be seen with the "naked eye," this should have been done, and emphasizes that these employees have all had good records and long service.

On the other hand one cannot overlook or ignore certain indisputable facts, namely that the timecards were all altered either by pen, by jiggling, or by erasure; that each of the alterations was in favor of the employee affected; that if any employee has 15 minutes of accumulated lateness, he is docked one-half hour at the end of the week, and therefore that there is a clear and obvious advantage to the employee in making these alterations. Of course, the Hospital concedes that there are no witnesses who saw the changes being made, but observes that an Arbitrator must "dispense industrial justice without parking his common sense at the door."

I note that no Supervisor was even charged in this proceeding with any "ill will" against any of the grievants and that since the grievants all had good records there could be not even a scintilla of advantage to the Hospital in fabricating or having a motive so to do.

Supervisors in this matter, as had been their long and consistent practice, only cursorily examined the cards. They cannot be faulted for so doing; they are neither sleuths nor detectives and their examination of the card only for the purpose of noting latenesses and calculating time cannot give rise for the "bootstrap" conclusion that the Union here seeks. Especially is this so in view of the concededly "skillful" alterations. These were hardly clumsy modifications, easy to catch or see.

The "work place," as Supreme Court Justice Douglas had observed, must be comprehended, not theoretically but rather in a practical way based upon industrial realities. Unlike Unemployment Insurance decisions, the end product of an arbitral evaluation is based upon "just cause" considerations weighed, as in this case, in the light of industrial common law and the mores of the work place.

A statutory approach based upon the broad public policy of the specific statute involved is not coexistent with the approach and decisions required in the light of the parties' collectively bargained agreement. The "public interest" set forth in the preamble of a socially desirable statute, for example granting unemployment compensation payments, is hardly the same as the "private interest" requiring the application of "just cause" criteria. Thus, arbitrators have universally and consistently held that Unemployment Compensation awards cannot be binding in Arbitration.

Again, a most careful evaluation of the evidence in this case conclusively establishes that the timecards in evidence were indeed altered, that the tampering resulted in each grievant's favor, and, under all the circumstances, that each of the grievants participated in improper activity in his own favor. In so concluding, I have evaluated credibility and demeanor, as well as all the record evidence before me. I am constrained to conclude that what has happened here provides "just cause" for the action taken by the Hospital. Cardinal infractions have occurred which must be placed "at the door" of each grievant; the evidence is overwhelming. I find, as did the Arbitrator in the A.C. case, that the discharges herein were indeed for "just cause."

Accordingly, the Union's grievances on behalf of its members must be, and are, denied, as each has repeatedly committed dischargeable infractions.

I regret exceedingly that the efforts made during the course of the proceeding to settle and adjust this controversy on a mutually agreeable basis were not successful and that this adjudication, difficult as it is, must be made.

One final word: All six of these grievants have good records otherwise; all six are long-term employees.

Although rarely invoked for understandable reasons, an application of equitable considerations permits that each grievant, as in the T.T. and M.P. cases, here be given one final chance to resign, even though, as in the A.C. case, both parties have necessarily had to expend large sums and considerable time in processing their cases. Accordingly, solely as a compassionate matter, without prejudice to either party in the future, and certainly without any precedent value, lest others be encouraged to insist on the processing of grievances lacking in merit, I will provide that "last chance" in the appended Award.

AWARD

The Arbitrator, having been designated in accordance with the Arbitration Agreement entered into by the above-named parties, and having duly heard the proofs and allegations of the parties, awards as follows:

I. The discharges of F.A.F., N.C., O.G., D.V., T.W., and H.H. are each supported by "just cause." Accordingly, the Union's grievances on their behalf must be, and are, overruled.

II. For reasons set forth in the attached Opinion, each grievant may resign within ten (10) days of the date of this Award, effective April 24 of last year. For those who do so, the Hospital's records shall so state, notations regarding discharge shall be physically expunged, and references and inquiries shall reflect a resignation. For those who choose not to resign within the next ten (10) days, the Hospital's records are to reflect the arbitral determination made in Decretal Paragraph I above, namely, that the grievants' employment terminated by discharge, adjudicated to be grounded upon just cause.

Analysis of the Case

In this case of employee dishonesty, the Union bases its defense of the accused six on the following four points:

1. None of the accused employees was actually seen by anyone tampering with his or anyone else's timecard.
2. Supervision was responsible for checking and approving employee timecards. The cards in question were checked and approved when originally submitted, with supervision giving no indications at that time of changes to time entries made by employees.
3. All of the accused were long-service employees with clean records.
4. Most of the accused employees were granted Unemployment Insurance compensation (although those standards are quite different and are not binding on the arbitrator).

These are significant points that, if not for the lack of credibility of the grievants' testimony, would have had substantial weight in deciding the fate of these employees. In addition, the decision to discharge all six was impacted to a great extent by the previous two resignations and one discharge generated by timecard frauds.

Supervisors no doubt will encounter situations where employee discipline should be administered for unacceptable behavior absent corroborating witnesses. Such action may be necessary even without such eye-witnesses; therefore, it is one person's story against another's. Such cases are the toughest kind to adjudicate, especially where the involved employee has an unblemished record.

The arbitrator concludes, with regard to the union's suggestion that supervision should have discovered the alteration when the timecards were submitted originally, that supervisors are not detectives. In this case, management's longstanding practice was to check for lateness and to calculate time only. In fact, as the arbitrator points out, had the timecards not been subpoenaed by the union in its defense of one of the offenders in a prior case, management's scrutiny in this instance more than likely would not have occurred at all.

In affording the "last chance to resign" option, the arbitrator recognized that the six were long-term employees who until this situation had essentially good records, factors very important to arbitrators in their determinations.

In cases of dishonesty, as pointed out earlier, arbitrators require a higher standard of proof since an employee will be stigmatized as "discharged for theft" with the potential this has for causing a permanent loss of employment. Altering timecards is considered as theft of the institution's money. The evidence required to support a discharge for dishonesty frequently is stated by arbitrators as "proof beyond a reasonable doubt," as compared to a lesser degree of proof in other cases where all that is required is "preponderance of the evidence." Arbitrators generally agree that discipline may be enforced where employees have falsified work records.

Finally, it is well to note the arbitrator's clear distinction between arbitration and Unemployment Insurance proceedings. If after careful review of the facts an employer who is convinced that the decision to discipline meets "just cause" criteria should not hesitate in implementing that decision. Awards for Unemployment Compensation eligibility, in most cases, do not influence the arbitrator's decision, which is based strictly on just cause merits.

NOTE

1. Grievance Guide, 6th ed. (Washington, D.C.: The Bureau of National Affairs, Inc., 1982), pp. 4–5.

Chapter 9

Arbitration Cases: Patient Abuse

CASE 7: ALLEGATIONS BY FEMALE PATIENT

Opinion and Award

Pursuant to the provisions of a collective bargaining agreement, the undersigned was selected under the rules of the American Arbitration Association to hear and decide a dispute between the parties. Hearings were held on December 10, and January 12 and February 8 of the following year, at the offices of the American Arbitration Association in New York City. Both parties attended and were represented by counsel. The Union and the Employer were represented by counsel. Based upon the evidence introduced and the arguments made, the Arbitrator issues this Opinion and Award.

Issue

At the outset of the first day of hearing, the parties agreed to the following issue:

1. Was T.S. discharged for just cause?
2. If not, what shall be the remedy?

Facts

On July 9, Dr. L., Director of Psychiatry at the Hospital, was informed that a patient, L.S., had reported that a mental health worker, T.S., engaged in intercourse with her on two occasions. Dr. L. conducted an investigation and, based on the facts presented to him, concluded that the evidence supported these allegations. To a large degree, the underlying facts are not in dispute.

Mr. T.S. has worked at the Hospital for 15 years, except for three years' service in the armed forces, and has been a mental health worker for 12 years. Ms. L.S. has been a patient off and on at the mental health center at the Hospital for a number of years and has known Mr. T.S. for about four years. Ms. L.S. was part of Mr. T.S.'s therapy group at the Hospital and she had great trust in him.

In May of last year Ms. L.S. was being treated at the day hospital service, a service for persons who do not need 24-hour attention. These persons come to the Hospital five days a week but go home evenings and weekends. Towards the end of May, Ms. L.S. broke up with her boyfriend with whom she had been living for over two years and decided to get her own apartment and to look for a job. She found an apartment near the Hospital and moved in during early June.

However, at this time Ms. L.S. was readmitted to the Hospital as a result of an incident that occurred in the apartment and she was concerned about the apartment's security as the result of this incident. Consequently, Ms. L.S. discussed her concerns about leaving the Hospital and about the security of her apartment with Mr. T.S. In that conversation he told her that it was a simple matter to change the cylinder of a lock and he tried to explain it to her. She told him that she had no money to buy a new lock and that she did not want to borrow any more money from her father. In order to be helpful, Mr. T.S. told her he had an extra lock and that he would bring it in and exchange it for her lock.

On Monday, June 22, at about 4:30 P.M., Ms. L.S. approached Mr. T.S. and asked him if he had the lock with him. He said yes, and that she could change it. However, she prevailed upon him to change the lock for her and he agreed. They left the Hospital together and he drove her to the apartment where Mr. T.S. changed the lock. At this point the testimony diverges. Ms. L.S. claims that Mr. T.S. stayed; they talked and engaged in intercourse. Mr. T.S. states that he returned to the Hospital immediately after changing the lock. Similarly, the stories differ with regard to events on July 6. Ms. L.S. testified that she saw Mr. T.S. at the Hospital, invited him to her apartment and they engaged in intercourse again. Mr. T.S. denies ever being in Ms. L.S.'s apartment again or ever having intercourse with her.

Following the second alleged incident, Ms. L.S. became upset and mixed up about what had occurred with Mr. T.S. and she related the allegations to various personnel at the Hospital. Thereafter, Dr. L. was informed and conducted the investigation which uncovered these facts, among others. On July 21, Dr. L. concluded that the allegations were supported by the evidence, and Mr. T.S. was informed that he was discharged. The Union grieved the decision to this arbitration.

Positions of the Parties

The Hospital argues that the testimony of Ms. L.S. is credible, is corroborated by other evidence, and supports the Hospital's decision to terminate Mr. T.S. The Hospital asserts that Mr. T.S. visited Ms. L.S.'s apartment by himself in violation of Hospital policy, failed to report his visit to anyone either orally or in writing, and failed to punch out his timecard on July 6, the date of the second incident. According to the Hospital, Ms. L.S.'s testimony was consistent and believable because there was no reason for her to implicate Mr. T.S. unless her story was true.

The Union urges that a comparison of Ms. L.S.'s testimony with Mr. T.S.'s can lead only to the conclusion that Ms. L.S.'s allegations are consistent with her prior problems and past history of hospitalizations. The Union does not contend that Ms. L.S. was purposely telling untruths but that she has a history of dealing in fantasies, hallucinations, and other delusions. The Union notes that Mr. T.S. not only has an unblemished record for over fifteen years but has received commendations for his work. According to the Union, these factors, plus the fact that the Hospital did not conduct a full investigation into the facts, support the proposition that the Hospital has failed to meet its burden of proof in this case.

Discussion

As both parties have urged, the basic issue in this case involves a determination of credibility. Two persons have testified under oath and their testimony is diametrically opposed on the crucial fact—whether Mr. T.S. and Ms. L.S. engaged in intercourse on June 22 and July 6. (The Hospital conceded at the hearing that Mr. T.S. was discharged for engaging in intercourse with a patient and not for visiting her by himself or failing to punch his timecard.) There are no other eyewitnesses to the events, and there are no compelling assertions or contradictions which lead the way to a definitive result. Instead, the evidence presents the most difficult type of case for an arbitrator to decide, one dependent solely on the credibility of witnesses.

It would be extremely difficult and it would serve no purpose (in fact it might be harmful) to detail and analyze the specific aspects of testimony and circumstantial evidence which have led to the result reached in this case. It is sufficient to state that the weight of all the circumstances, evidence, and testimony leads me to believe that while the Hospital's actions were understandable, its decision to discharge Mr. T.S. is not supported by the record.

Therefore, based on the evidence presented and the arguments made, the Arbitrator issues the following.

AWARD

There was not just cause for the discharge of T.S. Mr. T.S. shall be reinstated with full back pay, seniority, and all other benefits, less any earnings during this period.

It is so ordered.

Analysis of the Case

"It is sufficient to state that the weight of *all the circumstances, evidence, and testimony* leads me to believe that while the Hospital's actions were understandable, its decision to discharge Mr. T.S. *is not supported by the record*" (emphasis added).

This sentence immediately preceding the Arbitrator's Award is restated here because of its critical importance to decisions regarding employee discipline. When management asks itself if the record supports the decision in discipline cases, it must fully understand what the record is. It is not merely the charge against the employee or the testimony in the hearing. It is not solely the length of time the person has worked in a particular classification, or for the hospital. It is all of these, and more.

Granted, the patient abuse charge in this case is serious and, in different circumstances, could have resulted in the discharge of Mr. T.S. even in the face of a clean record plus 17 years of service. Managements may act hastily, take swift action to terminate, and not thoroughly investigate the charges of patient abuse in their efforts to still the cries of outrage and indignation from staff or others. In this case, the hospital made its decision based on the allegation of the patient, who may not have been truthful or able to discern fact from fantasy.

The hospital should have reasoned, given the one-to-one nature of the incident and in view of the patient's medical history, that determination of guilt or innocence must be made from facts established from other sources. The totality of the employee's record must be considered. Were there any such previous allegations from patients, employees, or others in Mr. T.S.'s 17-year work history? Did Mr. T.S. have a criminal record of sex offenses? The written record shows an unblemished work history with commendations for superior work performance. The hospital offered no testimony as to behavior, work patterns, or actions that would give credence to the patient's allegations.

It is clear that management must proceed with extreme caution in discharge determinations. This is especially true in patient abuse cases, since the most difficult problem in such cases arises where they deal with sexual molestation or assault. Evidence of bodily injury is not always apparent. The employee may—and often does—charge that the "abused patient is venting the fantasies of a sick or senile mind."[1] In such cases, arbitrators insist that the evidence required to support a discharge display proof beyond a reasonable doubt, while a lesser degree of proof, such as preponderance of evidence, may be acceptable in other types of cases.

Charges injurious to a worker's reputation have the potential of causing a permanent loss of employment. Management must be mindful that such charges, if unfounded and unsupported by evidence, may lead to lawsuits. Finally, in most one-to-one situations (employee vs. patient), arbitrators lean heavily on the credibility factor: who is the more credible witness.

CASE 8: SEXUAL CHARGES BY MALE PATIENT

The parties were heard on July 5 in regard to the following stipulated issue:

1. Was there cause for the discharge of N.W.?
2. If not, what shall the remedy be?

The grievant is a transporter who when not transporting patients to and from the department is assigned miscellaneous jobs there. He was discharged for sexually abusing a patient on March 17.

The patient is 27 years old, is mentally retarded, with a 9 to 14-year-old mental age level, according to his doctor. He knows what an oath is and truth from falsity.

The patient suffers from epileptic seizures and ataxia, and his movements are uncoordinated. He can, however, sign his name, urinate into a bottle without help, and adjust his clothing. When questioned, he may ramble at times, but he can slowly and laboriously speak, explain, and describe.

Though he can walk with a cane, during the month of March while he was in the Hospital, 5 North, he moved or was moved in a wheelchair. On March 17th he was in a wheelchair, tied there because of his seizures, and because of its low wheels required help of a second person for movement.

It is the patient's testimony that on March 17 the grievant sexually abused him in the toilet near the TV lounge. Allegedly, there were four assaults, and the grievant, per the patient's testimony, committed these at two different points in time when he twice took him to the lounge.

It is the grievant's testimony that he only took the patient to the lounge once with the Head Nurse's knowledge. (That he did take the patient once to the lounge with the Nurse's knowledge is not in dispute.) There they talked about sundry matters for about 12 to 15 minutes, when the patient said he had to urinate. The grievant took the patient to the toilet, and helped him urinate. They returned to the lounge, spoke for some nine minutes more when again the patient had to urinate, and the process was repeated. At no time, according to the grievant, was there any sexual abuse; all he did was help the patient.

Examination by the police laboratory showed semen stains on the pajamas the patient wore on March 17th. Whether the stains on the March 17th pajamas were due to patient abuse by the grievant is to be determined.

Discussion

The number of incidents and whether some took place before lunch or all after lunch is not determinative in the issue before me. Nor are the questions whether the patient enjoyed sexual play by another, whether he called on God in ecstasy or for protection, or whether he called on God at all. The only question is whether the grievant committed the act claimed.

In a case such as this, corroboration can only result from either happenstance or perjured witnesses. Failure to produce corroboration neither proves nor disproves the allegation. If the acts claimed were actually committed, they would not be performed in the presence of noninvolved witnesses; if not done, they would not be claimed if impartial witnesses were present. Whether in fact they did take place can only be determined by assessing credibility on the basis of the evidence as a whole.

The patient testified that he tried to speak to the Head Nurse before the grievant returned with him to the TV room the second time. He was agitated, and his doctor witnessed this immediately after the grievant left the lounge when the patient related what happened. Later in the day, an attempt to get details from him was terminated due to his agitation. This followed an expressed intent by the grievant to the Head Nurse to cheer the patient, because he looked lonely, and did not expect visitors that day.

Whether the grievant reported two bathroom trips, as he testified, or several, as the patient's doctor testified, because the patient was urinating frequently, telling this to the patient's doctor could have been either a helpful afterthought or forethought in the event of later accusations. The condition ascribed to the patient was unusual for he had no urological problems, and there had been no reports or observations of such a condition in the more than two weeks the patient had been hospitalized.

Unusual too would be the fact that the patient would need someone to assist him in relieving himself. The grievant testified that he hesitated when the patient claimedly asked to go to the bathroom. He helped him in the process, though the patient did not ask. Why he did not hesitate here too when he was not involved in patient care is not understandable, and his account is hardly credible in view of the fact that the patient urinates without help.

Some allowance must be made for failure of memory, and this often explains contradictory testimony by a witness. Where, however, there is a discharge based on such serious charges, I cannot accept a failure to recollect what brought the grievant to 5 North, the area where the patient herein involved was hospitalized, as anything but an evasion, particularly when the record shows that he did not transport anyone from his department there. The grievant must have given March 17th a good deal of thought; there was a grievance session since then, and though the arbitration was held on July 5th, the time lapse should not lead to a memory lapse on so basic and obvious a question.

At approximately 11:00 A.M., after delivering a patient from and to another hospital floor, the grievant could not be found. He returned at noon to sign out for his 45-minute lunch period. After lunch, he picked up a patient from the floor where the incident in this case occurred, at 1:00 P.M., and delivered her for therapy. The log does not contain his initials showing that he returned her there. His supervisor, who witnessed his 11:00 A.M. absence, also testified that this was the second time he was missing that day, and the 5 North patient in therapy was returned by another transporter. The grievant did not return for a 1:30 P.M. new pickup until 2:00 P.M.

The grievant's absences and his lunch period were within the time frame of the alleged sexual abuse. It makes credible the patient's testimony that the grievant was twice, not once, with him in the TV room. Unexplained absences, longer than some 15 minutes he claimed he was with the patient, combined with the patient's ability to urinate unaided, to dress and adjust his clothing make the grievant's testimony incredible where excessive patient urination was never noted during his hospital stay.

Involved here is not discipline for failure to meet time-work obligations, but for far more serious reasons. It was obligatory on the grievant to explain what he was doing during a time which, even without lunch, greatly exceeded the approximately 15 minutes he claimed only to have spent with the patient. He neither explained the time gap nor what he was doing on the patient's floor when he transported no one back to there.

I am fully cognizant of the fact that the grievant is a long-term employee and that the charges against him are extremely serious and reputation damaging. Though there may be some question as to whether the first time he removed the patient to the lounge he played with his privates there or masturbated him in the bathroom, I am convinced that the charges are substantially true. Any employee, regardless of length of service, merits discharge for sexual abuse of a patient in violation of the hospital's duty of care.

After considering the evidence, argument, testimony, and allegations, I, as arbitrator designated by the parties

AWARD

N.W. was discharged for cause.

Analysis of the Case

Patient abuse disciplinary cases require particularly skillful handling by supervisors. As the primary business of any medical facility obviously is patient care, abuse by the employees hired to provide comfort and treatment is a cardinal offense. In patient abuse allegation situations, the atmosphere generally is charged with emotion.

In the face of serious charges filed by a patient or a patient's family against the institution, and/or to quell the outburst of public indignation generated by publicity of the abuse or alleged abuse, management may move hastily and may take swift action to terminate without a thorough investigation of the incident. This is especially true in sex-abuse cases such as that involving N.W.

The facts and allegations with which management was confronted are worth examining:

1. N.W. was a long-term employee (nearly 20 years of service) with a clean personnel record.
2. He was accused of a heinous offense by a patient with a serious and medically documented mental impairment.
3. There were no witnesses to the actual assault (if there was one) as alleged.

4. It could easily be assumed, given his condition, that the patient might have some serious judgmental limitations. Did the assault actually occur or was it a figment of his imagination?

Action Taken by Management

The employee was suspended pending investigation. (The authors believe this was an excellent move. It provided the opportunity to investigate, with the added protection of removing the accused employee from the institution.) Management was visited at once by union officials demanding N.W.'s immediate reinstatement.

Management explained its suspension action as logical, unemotional, and nonjudgmental. It assured the union that the decision to suspend was generated by a desire to have the institution conduct an effective investigation absent an atmosphere laden with emotion and fear. Management assured the union of reinstatement, with back pay, should the investigation reveal the allegations to be foundless. The investigation proceeded expeditiously and the union was assured of its rights to grieve outside the filing time limitations.

Given the circumstances involved, i.e., an employee with nearly 20 years of service and a clean record, no witness to the alleged attack, and the serious nature of the allegation, management was confident at the start that such a matter, if grieved and upheld in its favor through the internal grievance process, would end in arbitration. Management fully appreciated that in a case of a grievant with a spotless employment record and no history of related prior activity, the arbitrator would be forced to make judgment solely on the basis of grievant and patient testimony and the credibility of such testimony.

In acting as it did, management had developed:

1. a course of immediate action
2. a plan and time frame for investigation
3. a follow-up to the investigation

The arbitrator's award in the case of N.W. is based largely on the following factors:

First, management was able to clearly identify through the testimony of expert witnesses that although severely retarded, the patient was capable of competently testifying at the age level between 9 and 14 years, an age legally acceptable in proceedings of this kind.

(An expert witness is defined as one possessing scientific or specialized knowledge and experience. Expert witnesses frequently testify when disputes concern a subject requiring scientific or specialized knowledge and experience and cannot be determined intelligently merely from the deduction made and inferences drawn on the basis of ordinary knowledge, common sense, and experience.) The patient could urinate and adjust his clothing without assistance. He had a communication problem when agitated. His agitated condition was witnessed at the time of the alleged incident by a physician. Attempts to solicit details from the patient on the day of the incident failed because of this condition, yet at the arbitration hearing, the patient could communicate, albeit slowly and laboriously.

Second, as is clearly indicated in the arbitrator's decision, the key determinant of the lack of credibility of the grievant's testimony was his inability to recall the reason for his presence on the patient's floor on the day of the incident. This obviously highlights the necessity of an effective employee activity logging system. Had there been no such system in effect to identify the grievant's absence from the actual transport division for two one-hour periods at 11 A.M. and approximately 1 P.M. in addition to his scheduled lunch break, there would have been no evidence whatever to support the allegations of the patient as to the period during which or the number of times he had been victimized. There would have been no evidence to discredit the grievant's testimony that he had been missing from the duty station in addition to his scheduled lunch for only 15 minutes.

The log was excellent evidence; it refuted the grievant's account of the reason he was on the floor, the number of times, and the amount of time he spent on the floor. It was a credible management exhibit.

NOTE

1. Jesse Simons, "Arbitration of Patient Abuse Grievances: Proposed Changes," in Norman Metzger, ed., *Handbook of Health Care Human Resources Management* (Rockville, Md.: Aspen Systems Corporation, 1981), p. 793.

Chapter 10

Arbitration Cases: Alcohol Abuse

CASE 9: DRINKING ON THE JOB

Issues

1. Did the Company discharge Mr. J.L. on February 14 for just cause?
2. If not, what shall the remedy be?

Mr. J.L.'s Background

J.L. was hired five years ago as a porter. Prior to his discharge, he had a somewhat checkered history. It ran something like this:

2/2:   Came back from lunch one hour late.
4/7:   Insubordination—addressed two supervisors in a surly manner.
8/14: (two years later) "Poor work habits" (Extra long lunch hour—second warning).
9/6:   Came back late from lunch. Suspended for five days.
9/14: "Poor work habits"—Insubordination—Final warning.
10/19: One hour late from lunch. Discharged. Reinstated after a conference (10/23). Changed to suspension for five days.

However, he had no record of drinking or of alcoholism. Mr. O., Personnel Director, testified that he never saw J.L. intoxicated, or smelled liquor on his breath. The warnings for "poor work habits" had reference to lateness or to an "insubordinate" manner of speaking to one Mr. N.

Mr. J.L.'s Duties

J.L. was overseer of garbage disposal. All garbage was funneled down into the room where he worked, known as the "compact room." There the garbage was mechanically pressed into more compact form and then disposed of. J.L. had to watch this operation for possible malfunction and to keep the room clean generally.

Events of February 14

E.B., a new Executive Housekeeper, walked into the compact room around 4 P.M. She testified that she found J.L. sitting on a wooden box with a radio playing; that he was pouring from a liquor bottle into a cup. She further testified that she took the bottle (a pint bottle, almost completely empty); that J.L. said to her, "Give me the bottle and I'll throw it away." She locked up the bottle in her desk, and the next morning called the personnel office and spoke to Mrs. C. She and Mrs. C. then went to the director, (Mr. C.), and he agreed that J.L. should be discharged. (The bottle definitely contained the remnants of an alcoholic beverage.)

Three days before this incident, E.B. testified that she had passed by J.L. and smelled liquor on his breath. She did not mention this to J.L., but instead testified that she spoke to the shop steward, G., about it. G. denied this.

On cross-examination, E.B. was asked why she didn't mention the incident, three days previous, to J.L. Her reply was, "I didn't feel I should." She explained that she had intended to call a meeting of all the employees under her jurisdiction, at which she would include discussion of the liquor problem.

When asked by the arbitrator why she took the bottle from J.L. and not the cup, into which she had testified he poured the contents of the bottle, she replied that she was "too perturbed."

She also testified that at the time, J.L.'s speech was not thick; he arose and walked, and he did not lurch or stagger.

In summary, therefore, E.B. did not see J.L. take a drink, nor did he appear to be drunk. Furthermore, the best evidence on which she could rely, to support her testimony, the liquid in the cup, she did not take from him.

J.L. denied that he had been drinking at all, or even that he had the bottle in his hand. He testified that the bottle was lying on the floor between two boxes and that E.B. picked it up. (He testified without contradiction that it was impossible to lock the compact room and that other employees utilized the room to dispose of their empty liquor bottles.) J.L. further testified that what he actually had in the cup was coffee, into which he had poured a medicine called "666." He takes this for nosebleeds as well as for colds and sinus. He never utilized the services of the Union's Health Plan because he said he "doesn't like doctors." He had originally gotten the coffee from the kitchen at about 2:30 P.M.

He testified that he offered his full cup to E.B. but she wouldn't take it from him. Apparently she didn't even smell the cup.

J.L. admitted to being a regular drinker of beer, but at night only, in his home.

The Book of Rules

The employer publishes a small booklet of approximately 30 pages, pocket-size, which contains the benefits the employees are entitled to and the rules they must obey. On page 21 appears the following:

> The Home may discharge or otherwise discipline an employee for just cause. Just cause is deemed to include, but shall not be limited to . . . *drinking or being under the influence of alcoholic beverages while on duty . . ."*

Analysis

Normally, an arbitrator will sustain a discharge for drinking on the job where one or more of the following additional factors are present: (a) frequent absenteeism as a result of drinking; (b) other serious improper behavior; (c) inability to perform the work; (d) overt evidence of intoxication; (e) a destructive effect on the morale of the other employees; (f) chronic alcoholism with no effort at rehabilitation; (g) where the employee is in personal contact with the public; (h) when the job is such that drinking will endanger the safety of others (e.g., driving a truck); or (i) past warnings about drinking on the job.

None of the above factors is present here. There isn't even the basic proof that J.L. was actually drinking. If there were any proof at all, it would be in the contents of the cup, and for some reason Ms. E.B. did not confiscate it.

Possibly, this failure on her part resulted from her being "perturbed," as she testified. E.B. appeared to be an extremely capable, confident person. Nevertheless, one must accept her statement that she was "perturbed" at the sight of a porter sitting and listening to the radio and seemingly drinking.

The fact is that her error in judgment destroyed any possibility that the company might have had to prove that J.L. had poured liquor into the cup. Such proof would also have been supplied by testimony that J.L. lurched or staggered or spoke with thickness of speech. But E.B. testified to the contrary. Referring again to the Rule Book, we therefore have no proof here that J.L. was either "drinking" or was "under the influence of" liquor.

The company argues that it really makes no difference whether E.B. appropriated the cup or the bottle since they each implicate J.L.

I disagree. This whole case depends on whether or not J.L. was pouring liquor from the bottle into the cup. This could have been shown, not by an examination of the bottle, but of the contents of the cup—or else by J.L.'s demeanor, which we have seen as thoroughly unobjectionable.

I agree that E.B. would have no motive to consciously fabricate. However, in view of her emotional state, one possibility is that, in her mind, the porter, the empty bottle, the cup, the inactive, seated position and the radio, all kaleidoscoped into one picture—of an employee drinking on the job. J.L., not intoxicated, is more convincing in that he urged her to sample the cup, an offer she didn't accept. A guilty man would not be likely to have acted in this manner.

Conclusions

The following factors tip the scales in favor of J.L.:

(1) He had five years of seniority, with a perfectly clean slate as far as drinking or alcoholism are concerned (this is probably why the alleged incident which occurred three days previously was never mentioned to J.L.; there must have been serious doubt as to what E.B. had smelled, or whose breath it was on). (There is a conflict as to whether or not the incident was mentioned by E.B. to the shop steward. It is of no importance. The Home has the responsibility of notifying employees directly of any alleged violation of rules, and it has no right to depend on the Union to carry the message. No one from the Home spoke to J.L. about it.)

(2) Even according to E.B., J.L. was definitely not intoxicated on the 14th.

(3) E.B. could not even testify that she saw him take a drink.

(4) J.L. offered E.B. the cup as proof of his innocence and

(5) E.B. refused the proffer of what would have been the best evidence of J.L.'s innocence or guilt.

(6) None of the aggravating factors which I have mentioned *supra,* under "Analysis," was present in this case.

Thus I find the evidence herein insufficient to constitute "just cause." Surmise and suspicion are too flimsy a basis on which to predicate a discharge.

AWARD

I find and decide that the Company did not have just cause in discharging J.L., and I order him reinstated to his former job, without loss of seniority, and with full restitution for his net loss of earnings from the date of his discharge.

Analysis of the Case

The arbitrator in this case, like many fellow practitioners, listed factors that added to the persuasiveness of management's action of terminating an employee for drinking on the job:

1. frequent absenteeism as a result of drinking
2. other serious improper behavior
3. inability to perform the work
4. overt evidence of intoxication
5. destructive effect on the morale of other employees
6. chronic alcoholism with no effort at rehabilitation
7. where the employee is in personal contact with the public
8. where the job is such that drinking will endanger the safety of others (e.g., driving a truck)
9. past warnings about drinking on the job

In most of the cases that involve terminating for intoxication, arbitrators direct their attention to the question: Was the employee drunk on the job? If the answer is in the affirmative, the discharge usually is upheld. Slowly, but perceptively, arbitrators have followed the lead of the courts in accepting the idea that intoxication on the job may indicate that the employee is an alcoholic. If such a determination is made, arbitrators again, similar to the pattern being established in the courts, will come down for rehabilitation, i.e., treating alcoholism as an illness rather than simply as misconduct.[1]

In discharge cases, arbitrators have required that the employer establish a quantum of proof to justify its action, not that the employee establish innocence. Assuming it were to be believed that J.L. had been caught red-handed drinking on the job by supervisor E.B. and that all of the allegations regarding the incident and the porter's actions were true, not one scintilla of proof has been presented to support the charges. As the arbitrator points out in his summation, "Surmise and suspicion are too flimsy a basis on which to predicate a discharge." Even if the arbitrator believes management's allegations, to find "just cause" in the decision to discharge, sufficient evidence must be presented on which to base a decision in support of the employer's position.

From the very first contact with J.L. on February 14, management began construction of a weak framework on which to build a case for discharge. Why, for instance, did supervisor E.B. confiscate the liquor bottle and not the cup into which J.L. allegedly poured the contents of the bottle? The arbitrator stresses the cup as important evidence that should have been collected by the supervisor. If any materials were to be confiscated, then the supervisor should have taken both bottle and cup, not merely the bottle (as the Home suggested as sufficient) or the cup (as the arbitrator indicated as sufficient).

J.L. was accused of pouring liquor from the bottle into the cup. Both make up the evidence, not either/or. More importantly, a blood test could have established an alcohol level discrediting J.L.'s emphatic denials of having consumed any alcohol that day (it should be noted that he did not claim that he had had a drink at lunch, which he could have done to cover possibly damning results of a blood test had one been ordered).

The decision made by three management persons the next day to discharge J.L. for drinking on the job without hearing the grievant's side was an error of significant proportions. It automatically assumed that the employee was guilty as charged without a thorough investigation. The employee thus was being denied very basic rights in not being afforded an opportunity to explain his side of the story. Arbitrators are sensitive to the quality of investigation of employee wrongdoing. No arbitrator will sit idly by and allow an employee to be railroaded out of a job.

Personnel Director O.'s testimony that he had never seen Mr. J.L. intoxicated or that he had ever even smelled liquor on his breath, certainly was a decisive point and was deemed important by the arbitrator.

Even though an employee's work record over a protracted period might be less than commendable and prior disciplinary action had been handled progressively and documented as in the case of J.L., termination for something that cannot be proved will not stand up in arbitration.

One arbitrator set forth principles as to the sufficiency of evidence regarding an employee's state of sobriety:

1. Mere opinion evidence is not sufficient proof of a drunken condition. The evidence must be sufficiently specific in describing various details of appearance and conduct so that it is clear that the person accused is under the influence of liquor.
2. Supervisors who have no medical training nevertheless are capable of recognizing when an employee is intoxicated or under the influence of alcohol if they objectively compare an employee's normal demeanor and work habits with those at the time his sobriety is questioned.
3. Results of blood alcohol tests may be accepted as conclusive proof of guilt or innocence of intoxication. However, it is not required that management give such a test in order to prove intoxication, since it is recognized that requiring such a test might cause undue delays and disruption of production.[2]

CASE 10: DRINKING ON THE JOB

Pursuant to the rules and procedures of the American Arbitration Association and the Collective Bargaining Agreement between the Hospital and the Union, the undersigned was designated as Arbitrator to hear and render a final and binding Award concerning the following issues:

1. Was the discharge of A. and B. by the Hospital for just cause?
2. If not, what shall the remedy be?

On written notice to both parties, a hearing was held before me on May 7, 1980, at the offices of the American Arbitration Association. The parties were afforded full opportunity to develop respective positions by examination and cross-examination of witnesses, by presentation of evidence and by argument.

Background

Grievant B. was employed by the Medical Center (including military service) for about 12 years, the last four as a pharmacy attendant. Grievant A. was employed by the Employer for about eight months as a building service attendant, assigned to the Pharmacy. Both employees were discharged by telegrams sent December 21, 1980.

The Employer's primary witness in support of just cause was Chief Pharmacist F.

Mr. F., who has held his position for some 12 years, testified as follows: At about 3:45 P.M. on Wednesday, December 19, 1979, he had occasion to enter the infusion room (also called the IV room), a room maintained for storing various solutions, and there observed grievants seated on skids opposite each other. Each grievant "had a paper cup containing a purple fluid" and on the floor between them was a paper bag. Another employee, D., was also present in the room. D. was filling a truck with IV solution. All were engaged in conversation.

F. asked A. and B. what they were drinking. Grievant A. replied that he was drinking orange juice. F. quipped, "By the color of it, you should have said grape juice." Thereupon, grievant A. drank the contents of his cup. At the same time grievant B. said, "Now you'll make us take a blood test." B. also volunteered that he had been to a party at lunch time, and that he had drunk some alcohol.

When F. asked the grievants what was in the paper bag, B. tried to push it under one of the skids. F. then picked up the bag and produced a bottle marked "Night Train Express" (alcohol content, 19 percent by volume). The bottle contained a small amount of wine. F. does not recall asking the grievants whether it was their bottle.

F. then told the grievants to go to his office, that he would be there in five or ten minutes. Thereupon, F. went to see the Employee Relations Assistant, R., and asked him what to do. R. advised F. to go back and "try and get the cups," and to try and get statements from the grievants.

Returning to the infusion room, F. found one cup containing a quantity of wine. The cup was found "in the place where B. was sitting." Employee D. was still working in the room. He pointed out to F. some beer cans lying under the skids. F. then left the infusion room, and delivered the cup containing the wine, to R.

From R.'s office, F. proceeded back to the pharmacy area to speak with the grievants. He spoke first with grievant A. In addition to B. and A., E., the Pharmacy Supervisor, was also present.

Asked what he was doing in the infusion room, A. replied he was cleaning it and drinking grape juice. A. looked "glassy-eyed," said F.

When asked whether he was familiar with the rule against drinking in the Hospital, A. replied "no," he was not, and did F. see him drinking? F. said "yes," he did. A. refused to sign a handwritten record of the conversation, as prepared by Mr. F. F. then suspended A. and told him that he would let him know on Friday, December 21, whether or not he had a job.

A. refused to leave, despite a number of requests by F. F. thereupon called Security, but before an officer arrived, A. in fact left.

Grievant B. was then questioned by F. in the presence of E. and N., a Pharmacy Aide who B. had asked to accompany him.

Asked what he was doing in the infusion room, B. stated that he thereafter planned to take certain "stock from the infusion room to the main pharmacy" to replenish supplies. B. produced a small slip containing notes on certain inventory items. F. testified that B. then "talked about a party," but "kept changing his story."

When asked by F. whether he knew about the rule against drinking, Mr. B. answered that he did, but asked "is it OK to drink at lunch?" Mr. F. replied that this was OK, but drinking on the premises was not, except at an official party. F. told B. that he would notify him by Friday as to what action would be taken, and asked him to sign a "transcript" of the interview prepared by F. Grievant did so, and asked F. for a copy.

F. then went to his office to copy the statement. As he was copying the document, B. entered, closed the door behind him, and said, "If I get fired, your ass is mine." Upon further questioning, F. testified that B. may have said, alternatively, "your ass is mines," or "Your ass is minus."

Grievant B. then opened the door, and F. said that grievant's statement would be made "part of the official record." Grievant answered that he (grievant) would make his "own record," and that F. had in fact threatened him.

It was not contested that there was an employee handbook which "forbids drinking on the job."

Grievants were terminated by telegrams sent on Friday, December 21, 1979. Although they were suspended, pending notification, both grievants reported to work on December 21. They were sent home.

Grievants' versions of what happened on December 19 were quite different from Mr. F.'s.

Grievant B. testified to the following: On the day in question he was on his break in the infusion room, having gone there to discuss payment for a movie camera and projector he had purchased from Mr. A. Shortly after the grievant had begun speaking to A., Chief Pharmacist F. walked in. B. testified that there was "no discussion about drinking" in the infusion room.

B. related that F. confronted both grievants with the bottle and an accusation of drinking not in the infusion room but at a location outside that room. Both grievants reacted to the confrontation by requesting a blood test. F. replied, "that's not necessary." Then F. separated them for questioning.

Grievant B. was then questioned by F. in the presence of N., a Pharmacy Aide (whose presence B. had requested) and E. On direct examination, B. testified that he had "denied everything," and had asked F. only if it was "OK to drink at a Christmas party," since he was planning to "go to one." As to what transpired in F.'s office, B. denied threatening F. After the copy was made, B. testified, he "said good-night" and "that was all."

D. testified as follows: On the afternoon in question, grievant "went to the IV room to clean it." As he sat on a skid, waiting for Mr. D. to finish and get out of the way, F. came in and, without more (sic), asked grievant to go to the office.

A. testified that he "saw no cup and no bag" that day. He stated that F. "pulled out a wine bottle" that he had "never seen before." He went on to state that he "does not recall all the questions that day," that he was "asked to sign a statement," and he was "asked nothing about a cup."

On cross-examination, A. denied saying to F. that he had been drinking grape juice. He stated that he routinely cleans the infusion room two or three times a week, and that he did not sign the statement F. had prepared because he "didn't understand the question." Finally, A. recalled that he "was confused at the time" he saw the bottle, and that he had consumed "a cup or a cup and a half" of wine at lunch.

Called as a rebuttal witness, F. testified that on December 19, 1979, after B. was sent home, he went to the infusion room to see if the items listed on the slip produced by B. were needed in the pharmacy. The slip (a copy of which is annexed to this decision) noted three different items, each identified by a numerical "code."

As to the first item, there was "room for two" as noted on the slip. As to the second, although the slip called for three, there was "only room for two." The third item was fully stocked in the Pharmacy; there was "no room" for more, and "none was needed." F. went on to state that "normally a list (such as the one grievant B. produced) contains many more items; 25 to 30 items." He testified, moreover, that the "usual practice in cleaning the infusion room" is to do it "on Friday;" that it was "not usual on a day other than Friday unless specifically assigned."

F. also stated that grievant B. "appeared normal" on December 19, 1979. The Hospital stipulated that it had not had attendance or lateness problems with either grievant. With the exception of a five-day suspension for refusing overtime in 1977, B. had a clean employment record over ten years at the Medical Center.

D. has been employed by the Medical Center as a Pharmacy Aide since 1971. One of his duties is to keep the Pharmacy stocked. He works periodically in the infusion room.

D. recalled the afternoon of December 19 when B. and A. entered the infusion room. D. had been there about a half-hour filling a truck with IV solution. He observed grievants entering the room, noting that B. "had only a small piece of paper," and that A. had nothing.

Mr. A. testified that he had a conversation with Mr. B. about movie equipment he had sold to B. B. asked A. whether he could wait until the next payday for the amount owed. A. agreed to wait.

Five minutes after grievants entered the room, F. came in. He "had nothing with him." When F. entered, D. turned his back "and went back to work."

Then, D. recalled, F. asked B. what he was doing there. "I'm taking my break," B. replied, adding that he had with him a list of items for the Pharmacy. A., when asked by F. what he was doing in the room, answered that he was cleaning the room. F. then asked both employees to wait for him in his office.

D. testified that "nothing was said about drinking." F. remained in the room another minute or two. When he left, he "had nothing in his hands."

F. returned five to seven minutes later. He had an inventory card of a kind used for IV solution inventory. D. asked F., "can I help you?" F. replied, "no, I'm just looking to see if I can order some additional items."

D. testified that F. then "bent over a skid while looking," that the skid moved, and that only then did F. find another bag with the wine bottle lying among some empty beer cans. As F. removed the bottle from the bag, D. pointed to some empty beer cans and asked, "do you see them?" F. answered that he was "not interested in empty beer cans." D. did not recall any cups. F. then left the room.

D. also stated that five minutes later, employee H. came and said that F. wanted D. to go to his (F.'s) office.

D. told the hearing that he had seen bottles in the infusion room before, that he had thrown them away so he wouldn't be suspected of drinking. Also, on Monday, December 17, 1979, D. had found the door to the IV room unlocked and the lights on and reported to F. that this was the third or fourth time he had found the door open. F. remarked that "maybe it is the night security guard."

In his office, F. asked D. whether he "was aware of drinking." D. said, "Yes, but not me. I don't drink or smoke." He said he had seen B. and A. but that he didn't see them drinking. In fact, said D., employees don't drink in front of him because he is a minister in the Pentecostal Church. D. said that despite an apparent prohibition, employees do take lunch breaks in the infusion room.

On cross-examination, D. testified that he had seen other employees having lunch in the infusion room. This worried D. because "they might think" he was drinking.

Also on cross-examination, D. recalled, before F. arrived, having seen A. "pick up empty bottles" and "throwing them in the disposal." He explained that he pointed out the empty beer cans to F. because he thought F. was "looking for something else—not liquor." He said that he would have pointed out empty fruit juice cans as well.

Asked whether it was possible that grievants might have been drinking without D. noticing, D. did not answer.

Discussion and Opinion

The Union argued, with regard to grievant B., that there was no evidence presented to show that this employee was drinking on the job on December 19, 1979. The Union pointed out that B. admitted having wine during his lunch. No closing argument was made about the alleged threat uttered to Supervisor F. Given B.'s 12 years of service, said the Union, and his almost clean employment record, no just cause existed for his termination.

The Union also submitted that, on the record, no just cause existed for termination of A. It requested reinstatement with full back pay for both grievants.

The Employer, in its closing argument, submitted that grievant B. was shown to have:

a. been in possession of an alcoholic beverage;
b. been drinking on the job;
c. threatened Mr. F.; and
d. been insubordinate on Friday, December 21.

Mr. A. committed all of the above infractions except the threat, said the Hospital.

The Employer argued that the serious credibility questions emerging from the testimony should be decided in its favor. As to the testimony of D., it was argued, the record suggests that D. was concerned with discipline against himself, and was, therefore, naturally defensive. In addition, there were times when D. could not observe grievants. An additional shadow was cast on D.'s testimony, counsel submitted, because D. testified at the "Step 3" hearing that he saw F. "take the bottle and the cups together and leave the IV room."

The Employer submitted that both grievants displayed a disregard for authority. Any consideration of mitigation in favor of grievant B. should disappear, it argued, because of his threat against F.

I have carefully studied the testimony of all witnesses. On the question of what grievants did in the infusion room, the testimony of D. is of little help because, by his own testimony, he was not in a position to observe grievants at certain times. What remains is the testimony of grievants and that of F., diametrically opposed on the key charges, possession and consumption of alcohol while on duty in the Hospital and threatening the supervisor.

On the entire record, I credit the testimony of F. that A. was drinking in the Hospital during working hours. There was no evidence, direct or implicit, that the supervisor was motivated to fabricate a story about A. and indeed A.'s memory of the events of December 19, 1979, was very hazy at best. F. saw A. drink the wine.

A Hospital Employer has a vital interest in maintaining clear-minded and unimpaired functioning by its employees. The consumption of alcohol (A. by his own admission had already consumed a quantity of wine at lunch) impairs job performance. The Hospital's rule against drinking on the job was laid down for that very reason. A. had been made aware of that rule and he violated it. Drinking while on duty in a hospital, where patients depend on alert and sober conduct of personnel, is an extremely serious offense. The discharge of A. will, accordingly, be upheld.

As concerns B., the Employer contended but failed to show that this employee was drinking on duty. However, I again credit the testimony of F. who testified that he saw B. holding a cup containing Night Train Express, and thereafter attempting to secrete the paper bag containing the bottle with the remaining wine. I therefore find that B., in violation of the Hospital rules, was in possession of an alcoholic beverage in the Hospital during working hours.

Did B. also threaten his supervisor, as alleged? On this record, there is no doubt that B. used improper and abusive words to F., his supervisor. The record is not clear, however, on precisely what was said. F. was not sure of the words spoken, and in fact testified to three alternative versions. The supervisor was not certain whether B.'s statement ended with the word "mine," "mines," or "minus," and F.'s doubts existed when the statement was originally uttered.

In a discharge case, particularly one involving an employee with 10 or 12 years of service, the standard of proof must be the highest properly applicable in industrial justice. On this record, I cannot be certain of what was said, and I am not permitted to guess. It is clear, however, that B.'s language was improper in an employment setting and abusive to Mr. F.

An employee's abusive language to a supervisor, even if it falls short of a threat, may so alter the relationship that supervisory control is impaired. It is noted that F. did not call security after B.'s statement, although he had called security previously that day. The record as a whole does not lead me to believe that B.'s statement or his conduct placed the supervisor in actual jeopardy or so disrupted the employment relationship as to require or justify the removal of the employee.

Considering the serious nature of the other charges, the grievant's insubordination in reporting to work on December 21 does not require discussion.

The charges proven against B. are extremely serious, and I am giving him the benefit of the doubt primarily because of his 10 or 12 years of service at the Hospital. Given B.'s serious misconduct, it would be inequitable to the Employer to require payment of any back pay. I shall therefore direct B.'s reinstatement without back pay.

Mr. B. should now be on notice that any further misconduct on his part may result in his immediate termination. This award should be placed in grievant's personnel file as a final warning against such misconduct in the future.

AWARD

The employer had just cause to terminate A. As to this employee, the grievance is denied.

The Employer did not have just cause to terminate the services of B. The Employer is directed to reinstate B. without back pay. This award finds that on December 19, 1979, B. was in possession of an alcoholic beverage while on duty in the Hospital, and that he used abusive language to his supervisor that day. This award is to serve as a final warning to Grievant against any further misconduct.

Analysis of the Case

It has been stated several times earlier that arbitrators will go to excessive lengths to avoid terminating long-term employees (long-term generally is considered tenure greater than five years). This is especially true in cases where evidence is either nonexistent or "soft." In his award the arbitrator states that "In a discharge case, particularly one involving an employee with 10 or 12 years of service [grievant B.], the standard of proof must be the highest properly applicable in industrial justice." With reference to alleged threats made to the supervisor by grievant B., the arbitrator reasoned that he could not be certain of what precisely was said.

Management must take careful notice of just how exacting is the task of presenting evidence in arbitrations concerning terminations of long-term employees. This is not the exception, it is the rule. In this case, the threat aspect of grievant B.'s total conduct on December 21 was not handled well by the supervisor. This fact significantly weakened the use of the threat as a reason for discharge of B.

If, as the supervisor contended, grievant B. entered his (the supervisor's) office, closed the door behind him, and threatened him, then the notice of discharge should have included this as a major reason for the discharge. Instead, the threat was presented at the third-step grievance hearing and at arbitration in testimony by management, but it was not included in the discharge notice as a reason for discharge. This diminishes the validity of the charge; it appears to be an afterthought.

It may be difficult to understand the arbitrator's differentiating between grievant B.'s and grievant A.'s culpability for drinking on the job. From what was presented in the hearing, B. was merely in possession of an alcoholic beverage. The rule was against drinking on the job, not against possession. It may be concluded that the preponderance of the evidence, albeit circumstantial, pointed to violation of the drinking-on-the-job rule by both A. and B. It is important to note that circumstantial evidence is considered ''soft'' evidence and not given much weight by arbitrators.

This case is presented as one in which management prevailed in its discipline decision. That it did in the case of grievant A., caught drinking on the job, is clear. There existed a clearly communicated rule against drinking (it was in the published Employee Handbook). A., however, (as compared to 12-year employee B.) had been employed for less than one year. This is not to imply that tenure is a license for rules violation and poor performance/behavior; as can be seen, B. did not go undisciplined for his part in the December 21 episode. It is clear that B. deserved to be disciplined but where lengthy years of service and clean employee records are factors, the degree of discipline should be considered carefully prior to implementation.

One important note in closing. Both grievants B. and A. testified that they requested their blood be tested for alcohol content and that the supervisor dismissed the request as unnecessary. Where employees appear to be drinking on the job, such tests are always important to management in the development of its case. The employee has an obligation, especially in the hospital setting, to be, as was stated by the arbitrator, ''clear-minded and able to function unimpaired.'' Furthermore, whether an employee drinks at lunch or at home before reporting for work, the individual may not be able to perform effectively and should not be allowed to do so. The supervisor was remiss in not making this perfectly clear to grievant B. in answer to the latter's question regarding drinking at lunch.

NOTES

1. *Grievance Guide*, 6th ed. (Washington, D.C.: The Bureau of National Affairs, Inc., 1982), p. 61.
2. Charleston Naval Shipyard 54 L.A. 145.

Chapter 11

Arbitration Cases: Theft

CASE 11: AMBULANCE DRIVER ACCUSED

On October 30 a hearing in the matter of T.D.'s discharge was held before the Arbitrator.

At the outset of the hearing the parties agreed to submit the following issue to the Arbitrator for his decision:

1. Was there just cause for the discharge of T.D.?
2. If not, what shall be the remedy?

Mr. T.D. is an ambulance driver for the Hospital; he started to work for the Hospital six years ago. He was suspended pending investigation of an alleged rule violation on July 2 and on July 8 was discharged for violation of rule 6.15 of the "Manual On Procedures and Operations Governing Ambulance Service Operated Under the Emergency Medical Service" which says in part:

" . . . ambulance crew members are not authorized at any time to search a patient or his possessions or remove his personal property . . ."

On June 20 T.D. and N.C., an ambulance attendant, responded to a call in Brooklyn regarding a probable D.O.A. [dead on arrival]. When they arrived at the apartment building, they were led into the third-floor apartment of the dead person by a neighbor, Mr. K., from the first floor, who had been given a key by the deceased for purposes of letting in the deceased's daughter should the daughter ever come when the mother was not in.

According to the Hospital, the daughter complained by telephone on June 23 to P.N., the Ambulance Supervisor (who for 21 years prior to his employment by the Hospital as an Ambulance Supervisor had worked for the city Police Department as a detective and patrolman). The daughter told P.N. that the ambulance crew were ghouls; that she had been told by Mr. K. that he had seen them searching her mother's property and that $50 in cash and some jewelry were missing.

P.N., together with another administrative employee, visited K. at his apartment the next afternoon and obtained his signature on a statement prepared by P.N. from what K. told him. P.N. reported what he had found and showed K.'s statement to M.B., the Director of Personnel, that afternoon, at which time, according to M.B.'s testimony, M.B. decided that a discharge was warranted on the basis of the eyewitness account unless the Union would be able to change his mind by producing other information. He called the Union office trying to reach the Union Organizer, B., who was assigned to this Hospital; B. was not in, so M.B. left a message. He finally had a meeting with B. and the grievant on July 2nd.

Meanwhile, on June 24th, P.N. told T.D. and N.C. about the telephone complaint of the daughter. He did not tell them about the statement signed by K.; he simply asked them what had happened and when they reported that it had been a routine D.O.A. case, he asked them to make out incident reports, which they did in virtually identical language.

On July 2nd, P.N. told T.D. that Mr. H., the Assistant Administrator who was P.N.'s immediate Supervisor, wanted to see him. According to T.D.'s testimony, which was not contradicted in regard to this, Mr. H. asked him to resign because K. had reported that he saw him going through the dresser drawers of the dead woman on June 20th. T.D. gave Mr. H. a detailed and circumstantial account of what had taken place on the 20th, according to him, which indicated that he had not done what K. accused him of; but Mr. H. persisted in asking that he resign. T.D. refused, telling Mr. H. he had done nothing wrong, whereupon Mr. H. told him he was suspended pending further investigation.

However, there was no further investigation before a meeting was held on the next day, at which were present M.B. for the Hospital; B. the Organizer, and the Shop Steward for the Union, together with T.D. M.B. said that the Hospital intended to discharge T.D. and made clear, in response to T.D.'s question as to whether he was being accused of taking money and jewelry from the apartment, that there was no accusation of theft—that the discharge would be because T.D. had been seen going through the dresser drawers. M.B. told the Union that the Hospital would proceed with the discharge unless the Union brought in evidence to make him change his mind about what had happened.

T.D. denied going through the dresser drawers and pointed out, as a possible explanation for whatever was missing, that K. had a key and could have gotten into the apartment. T.D. said that he would not "take the rap" for the missing things. T.D. told M.B. that he had been in the apartment only long enough to help his partner, N.C., open windows.

M.B. and B. then went to the apartment, spoke to K., and according to M.B.'s uncontradicted testimony, K. repeated substantially what was in his signed statement. M.B. and B. took turns standing, one at the entrance door of the apartment and one at the dresser at the other end of the passageway and both confirmed that they were able to see the opening of the dresser drawer from the apartment entrance doorway.

No attempt was made on this occasion or at any other time up to the date of the hearing to check out the specific circumstances recited by T.D. in his denial first given to Mr. H. on July 2nd.

The statement signed by K. on June 24th is as follows:

> I, Mr. K., on June 20 did call 911 for an ambulance because I had discovered Mrs. N. in Apt. 11 of the premises dead. I found her on the couch in the living room.
>
> I returned to my apartment and called 911. The ambulance responded and I took Mr. T.D. and Mr. C.N. to the apartment. I then saw the man in white enter the apartment and he told me I should not enter the apartment because of the smell. The door was ajar and I saw the man in blue going thru a drawer in the rear room and again the man in white said 'I advise you not to come in here.' At this time there was no policeman on the scene. They stayed up in the apartment approximately 20 to 25 minutes. I saw them leave but they didn't stop at my door. They left before the police arrived.

K's testimony at the arbitration hearing differed in some details. K. is a man of 77 years who, it was conceded, has a failing memory. His testimony was emphatic, however, that he saw through a wide-open door the man in the dark uniform open the top dresser drawers with both hands and that he had not, as set forth in his signed statement, seen through the door which was "ajar" "the man in blue *going thru* a drawer." K.'s statement and testimony were consistent in indicating that the ambulance crew stayed in the apartment for 20 to 25 minutes, but in his testimony he was specific that he did not see them leave the building, that his wife told him that she saw them leave; but the signed statement is specific to the contrary:

> I saw them leave but they didn't stop at my door. They left before the police arrived.

P.N. explained in his testimony that he had used the word "ajar" to mean wide open because that was the usage he had become accustomed to in his work in the Police Department; but even if that is so, it does not explain the differences between K.'s testimony and the signed statement on other questions of fact.

No explanation was offered by the Hospital as to why nobody bothered to check with the other tenants in the house who were said by both K. and T.D. to have been present at various times during the incident. For instance, T.D.'s story was that he (who was the man in the dark blue uniform) remained outside the apartment talking with K. and at least two other tenants most of the time that K. was there; and that he, and not N.C. (who was called by K. the "man in white" and "the doctor") had asked the tenant who had come down from the fourth floor for a piece of cloth to wrap around his face so that he would be able to stand the stench of the maggotted and gas-filled body.

No effort was made to confirm either K.'s or T.D.'s story by asking the lady from the fourth floor: she may have been able to identify which of the ambulance crew asked her for the cloth (which, in fact, she supplied). No effort was made to interview other tenants who might well have thrown light on the question of whether it was the man in blue or the man in white who remained outside the apartment with K. Nor did the Hospital check T.D.'s story to Mr. H. that included the circumstance that he went into an apartment on the third floor, across the hall from the apartment of the deceased, and spent ten minutes talking to the lady in that apartment and calling on her telephone to the dispatcher in order to speed up the arrival of the police so that the ambulance crew could get back to the Hospital.

Nor, according to the testimony, was any effort made to get any detailed information about the incident from N.C. (who had also originally been accused by the daughter); the only information obtained from N.C. was in the routine incident report. (The fact that the reports of T.D. and N.C. are virtually word-for-word identical does not transfer the burden of proving that T.D. was guilty from the Hospital to the Union: it is the initial burden in a discipline case for the Employer to present evidence adequate to convince the Arbitrator that the employee being disciplined committed the act for which he has been disciplined.) Apparently the Hospital elected simply to accept K.'s statements as against T.D.'s denials.

Because of this failure of the Hospital properly to investigate the differences between T.D.'s categorical and circumstantial denial and K.'s eyewitness account, the Hospital was unable to prove that K.'s observations, either as recited at the hearing or as recited in the signed statement, were correct. While it was apparent that K. was not deliberately testifying falsely, it was equally clear that his memory was less than sharp and might well have been confused with regard to the essential facts in this case.

Article XXVI of the Agreement provides not only that the Hospital shall have the right to discharge for cause but:

> 2. The Hospital will notify the Union in writing of any discharge or suspension within forty-eight (48) hours from the time of discharge or suspension. If the Union desires to contest the discharge or suspension, it shall give written notice thereof to the Hospital within five (5) working days, but not later than ten (10) working days from the date of receipt of notice of discharge or suspension. In such event, the dispute shall be submitted and determined under the grievance and arbitration procedure hereinafter set forth, however, commencing at Step 3 of the grievance machinery.

> If the Union notice of contest is given from six (6) to ten (10) working days after receipt of notice of discharge, the days beyond five (5) days shall be deemed waived insofar as back pay is concerned.

In this case the Hospital never notified the Union in writing of either the discharge or the suspension. According to the testimony of M.B., the Hospital has often discharged and/or suspended employees without giving such written notice and without any consequent complaint by the Union. No witness for the Union denied this assertion (although M.B. was unable to specify the name of any employee involved in any such incident) and the Union did not deny that in this case this procedural lapse had not been raised at any time prior to the arbitration. However, in the circumstances of this case, my conclusions have not been affected by the procedural lapse.

AWARD

The undersigned hereby makes the following Award:

1. There was not just cause for the discharge of T.D.
2. The Employer shall eliminate from the record any reference to this incident as a dereliction by T.D.

3. The Hospital shall immediately on receipt of this award restore T.D. to the position as ambulance driver he had immediately before his suspension and with no loss in seniority or any other right or privilege previously enjoyed by him. The Hospital shall make T.D. whole for any loss in earnings he suffered as a result of the suspension and discharge by paying to him a sum of money equal to what he would have been paid by the Hospital had he not been suspended and discharged less any monies he may have earned in the interim between the date of his suspension and the date of his reinstatement.

Analysis of the Case

Charges of misbehavior must be accompanied by exhaustive investigation and clear evidence, often supported by eyewitnesses. An employee, like any other citizen, is innocent until proved guilty. The case of Mr. T.D. is an important one to present in this review of arbitrations since major errors in sound disciplinary procedures destroyed management's position.

The grievant was discharged solely on the basis of an accusation by one alleged eyewitness. In questions of serious offenses, one-to-one situations present management with the most difficult position in sustaining an action on the basis of "its" witness. The arbitrator states: " . . . it is the initial burden in a discipline case for the Employer to present evidence adequate to convince the Arbitrator that the employee being disciplined committed the act for which he has been disciplined. Apparently the Hospital elected simply to accept Mr. K.'s statements as against T.D.'s denials."

In a one-to-one case, credibility is the key. Mr. K. was less than a credible witness. At his age, he was subject to failing memory. There were inconsistencies between his testimony and his written statement. There is reason to question management's decision to base its case on the single witness, whose motivations could be questioned and whose memory was less than accurate.

The failure of the hospital to investigate thoroughly, but instead to base its case on one witness, weighed heavily in the arbitrator's decision to reverse the discharge. As the arbitrator stated, no attempt was made to check out the specific circumstances offered by T.D. in his first denial of the charges. It is incomprehensible that management did not interview other tenants, who obviously were material to the complete development of an accurate view of the incident.

As pointed out in an earlier chapter, one of the tests for determining whether an institution had just cause for disciplining an employee was whether or not management investigated before administering the discipline, whether the investigation was fair and objective, and whether it produced substantial evidence of proof of guilt. The arbitrator in this case concluded that none of these tests were met.

Hasty decisions based on alleged misconduct will produce poor cases in arbitration. Management's first duty is to investigate. This includes interviewing other employees who may have been involved, other witnesses, the reviewing of relevant records, and a general stepping back from the problem to gain an objective view. These are worth repeating, and certainly pertain to this case. As stated earlier, a hasty or careless decision will produce unsupportable management actions. Therefore, it is essential that supervisors investigate before action is taken.

In analyzing this case and the evidence presented, the fact that a second man, N.C., was involved would have directed attention to the evidence assembled from interviews and statements from that individual; yet all that is provided is that the only information obtained from him was in the routine incident report. The arbitrator comments that "The fact that the reports of T.D. and N.C. are virtually word-for-word identical does not transfer the burden of proving that T.D. was guilty from the Hospital to the Union." It is clear that a more thorough investigation would have directed attention toward ascertaining N.C.'s account of the occurrence. Was he acting in concert with T.D.? Was N.C. the guilty one, and not T.D.? All of these questions remained unanswered.

The arbitrator, in his preaward discussion, writes: "Because of this failure of the Hospital properly to investigate the differences between T.D.'s categorical and circumstantial denial and K.'s eyewitness account, the Hospital was unable to prove that K.'s observations . . . were correct."

This is a classic case that serves as a lesson for management as to the appropriateness of taking action that cannot be substantiated in arbitration. The authors believe that such action, in this case, was precipitated by an emotional reaction to pressures, which are common in health care institutions.

When employees are accused (and the line between accusation and proof is a broad one) of patient abuse, theft, or gross acts inimical to proper patient care, personnel executives often overreact in haste to rid the institution of the culprit. There is no substitute for proof in civil or criminal actions or in labor relations. Pressures for disciplinary actions short of complete investigations must be resisted. The embarrassment and the cost of a reversal in arbitration is a lesson that need be learned only once, and not repeated.

CASE 12: MISAPPROPRIATION OF HOSPITAL FOOD

This case was heard on March 10 and April 17 at the American Arbitration Association, New York.

The Issues Presented

1. Did the Employer have cause for the discharge of grievant, E.S.H., which took place on June 20 of last year?
2. If not, what shall be the remedy?

Facts, Contentions of the Parties, and Discussions

Grievant has a date of employment of June 22 ten years ago, and was a Food Preparer in the Food Services Department at the Hospital. The Hospital discharged her because it contends that she attempted to misappropriate food, Hospital property, upon leaving work on June 17th of last year. It also contends that this type of offense, if proved, constitutes cause for discharge even on a first occasion because it violates the employee's duty to act with basic honesty toward the Employer.

The Union contends on behalf of grievant that she did not take anything from the Hospital; she had purchased items and brought them in to work with her; because she took no Hospital property, there is no cause for discharge and she should be reinstated with full back pay and other benefits.

The arbitrator has reviewed all evidence and arguments in the detailed record in this case in arriving at this decision.

Security Supervisor Lieutenant V.K.G., an 11-year employee then, testified that while on duty at about 7:45 P.M. on June 17th, about 15 minutes after the end of grievant's tour of duty, he saw her approach with a shoulder bag and a large brown envelope in her hand. When asked what she had in the envelope, she replied that it was "leftover cake." When asked whether she had a pass to take it out, grievant answered "No." The officer looked in the envelope and saw two cooked steaks and eight pieces of pound cake, both wrapped in aluminum foil. The evidence shows that both items were part of the menus for patients' meals that day.

Per Lieutenant V.K.G., when he stopped her, grievant said, "Why do you do this to me? I'm your friend." Then the officer looked in the grievant's shoulder bag and saw other foods; he asked for her ID card; she said she did not have it; Ms. E.S.H. testified that in fact it was in her wallet, but that she thought she had left it in her uniform.

Supervision was called to identify Ms. E.S.H.; per Lieutenant V.K.G., on the way to the Security Office, she asked him to give her a break, saying she would do anything for him. Once there, Lieutenant V.K.G. opened grievant's handbag and took out the balance of the food found; in all, it totalled seven cooked and seven raw strip steaks, a plain plastic bag containing 3½ pounds of peanuts, eight slices of pound cake, four large rolls of the type sold in the Hospital cafeteria, two quarts of milk, two grapefruits and three lemons.

At that point, grievant handed over her ID card; Ms. E.S.H. testified to one piece of pound cake with label and price on it; neither Lieutenant V.K.G. nor anyone else involved for the Hospital saw store labels or prices on the food items. The food was put in a refrigerator in a plastic bag; later it was discarded by the Hospital. Department Supervisor R.A.S. weighed the peanuts; Mr. R.A.S. gave Lieutenant V.K.G. an itemized receipt for the food.

At that time, Ms. E.S.H. did not produce a receipt for the food nor give an account of how she obtained it such as she later offered.

The evidence shows that the Hospital put out rules while Ms. E.S.H. was an employee requiring that employees obtain passes to remove property from the premises; so did a statement on the back of grievant's ID card. Her experience in her job over nine years also should have led to her understanding that taking Hospital property without authorization, which she did not have in this instance, would be a serious employment offense.

Some questions pointed out by the Union about the Hospital's case, such as lack of identification of the brand of the milk and uncertainty about the size of the bag holding the peanuts (Hospital witnesses were clear on their weight) seem too much like small details to affect the credibility of the Hospital's case. On the other hand, explanations offered by Ms. E.S.H. conflicted, were uncorroborated, and in light of her changes in them and her need in the circumstances to make some explanation of her actions, came across as afterthoughts.

Mr. R.A.S. corroborated Lieutenant V.K.G.'s testimony as to the items taken and identified rolls, steaks, and milk as the types usually used in the Hospital. Peanuts are also kept in stock; and the evidence shows that the foods were wrapped in such a way, such as foil and plastic wrap, as to suggest that they came from there and were not purchased outside. Seven of the steaks were cooked; Ms. E.S.H. was unable to account for where they came from if not from the kitchen where she worked.

The Union contends that the food items should have been produced at the hearings. But in view of the positive identification of them at the time and at the hearings, and of grievant's knowledge at all times of what she was charged with taking, it was not necessary for the Hospital to produce them at grievance hearings early in July (although it probably could have done so then) or at the arbitration hearings. I note that most of the items were perishable.

Hospital Food Service Director J.G. testified that she saw the food items in an opaque tan bag; Union counsel contends that she must be in error because one cannot see through an opaque bag. Whether she meant to use another term or not, this discrepancy is too slight to affect the overall testimony in the Hospital's case because the items were fully identified by other witnesses and Ms. J.G. did not inventory them.

The Union points out that she did not go through the bag of food items; she testified that she made the decision to discharge grievant on the basis of the list, the availability of the items in the inventory of the Food Service Department, the service of steak and cake on the menu that day, the presence of aluminum foil which she said is not what one would obtain in a market, and the report from Security, together with the factual circumstances as to Ms. E.S.H.'s initial statements referred to above. All of that seems to amount to a reasonable basis on which to proceed.

Ms. J.G. stated that there was a rule in the Food Service Department that no food could be removed from the kitchen; a memorandum to that effect, referring to the requirement of package passes, and to risk of loss of employment for violation of the rule, was communicated to employees by being posted on the bulletin boards and at the time clock; it is dated March 13 five years ago. (An updated Employee Reminder not to take food from the kitchen without proper authorization is also in evidence. It was posted five years ago but not in June of last year.)

While Ms. J.G. testified that the notice was not posted in June of last year, there is no evidence that the rule was not in effect at that time. And grievant was employed at the time that the memorandum, and two others to the same effect dated in July of that year, were posted or given out to employees. It is difficult to see how Ms. E.S.H. could have not been aware of the rules about not taking Hospital property without authorization. It is basic knowledge for any long-service employee that such actions are wrong and disciplinable.

Ms. J.G. quoted grievant as pleading at the June 20th meeting that she not be terminated and asking Ms. J.G. to be her friend and stating that if she did, Ms. E.S.H. would not do it again; in addition to this apparent admission, Ms. J.G. testified that grievant offered no proof that any of the items listed in the security report had been purchased outside the Hospital. In the course of her investigation, she did not interview grievant, including when grievant came to the Hospital the next day; Ms. J.G. said that a telegram was sent to grievant advising her to contact the department as soon as possible, but that it was returned. But grievant's supervisor, J.B., did see grievant that day. The decision to discharge Ms. E.S.H. was made by Ms. J.G. on June 20th.

A discrepancy in a handwritten entry on the Incident Report dated June 19th that grievant was to be terminated per another employee was not accounted for, but Ms. J.G. said that only she could make that decision.

Ms. E.S.H. testified that on the way to work she went to see a friend who gave her four rolls and a few peanuts in plastic bags; she took them to work and put them in her locker until time to go home. While Ms. E.S.H. identified the friend by name and address, that person was not produced to testify that she gave grievant some of the food at issue.

Ms. E.S.H. said that at lunch time, between 2 and 3 P.M., she bought at a small Spanish grocery, at a location which she identified, four lemons, three pieces of boneless chuck steak, one piece of cake, three grapefruits and two quarts of milk for prices which she testified to; she got a receipt which she gave to Hospital Employee Relations Manager L.T. at a grievance hearing on July 5th.

The receipt is not dated and lists no store name. The meat items are not the same in quantity as those taken from Ms. E.S.H. She said she had never shopped there before, and that she did so with co-employee, D.K.; Ms. D.K. did not testify. She [Ms. D.K] was present at grievance meetings on July 5th and 9th but said nothing about accompanying grievant to the store. Ms. E.S.H. said she had never shopped with Ms. D.K. before. Ms. E.S.H. said that she put all the food except the meat, but including the milk, in her locker.

Ms. E.S.H. testified that she refused Lieutenant V.K.G.'s direction to open her handbag, claiming that was her personal business; that V.K.G. then snatched it away and opened it and took out food and put it on the table in the security trailer. Union counsel contends that this was a violation of her privacy rights, but all that is before the arbitrator is whether the Hospital violated her rights in such a way that it did not have cause to discipline her. Lieutenant V.K.G. had already seen what was in the envelope; therefore, he had reasonable cause to wonder at that point if more food was in her handbag. One of the formerly posted memos states that per the Employee Manual, individuals removing personal property continue to be subject to check by security guards.

In addition, grievant's statement about V.K.G.'s "snatching" is impliedly contradicted by V.K.G.'s testimony; he seemed a credible witness simply recounting an event as it happened. So it would be difficult to credit Ms. E.S.H.'s testimony that she told Lieutenant V.K.G. she had bought the items and her denial that she asked him to give her a break. She said that she kept the grocery receipt in her wallet in case she was asked about the goods, but then why did she not produce it right away?

Ms. F.B. testified that on the morning of June 18th grievant related her account of the events, saying that she had no proof of purchase but thought that she could get one; Ms. F.B. told grievant that was a good idea; but Ms. E.S.H. said that she could not get proof as to the grapefruits and lemons because she had bought them from a street vendor (and the milk in a grocery store) on the way to work. Ms. F.B. also quoted grievant as stating that when leaving work she saw a package which someone had left wrapped up on a warmer and that she walked by and picked it up, that it was wrapped in aluminum foil and contained some two or three steaks. Ms. E.S.H. denied saying all this, although she admitted telling Ms. F.B. what happened.

The Union argues that because the charges against grievant would amount to a crime, the Employer has the burden of proving her acts beyond a reasonable doubt; the Hospital that it has proved its case by clear and convincing evidence; whichever way the burden of proof is defined, I believe that the Hospital has met it; I find the Hospital's case convincing and grievant's explanations inconsistent and implausible.

While the Union points out Ms. J.G.'s failure to talk to Ms. E.S.H. before reaching the decision to discharge her, as part of the Hospital's overall investigation of the events, which it asserts was deficient, Ms. J.G. was not obligated to do so; I believe that Ms. E.S.H. had ample opportunity throughout to state her side and was not disadvantaged in preparing and stating her defense, with the Union's assistance, to the misconduct with which she was charged.

Ms. E.S.H.'s clear employment record over the nine years certainly counts in her favor, but under numerous arbitration decisions, even a first offense, when of the gravity of this one, is grounds for discharge. There are no other factors in mitigation. Otherwise, the Hospital would be exposed to a risk of repetition which it cannot reasonably be required to accept.

AWARD

1. The Hospital had cause for the discharge of grievant, E.S.H., which took place on June 20th.
2. The grievance is denied.

Analysis of the Case

Few management practitioners would disagree that administration has a right, if not a duty, to discharge employees who are dishonest. Why, then, are so many cases involving dishonesty reduced or reversed in arbitration? The effect of such a discharge is long term on the employee's ability to obtain other employment. Arbitrators demand a higher standard of proof—"proof beyond a reasonable doubt"—than would be required in other types of cases. An employee branded a "thief" will find it difficult to obtain other employment.

Keeping in mind this higher standard of proof required in cases of dishonesty, the case shows that Ms. E.S.H., a long-term employee of good standing, was caught in the act of thievery. Her excuse obviously was a weak one. Too often management rationalizes what is termed "small" pilferage. Small amounts of hospital supplies leave the premises in employees' handbags, pockets, and by various other methods. Pilferage can, if unchecked, become so severe that the very stability of an institution may be rocked.

The key to any procedure in controlling pilferage is an even-handed and firm approach. The need for antipilferage security policies, procedures, and systems is clearly evident. But those policies, procedures, and systems, in themselves, are not guarantors of success; rather, it is the people—supervisors and security personnel—who make it work. What is outstanding in this case is that the policy, the system, and the efficient security employee were all in place on the evening of June 17.

Arbitrators are adamant about one requirement in discharge cases: employees must know the consequences of their acts. The Food Service Department, in this case, conspicuously posted formal notices to all employees indicating that individuals removing personal property were subject to check by security guards. Other notices and memoranda to employees informed them that food could not be removed from the kitchen for personal use. The essential element of the communication was a notice stating that loss of employment would result for violation of this rule.

As the grievant was attempting to leave with a large envelope and handbag, she was detained, in accordance with policy. She was asked to disclose the contents of her package and to produce a pass authorizing property removal from the institution. She did not have the pass, so the incident was recorded in detail by the security department. Identification was essential, and this was provided by her supervisor. The thorough investigation produced clear evidence of the theft and, in accordance with institutional policy, the grievant was terminated.

Notwithstanding arbitrators' reluctance to discharge employees for dishonesty, theft usually is regarded as cause for termination if convincing proof of the worker's guilt is presented. This higher standard of proof was indeed presented by the management. The arbitrator had little room for determining mitigating circumstances. But arbitrators are persistent, and despite the preponderance of evidence offered by management, it was Ms. E.S.H.'s own testimony that was decisive.

Her defense was inconsistent and uncorroborated. Management's attorney, totally prepared for this possibility, made effective use of cross-examination of the grievant. The arbitrator concluded that the testimony of Ms. E.S.H. was generated by " . . . a need in the circumstances to make some explanation of her actions" that "came across as afterthoughts."

In preparing its case, management was able to prove that the stolen merchandise was part of the patient menu for that day. Other items were wrapped in such a fashion as to make it unlikely that they would have been purchased from a market, as the grievant testified. Management proved that the food items in the grievant's package were currently available in the inventory of the Food Service Department. Two witnesses for management offered damaging testimony against the grievant. She was quoted as pleading with them to give her a break, saying she would not do it again, telling Lieutenant V.K.G. she would do anything for him, and asking him, "Why do you do this to me? I'm your friend." This evidence was quite damaging since it clearly implied guilt.

Finally, in all arbitration cases the union will attempt to discredit management's witnesses. It is critical that witnesses be interviewed as close to the time of the occurrence of the incident as possible so that their recollections are fresh and accurate. Witnesses must be prepared carefully as to what to expect and, in general, how to present themselves. They should be told to listen carefully to all of the questions and to respond to only the specific points asked. They should not volunteer information not solicited by the question, or speculate, or venture opinions. If they do not remember a fact or detail, they should simply say so; witnesses are not expected to have perfect memories. They should be told that, if they become flustered or confused, they should simply take a moment to collect their thoughts or to ask that, if the question is not clear, it be repeated or rephrased.[1]

Management witnesses must be prepared for aggressive and often obnoxious cross-examination. In this case, the union's attempt to weaken the credibility of management's case did not have any effect. The arbitrator's final statement is worth repeating:

There are no other factors in mitigation. Otherwise, the Hospital would be exposed to a risk of repetition which it cannot reasonably be required to accept.

NOTE

1. Michael G. Macdonald, "An Overview of Arbitration," in Norman Metzger, ed., *Handbook of Health and Human Resources Management* (Rockville, Md.: Aspen Systems Corporation, 1981), p. 839.

Chapter 12

Arbitration Cases: Quality of Performance

CASE 13: POOR ATTENDANCE RECORD

Issues

1. Was there just cause for the discharge of Ms. M.H.?
2. If not, what shall be the remedy?

Opinion

The matter was heard by the Arbitrator on September 27, November 6, and December 19 (in a hearing room at the American Arbitration Association). The Medical Center and the Union were given full opportunity to present evidence and argument and to examine and cross-examine witnesses. The witnesses were sworn.

The parties agreed that the issue to be resolved is as stated above.

Ms. M.H., a Senior Clinical Technologist, was hired by the Medical Center 14 years ago. She worked in the Hematology Laboratory. Her hours as a part-time employee were from 11:30 P.M. to 8:30 A.M. on Friday and Saturday nights and from 4:00 P.M. to 11:30 P.M. on Sundays. She occasionally worked on other days when scheduled. On Friday and Saturday nights, she worked alone and was solely responsible for Hematology Department operations during that period.

Before considering the facts leading to her discharge, it is important to review Ms. M.H.'s disciplinary history. It constitutes a seriously deficient record. Over a period of two-and-one-half years, she was repeatedly tardy for work, even discounting those days on which she was called to work on an extra shift on short notice. There are many notices as to work performance deficiencies. Some disciplinary notices were for falsification of sign-in times. On January 16 of last year, she was suspended for one

165

shift for lateness, following a "final" warning on November 28 of the previous year. On May 16 she was given another Correction Notice for tardiness and was told in writing: "Any tardiness will lead to suspension and/or termination." (Medical Center Exh. No. 5).

Prior to the events of July 6 last year, which resulted in Ms. M.H.'s discharge, it is clear that she was on borrowed time as to her attendance and/or work performance. The Medical Center, over a period of years, had employed progressive discipline through counselings, warnings, and suspension.

The Arbitrator will find, however, that the penalty of discharge was excessive in view of the circumstances surrounding the events of July 6 of last year. To reach this conclusion, the Arbitrator has considered all the facts involved which differentiate this occasion from some or all of the previous instances.

On July 5, the Medical Center, through conference of several of its management personnel, determined that Ms. M.H. should receive a three-day disciplinary penalty *beginning with the July 6 shift* (a Friday night), for alleged failure to perform certain assignments and subsequent failure to reply to a supervisory memo concerning this work. Testimony in explanation of this event was given at the hearing by Ms. M.H. However, this suspension is *not* before the Arbitrator for resolution.

On July 6, Ms. M.H. was 40 minutes tardy in reporting to work. When she arrived, she was told she would not be permitted to work, since this was the first day of the above-mentioned three-day suspension, concerning which she had not been previously advised.

On July 9, the Medical Center sent and Ms. M.H. received the following telegram:

> Because of your most recent tardiness on July 6, records showing excessive lateness, suspension for same you are hereby terminated from employment at the Medical Center Hematology Laboratory effective July 6. (Union Exh. No. 1)

During the hearing, the Medical Center submitted a Correction Notice reading in part as follows:

1. Employee arrived 40 minutes late to her shift July 6.
2. She falsified her sign-in time on June 22. Actually she reported to work at midnight but signed in at 11:30 P.M.

As to the second charge, testimony was offered by the Medical Center. However, Ms. M.H. denied having received a copy of this Correction

Notice, and reference to it was not contained in the discharge telegram sent to her. No clear evidence was presented that Ms. M.H. was aware of the second charge until after her discharge was effected. The Arbitrator is constrained therefore not to consider this charge as part of the cause for discharge.

Now as to the July 6 tardiness. Ms. M.H. testified without contradiction that she lives in Staten Island; that her husband normally drives her to work; that, after several hours of searching, he was unable to get gas for his car (in the midst of the summer gas shortage); that she then called a taxi, which came late; that the ferry which she took to Manhattan was late; that she called the Hematology Department at 11:15 P.M. immediately upon leaving the ferry to report that she would be late (and was not then advised that she had already been suspended beginning that night); and that she took a taxi to the Medical Center.

In ordinary circumstances, this series of events, including her telephone report of impending lateness, would no doubt be considered an acceptable excuse. In Ms. M.H.'s case, and in view of her past record, the Medical Center did not see it this way. Nevertheless, it is a fact that on July 5 the Medical Center made its determination to suspend Ms. M.H. for three days. In essence, it can be shown that the Medical Center was discharging Ms. M.H. for arriving late on a day that was to be a nonwork or suspension day. Then again it is true that her unawareness of the suspension was a clear indication that despite warnings, the lateness problem continued.

Due to the unique nature of the circumstances surrounding the case supported by the Medical Center's position in its May 16 Correction Notice, that another instance of tardiness would lead to "*suspension* and/ *or* termination" (Medical Center Exh. No. 5, emphasis added), the Arbitrator finds the penalty of discharge inappropriate.

Based on all the testimony, evidence and argument, the Arbitrator makes the following

AWARD

There was not just cause for the discharge of Ms. M.H. The remedy shall be that she shall be given a disciplinary suspension of three days beginning with the July 13 shift and continuing through to July 16. She shall be promptly offered reinstatement to her previous position and shall be made whole for loss of earnings from July 16 to the date of offer of reinstatement, less outside earnings, if any, for Fridays, Saturdays, and Sundays she may have worked since July 16.

Analysis of the Case

Disciplinary decisions of managers and supervisors often are rescinded or revised significantly by arbitrators when it appears apparent that:

1. Management did not communicate clearly and concisely to the employee the ramifications of continued poor performance;
2. Management has attempted to correct weakness in an initial action against the employee through the retroactive revision of discipline or by retroactively changing the reason(s) for the discipline imposed; and
3. Discipline is punitive rather than corrective (where the latter is more appropriate).

Management decided on July 5 to suspend Ms. M.H. for three days for poor work performance. Before implementing discipline, it should have communicated this decision first to Ms. M.H. either by telephone or telegram on July 5. Instead management had her report to work, only to send her home. It should be noted that unions frequently identify such action as harassment.

In his decision, the arbitrator questioned the logic of effective discipline for tardiness on the first day of a suspension penalty. While management did not communicate the suspension prior to its implementation, it would have been more appropriate to merely effect the suspension as planned rather than to have administered more severe discipline. Had it done so, looking back, the Medical Center would have accomplished the same result as did the arbitrator's award at far less cost.

Inclusion of the record falsification charge of June 22 as an afterthought, in an attempt to strengthen its discharge decision, actually weakened the Medical Center's position. If, indeed, Ms. M.H. was guilty of falsification, why was this fact not included in the discharge telegram? Unsupported allegations are of no help in establishing guilt and tend to place management's credibility and motives in question.

Lastly, the Medical Center in its May 16 warning should not have stated "Another instance of tardiness will lead to suspension *and/or* termination" (emphasis added). Such a warning is nebulous, confusing to the employee, and illustrates a lack of management commitment and direction. The warning must be clear and state positively the ramifications of continued unacceptable behavior.

A more effective way of communicating such a warning would have been to state: "Continued behavior/performance of this nature will result in further disciplinary action.'' Written this way, management is enforcing its commitment to the progressive disciplinary system. In addition, it does not lock itself into a certain course of action that it may wish to alter later, based on considerations not before in existence such as an employee's good behavior over a protracted period.

CASE 14: NEGLIGENCE IN RESPIRATORY CARE

In this massive matter, tried over a period of time in 10 hearing days, the Union protests as not supported by just cause the discharge on August 24, 1978, of its member, H.L., employed as a Certified Respiratory Therapy Technician. The Hospital contends that the termination of the grievant is supported by just cause. The Union, to the contrary, maintains that standard has not been met and that its member should be reinstated and made whole.

Each of the parties was represented by able Labor Relations Counsel. Full opportunity to adduce evidence, examine and cross-examine witnesses, and proffer exhibits was afforded. The lengthy and complex testimony in this matter has been carefully analyzed, including the 65 exhibits produced by the Hospital and 16 exhibits received on behalf of the Union.

This is a "patient care" case. The Hospital through its seven witnesses adduced the following. On August 15 two years ago, 72-year-old F.C. had exploratory surgery to determine if he was suffering from cancer. He was later in the Recovery Room on a respirator and with a tube in his throat under intensive care—one of four patients there at the time—with two attending nurses. The respirator, a Bennett MA-1, was breathing for the patient.

At approximately 1:00 A.M., on August 16, the Surgical Resident instructed the nurses to place the patient on IMV, designed to effect a transition from controlled breathing to spontaneous breathing; that is, the patient is thus allowed to draw some breath on his own, and the objective is to take the patient off the MA-1 slowly.

Responding to a page, and at approximately 1:45 A.M., the grievant was instructed to make the necessary adjustment for a switchover to the IMV. In order to do this, a valve had to be placed with an arrow in the direction of the flow of air. The grievant allegedly set the valve backwards, and the result was, for the most part, to preclude the patient from easily drawing breaths, in effect, to create a condition like sucking on an empty pipe.

The patient began to thrash about agitatedly. The nurses became upset and asked the grievant, "What's wrong?" The bellows on the MA-1 were not moving and an alarm that was on the machine was not being heard, evidently because it had been placed in the "off" position. The patient's heart rate accelerated substantially. The grievant insisted it was "not the machine, it's the patient." Upon the therapist's insistence that the machine was not at fault and that the patient should be sedated, the patient was medicated with 50 mg of Demerol.

Although the grievant was asked not to leave, he departed, although the problem was not resolved at all. The grievant's excuse for leaving at this time was that a Code or Team 7000 relating to an emergency had been called at 1:45, and even though it was by then 2:00 A.M., or thereabouts, and a colleague of his, also on the "lobster shift," had answered that Code 7000, he said he had to go too.

At approximately 2:05 A.M., Respiratory Therapy was again paged. The grievant's colleague, W.M., answered the beep and was informed of the problem. He said he was attending a Code 7000 and could not respond promptly. Then, the "on-call" Anesthesiologist and the "on-call" Surgical Resident were likewise paged. The Anesthesiologist responded first and visited the patient who was still breathing abdominally and very agitatedly.

While he [the Anesthesiologist] was there, Dr. J.W., the Surgical Resident arrived. He discovered that the air valve had been connected in the wrong direction, and he corrected it. The patient's breathing then improved, and Dr. J.W., deeply disturbed, directed the nurses to prepare an "incident report" which triggered the subsequent events in the disciplinary process.

In this connection, the evidence of Dr. J.W., the Surgical Resident, is critical. He had been one of but nine students at a local Medical School who had, as an elective, worked for one month in the intensive Coronary Unit and had experience on the MA-1 and IMV. He had placed the patient on the Bennett MA-1 respirator with assisting ventilation after major abdominal surgery. In accord with standing procedure, at approximately 1:00 A.M., wishing to wean the patient from the ventilator, he directed that the IMV, Intermittent Mandatory Ventilation, be attached, which would permit the patient to breathe on his own for some part.

At the hearing, he demonstrated on the MA-1 the proper method of attaching the IMV, and also the wrong method. When he left the patient at approximately 1:00 A.M., he directed that a Respiratory Therapist place him on the IMV. The patient, he said, at that time was in good shape. He left the area of the Recovery Room at approximately 1:15 to 1:20 A.M. to proceed on his rounds.

After responding at approximately 1:45 to the Code 7000, which usually involves a cardiac or respiratory arrest, he later returned to the Recovery Room on a page from the nurse at approximately 2:20 or 2:25 A.M. The patient, he said, was now in "bad shape," with labored and shallow breathing, and in substantial distress, breathing some 20-25 times a minute, and the bellows on the respirator were not going up and down. The nurse informed [him] that the Respiratory Therapist, the grievant, had indeed placed the patient on the IMV, but he had become *immediately* distressed. After the grievant had been asked to check the machine, the patient was continuing to breathe very agitatedly and the grievant had insisted that it was "not the machine, it was the patient." Pursuant to standing orders, Demerol was administered.

Dr. J.W. examined the patient and then turned his attention to the machine, suspecting an air leak. He checked the humidifier, the hose, and then the IMV, and then found the arrow in the wrong direction which prevented the patient from drawing any appreciable air. The bellows were not working and the alarm was off. He turned the valve in the proper direction, the bellows worked at once, and in a few moments the patient was breathing in a better fashion.

Concluding that the negligence involved was "incredible" and "inexcusable," Dr. J.W. directed the nurses to prepare an "incident report." On cross-examination, he responded that the nurses had told him that the Respiratory Therapist had also left the alarm in the "off" position. He demonstrated again the proper method of attaching the IMV pieces to the MA-1 and stated that at "X" Medical Center there were normally 40-50 patients on an IMV, as against 2-3 at this facility and that he had never seen the valve "knocked off by a patient." He observed that in order to change the valve position, several motions have to be entered into, not just one. He observed that if the valve had remained in the incorrect position, and the MA-1 was still being used, the patient would be getting only 10 percent of the breath needed and in time he would suffer cardiac arrest and respiratory failure. He estimated that since the patient was "getting a rich mixture" there would be "slow suffocation rather than an immediate cutoff."

Staff Nurse V.O. then testified that Respiratory Therapist H.L. had arrived at approximately 1:15 A.M. on August 16 and had set up the IMV, that at once the machine began to emit a "strange sound," and the patient at once began to "thrash around." When she inquired why that was so, the grievant went over to the machine and the sound stopped, but the patient was still thrashing about agitatedly. When she asked the grievant what was wrong, he insisted that the problem was not due to the machine, but was because of the patient. When he was asked to wait while she medicated the patient, and observed his breathing, he said he had to leave, and he did leave, allegedly for the Code 7000.

Parenthetically, I observe that he never did arrive at the Code 7000 which was being attended to, as he knew, by the other Respiratory Therapist on the "lobster shift," W.M. After the grievant had left, Nurse V.O.

paged again for a Respiratory Therapist. W.M. answered the page, and said, "I'm the only one at the Code 7000 and I can only arrive at the end of the Code."

Significantly, she testified that the bellows were not moving at the time that H.L. was there, and that the machine's strange sound stopped after the grievant went over to the machine and adjusted something. She testified that she did not, nor did the other nurse in the Recovery Room, E.M., touch the valve and it was not until Dr. J.W. arrived that he observed that the arrow was in the wrong direction and corrected the situation. She also testified that Anesthesiologist Dr. S., who arrived shortly before Dr. J.W., did not touch the valve assembly, and had responded that he did not know what to do about the machine except to change the patient from the Bennett MA-1 to a Bear Respirator.

Nurse V.O. consistently testified that the problem began *immediately* upon the grievant hooking up the IMV and *continued* until Dr. J.W. repaired the improper installation. No one, she said, worked on the MA-1 or the IMV until Dr. J.W. arrived. She observed that the patient had a tube down his throat which he had not disturbed, and that a patient would normally do that rather than reach out for the valve, which he had not done in any case.

On cross-examination, Nurse V.O. unwaveringly responded that the MA-1, the moment that H.L. had put on the IMV, had made a sound she had not heard before or since, and that when H.L. adjusted the toggle switch or something, the sound stopped, but the patient, who was "thrashing about," was not helped. She observed that the nurses had not resorted to the "ambue procedure," that is, manually administering oxygen, and using the bellows, because the patient could breathe for himself "up to a point." She consistently averred under severe cross-examination that the problem commenced with the arrival of the grievant when he put together the IMV on the MA-1 and only ended with Dr. J.W.'s action.

Staff Nurse E.M. testified corroboratively. She observed that from approximately 1:50 A.M. when grievant H.L. started his activity, to approximately 2:30 A.M. when Dr. J.W. corrected the valve, the patient had been breathing in an agitated fashion. The sound that the machine made was, she said, "not the alarm" but a noise that she could not identify, and was stopped by H.L. by some adjustment.

The Hospital then called Staff Therapist W.M. from the Union's side of the hearing room. He testified that the Code 7000 occurred at approximately 1:45 A.M., was attended to only by him, in addition, of course, to physicians and other personnel, but not by the grievant. Then, under Union counsel's examination, he observed that the call for the IMV and the Code 7000 came at approximately the same time and that the grievant took the

IMV call and he took the Code 7000 call, saying to the grievant, "When you finish the IMV, come on back to the office and wait for my call because I may need an MA-1 set-up for the Code patient."

He observed that he had asked H.L. "if he knew how to put it together" referring to the small tube, the long tube, and the valve, which constituted the primary working parts of the IMV manifold set-up. The grievant said "yes," he did. He noted that the grievant was a replacement on this "lobster shift," since he normally works the 4–12 shift. Indeed, the grievant was working a "double shift" that night, and since W.M. has worked only once or twice before with the grievant, he asked the question whether H.L. knew the IMV procedure, and received the affirmative response. He observed, under interrogation, that if the machine is flawed, the proper procedure would be to ask the nurse to "bag the patient" (ambue the patient), and place a test lung on the machine and trouble shoot the parts, and that would include checking the valve.

Hospital witness G.M., Supervisor of the Respiratory Therapy Department on the evening shift, namely from 4:00 P.M. to midnight, testified that he was the only Supervisor on that shift as distinguished from the day shift, when three Supervisors are present. He observed that at the beginning of his shift on August 17, he was told by R.A., then the Acting Director of the Respiratory Therapy Department, what had occurred on the night of August 16 and had been asked to investigate. When the grievant arrived on Friday, August 18, G.M. spoke to him as part of the investigation and asked whether he had placed the valve incorrectly. The grievant, he testified, responded, "Yes, I'm sorry, I did." And G.M. said, "I'll talk to R.A. again. I don't know what will come of this."

He [G.M.] noted that some two weeks before the incident he had demonstrated to members of his shift, of whom H.L. was one, that the acceptable methods of setting up the IMV are two, and he described and demonstrated them, indicating that the arrow on the valve was extremely important and should be in the direction of the flow, and the valve should be inspected to see it was operating properly.

Thereafter, again on August 18, at approximately 10:30 P.M., G.M. had a second conversation with the grievant. It seems that an employee had called in "sick" and a replacement was again needed for the "lobster shift," the midnight to 8:00 A.M. shift. After going through the seniority list and not being able to get anyone, he [G.M.] asked whether H.L., the grievant, or Therapist F.G. would be willing to work. F.G. said, "No"; H.L. said "Okay," and G.M. told H.L., "If you finish by 11:00 P.M., go to dinner, and return at midnight." He also said, "Will you be careful?" At midnight, H.L. having left early, G.M. came to work. Grievant H.L. did not appear despite his promise to do so. Supervisor G.M. then remained for the night.

On Monday, August 22, Supervisor G.M. met with Director R.A. and informed him that H.L. had accepted the overtime assignment to work the "lobster shift," but had not appeared, and also reported that H.L. had failed to record and evidently therefore to perform the cylinder rounds for the second cylinder round check on the August 18 evening shift. This requires checking the pressure and the liter flow, if any, in the oxygen or compressed air tanks in the Hospital. He had asked Therapist W.M. to check immediately the condition of the cylinder rounds when he found that H.L. had not performed that duty and was told that the tanks were not in good shape; some indeed had to be changed, which was done at approximately 4:00 A.M. to 6:00 A.M. on August 18. A cylinder check, he observed, should take approximately 45 minutes.

The exhibits demonstrate that in fact the grievant had not recorded the second cylinder round. Union counsel observed that this did not prove that H.L. had failed to perform the activity. Company counsel's response was that the failure to enter the information, even if the round was made, is in itself improper and in view of the condition of the tanks, the clear inference is that the failure to record the information was accompanied by a failure actually to check the tanks.

In view of the concurrence of the failure to insert the valve correctly and the other incidents, Director R.A. told Supervisor G.M. to ask the grievant to transfer to the day shift for "closer supervision." The same evening, August 21, Supervisor G.M., with whom, as H.L. later testified, he had a "good relationship," suggested the change to H.L., stating that closer supervision would be to H.L.'s benefit. The response was, "I can't do it, I go to school." G.M. repeated the "request" several times during the evening. To the last two requests, H.L. just would not even respond. H.L. was also asked why he had not appeared for the "lobster shift" after agreeing to do so, or why he had not at least telephoned if there was some problem. There was no answer.

On Tuesday, August 22, G.M. reported to Director R.A. that H.L. had refused the offer to transfer to the day shift for closer supervision, and a meeting [was] convened with the Supervisors of the Therapy Department and H.L. as well as the Union delegate in attendance.

Regarding the valve incident, the grievant, according to G.M., again conceded that he had put it in backwards. Regarding the failure to show up on the "lobster shift," he stated that he did not come in because G.M. had told him "be careful" and this evidently hurt his pride. Regarding the cylinder rounds, he claimed he had performed the activity, and when asked why he did not enter the pressure of the various tanks, there was no answer. Again he refused to transfer to the day shift, and was told by

Director R.A., "You've got to do that or else there will be further action. Think about it and give me your answer, either tomorrow or the next day."

On Wednesday, the grievant reported for work, went to the Employees' Health Department, and was not seen thereafter. On Thursday, August 24, at 4:00 P.M., the parties convened in Director R.A.'s office and the grievant was read aloud a termination notice. In response to this, the grievant did not say he was prepared to work days, did not deny that he had placed the valve incorrectly, and did not deny the failure to show up on the "lobster shift," or to say that he called in, or that he had performed the cylinder rounds.

The Termination Notice, read aloud to the grievant, and then read by him and his Union representative, referred to "negligence" and a "willful act of conduct detrimental to patient care or to Medical Center operations." It read as follows:

On Wednesday, August 16, during the 12–8 A.M. shift, you incorrectly set up an I.M.V. valve on a patient in the A-6 Recovery Room. As a result, the patient experienced great difficulty in breathing, which was brought to your attention by a nurse in the unit. You left the Recovery Room area insisting that the problems the patient was experiencing with breathing could not be attributed to any equipment which you had set up on the patient. You had previously been instructed by a supervisor in the proper way to set up an I.M.V. valve. Your actions pertaining to the patient in the A-6 Recovery Room are totally inexcusable under any circumstances. In addition, on August 18, you did not complete your job assignment (cylinders rounds) or show up for the 12–8 A.M. shift on August 19, which you agreed to work. Your actions indicate a complete disregard for patients, co-workers, and your responsibilities as a Technician. Accordingly, because of your obvious negligence on 8/16 and your actions on 8/18 and 8/19, in view of previous infractions, you have left me with no choice but to terminate your employment at the Respiratory Therapy Department at the Hospital effective 4:10 P.M. August 24.

The reference to "previous infractions" relates primarily to an incident of May 3, three years ago, where the grievant was instructed to provide a 40 percent oxygen to "Baby Joseph." Allegedly, he had been negligent, and "the harm to Baby Joseph could have been catastrophic if not for the astute and timely intervention of the nurses on duty." A suspension of three days, together with a final warning, was administered, but after intercession on the grievant's behalf by the Union, the three-day suspension was rescinded, but the final warning remained.

In a later third-step meeting, held in the Labor Relations Office of the Hospital, the grievant for the first time said he had set up the valve correctly, contrary, say the Hospital witnesses, to other prior admissions; said that the Doctor had set it incorrectly; and led the Hospital officials to believe that his coworker Therapist W.M., had handed him the apparatus in an improper fashion.(sic)

Under rigorous cross-examination by Union counsel, Supervisor G.M. persisted in his testimony that the grievant had indeed twice admitted prior to the third step that he had placed the valve backwards. He acknowledged that he had no difficulty with H.L. during his tenure as his Supervisor, although he felt that H.L. was not "overzealous," and that he had told H.L. he should attend school and learn more when H.L. had come to him for "advice."

G.M. was an instructor in respiratory techniques at a local college prior to August, eight years ago, and thereafter. He averred that when the IMV valve is placed incorrectly it would inevitably lead to slow suffocation and therefore death after a period of time, and that the suffocation signs would be the patient thrashing around with the pulse rate up, the heart rate up, and his color white, and then blue.

Director of the Respiratory Therapy Department R.A. testified that he replaced a predecessor in June, 1978, and that the predecessor's relationship with the staff had been "tense and strained." As particulars, he observed that the staff had directed verbal abuse to his predecessor; that a rock had been thrown through his office window by an unknown person; that feces had been placed on his desk, again by an unknown; that discrimination charges had been commenced against him by several members of the staff; and that a libel action had been lodged. Indeed, he also noted that a prior Supervisor had received through the Hospital mail a death certificate with his name inserted.

Therefore, as a new Director, with a new supervisory crew, R.A. had emphasized that he wished to avoid the antagonism toward supervision that had flawed his predecessor's tenure. He had decided that he would bend over backwards for a "different style of leadership," hopefully leading to a "more cohesive staff." Accordingly, when presented with the "H.L. incident," only two months after his appointment, he determined to do all he could do to avoid discharging the grievant, even though he believed that the incident warranted a discharge. Accordingly, to avoid a harsh confrontation and all its ensuing difficulties, he offered the grievant a transfer to the day shift where he would receive "closer supervision." When the grievant adamantly refused to do so, he concluded he had no alternative and discharged the grievant, believing that his hopes for a more cooperative relationship were thus endangered.

R.A. averred that on August 22, at approximately 4:00 P.M., in his first meeting with the grievant, the grievant in the presence of other Hospital Supervisors and his Union representation, had conceded that "I set the IMV valve backwards" and said "Give me a verbal warning notice;" to this R.A. had responded, "This is much more serious than that. I want you to come on the day shift," and the grievant had refused that offer and again did so after being advised to think about it and give a considered response in a day or two.

The record indicates that the grievant at the time was in between school sessions and would not commence the fall session for several weeks, and that he had been told that there were certain courses that he could take at night. Director R.A. believed that H.L.'s infraction was "serious, inexcusable and merited discharge." He observed that in his experience no other Therapist ever had placed a valve backwards, had failed to make cylinder rounds, had agreed to work overtime and had not shown up.

With regard to schooling, he noted that he himself had dropped out of Long Island University for two years because of a personal problem and had then returned to school. He described the procedure followed on August 24. He had read aloud the termination notice and then asked the grievant to read it, which he did with his delegate. The termination notice quoted in full above was passed back without signature, excuse, or comment.

The Hospital's final witness, testifying in rebuttal on the final hearing day, was Dr. I.L.C., who had previously received a subpoena from the Union. However, he was called by the Hospital as a witness. He is Director of Respiratory Care Services and has been with the Hospital for many years. He testified that with the IMV valve in the wrong direction, a patient could receive only the volume of air that he could generate himself, and that it was impossible to say how long it would take before a patient would expire, especially if there was no chest surgery. In this case, he said, "it might take a couple of hours, but it was really impossible to say."

On cross-examination, he testified that in February two years ago certain Union personnel, employees of the Respiratory Department including the grievant, met with him. He believed that this was a "teaching session," and he told them that the bellows would not work because exhalation would not take place if the valve were placed in the wrong direction, and that depending upon the case involved, and the individual involved, there would be a death, either early or late, after a lot of "struggling." He was not told at the time that H.L. had been terminated and there was no discussion of competence or tenure, but only of IMV situations.

As "Medical Director" he said, it is not his function to tell the "Therapist Director" how to run his Department in regard to discipline. Although he has been Director of Respiratory Care Services at the Hospital for some six or seven years, and has been associated with the Hospital for some 22 years, this, he said, was the first "IMV backwards" incident that has been brought to his attention in this Hospital.

Under further cross-examination, Dr. I.L.C. answered that if an IMV valve is placed backwards the patient would *"immediately"* show the effects, and would begin to "struggle," which, incidentally, is what happened in this case, *but* that this struggle "could last a *fairly long* period of time."

The Union, in opening its case, maintained, as it did throughout, in excerpts from various learned works (analysis of these exhibits establishes that they are wholly distinguishable from the instant case) and with its six witnesses, that had the grievant inserted the IMV valve backwards the patient would have died within minutes, and that accordingly, H.L. could not have been guilty of this infraction. Accordingly, it maintained that if the testimony of the Hospital witnesses is credited as to the valve being placed in the wrong direction, then it must have happened *after* H.L. had been there.

The Union's first witness was A.B., a Union delegate, and a Respiratory Therapist. He maintained at the threshold that placing the IMV valve backwards had occurred on a number of occasions without any discipline having been imposed. He averred that Director R.A. did not wish to discharge the grievant for the incidents involved but was told to do so by "management." He said that although there are three Supervisors on the day shift, there are eight Respiratory Technicians. He believed that Day supervision was not as good as the Evening shift Supervision. There are four or five Technicians with one Supervisor on the Evening shift, and usually two Technicians on the "lobster shift," without any supervisor.

Then, H.L., the grievant, testified in great detail and for several days. He observed that he was attending college level courses preparatory to commencing a respiratory therapy course. He observed that in May, five years ago, he was accused of "killing a baby," and that he has a lawsuit pending for $2 million against the Hospital because of "defamatory words." This refers to the incident which the Union succeeded in having a three-day suspension rescinded to a final warning notice.

He stated that he learned from coworker F.G. and other members of the staff how to set up the IMV valve, which was new, and that no Supervisor had given him a lesson, in contradiction, of course, to Supervisor G.M.'s testimony. Nevertheless, he observed that prior to the incident of August 16, he had set up the IMV valve "about ten times" and could do it "with my eyes closed." He agreed that he and Supervisor G.M. "got along" and that G.M. would "explain things to me."

As to the incident in question, he said he had checked the MA-1, set up the IMV, and tested it, that the patient had pushed him away and seemed to be "in pain," and that the nurse had medicated the patient. Indeed, when he left the Recovery Room, he said the patient was "comfortable and breathing easily," totally contrary to the testimony of the two nurses in the Recovery Room. Although the nurses kept on telling him that it was "the machine, and not the patient," he said, "I must leave," "Call the doctor," and "I'll wait a few moments."

He insisted that the machine worked "perfectly" and that the patient was "in no difficulty." He agreed that if the patient were in difficulty, it was "not humane" to leave him, if, in fact, the valve had been placed incorrectly. Again, he observed the patient was "perfect" and that there was "no problem with the machine." This was reiterated in H.L.'s testimony time and time again. He maintained that Supervisor G.M. had told him that the nurses do not trust him, to which he had responded, "I want the names of those nurses, and I will get them." He insisted, as well, that Director R.A. had said the termination action was taken because "management" insisted.

With regard to his failure to work overtime after he had agreed to do so, H.L. said that G.M. had told him "not to touch the respirators" and "not to answer a Code 7000." To this he had responded, "Are you crazy? If you want that, write it up as an order, or else I won't work overtime." Believing that it was a dischargeable action to refuse a Code 7000, he did not work the overtime and G.M. "signed" him out and "told" him to "go home."

With regard to the cylinders, H.L. claimed that he did the work but "forgot to note the second check" because "I was upset with G.M." Yet, of course, the second check is normally between 9 and 10 P.M., and this was before he was asked to work overtime, or could get "upset." He then averred that he usually marks his second check on a "blue card" rather than on the "large sheet," and then "I enter it on a sheet thereafter." The sheet refers to the daily cylinder rounds record.

The grievant conceded that when he met on several occasions with Supervision and the Director to discuss his infractions, he did not exhibit or even refer then to this blue card. Even at the third step, this was so, although Union delegate A.B. allegedly said, "I have proof, but no one was interested in pursuing that."

H.L. then observed that he did not enter the second round of cylinder checks because he was engaged in a conference with his Supervisor. In fast succession, he testified that he did them at a certain time, at intervals, then that he did them simultaneously, and then that he did them at another time. He exhibited a "blue card" with some readings, but certainly not for the 26 cylinders, and denied that these were entered after the fact. He maintained that he had a number of blue cards, some had been ripped up, some were at home, and finally that all of them were in evidence in the proceeding.

He conceded again that he had never even offered to produce the blue card even though it was material, either on August 22 or August 24, although he maintained that he had told Supervision that he had performed the task. To the Hospital's attorney's question whether it was not indeed a fraudulent card made up after the fact, he said it was not. Finally, H.L. insisted that he had gone to lunch and not returned because Supervisor G.M. told him to "Get the f--- out of here and he would sign me out." He denied that he had ever admitted to G.M that he had placed the IMV valve backwards and insisted that the MA-1 and the IMV valve were both functioning properly, indeed, "perfectly."

He agreed that on August 24 the termination notice was read aloud to him and to his Union representation. Despite what he admitted were really "sincere" requests from Director R.A. to work days, to "give him a chance," he said he would not change.

Throughout, H.L. insisted that the patient was "calm and peaceful" and that he had not committed any error. Indeed, he went so far as to say that the nurse told him to leave and that was why he left. He conceded on cross-examination that Director R.A. mentioned that he thought he could get him into a local University Program at nights, but that he had responded that it is a four-year program and he was in a two-year program. Nor did he offer to go on days after the summer session which had just ended, even though he was between terms until mid-September. In continued conflicting and contradictory testimony, he observed that the nurse herself was "not stable," that the patient was "comfortable," and that he could not understand "why the nurse was creating a problem."

H.L. insisted that the valve was "set correctly," or else the patient "could not last," and indeed "would have died." Later on in his testimony, he stated that the patient would live only "two minutes" relying, he said, on Medical Director I.L.C.'s alleged estimate of "two minutes," when he had been asked in February two years ago about such a hypothetical situation. All Union testimony, incidentally, was *prior* to Dr. I.L.C.'s testifying, since I. L.C. testified at the very end of the case after both sides had presented their evidence. It is to be noted that Dr. I.L.C. had not so stated according to his testimony.

The Union's next witness was C.G., a member of the Respiratory Therapy Department, who had worked with the grievant on the same shift. He began testifying that he had asked the grievant on August 16, about 10:00 P.M., prior to the request to work overtime, "Have you completed the second cylinder round?" and that the grievant had said "yes." He [C.G.] also testified that depending upon "my mood," I write them on "Paper, cards, or the sheet," and that he had seen H.L. do the same except that H.L. never used "the sheet," and indeed had never carried it with him.

He corroborated H.L.'s testimony that G.M. had said, "When you work tonight," namely the double shift, "don't do the respirators," etc., and that H.L. had said "put it in writing." When G.M. refused to do so, H.L. said, "I won't work," to which Supervisor G.M. allegedly said, "Take your lunch and you don't have to come back." He said he heard the entire confrontation which lasted in an argument from 10:15 P.M. to 10:45 P.M.

He believed that the IMV valve had been tampered with on more than one occasion because nurses and residents were "curious." He insisted that Director R.A. had said that no discipline would be taken because one could not "pinpoint the responsibility for the IMV valve being back-wards," stating that Director R.A. had said "it happened so frequently that there is no way in which we can control it." He maintained that H.L. had always insisted that he had not done anything wrong. He said that he himself had twice committed the infraction of placing the IMV valve backwards and that he had not been disciplined. He maintained that Dr. I.L.C. had told his group in February two years ago that if the valve was set incorrectly a patient would last "no longer than two minutes."

Again, he maintained that he knew nothing about the valve incident until August 21 because H.L. did not mention it to him. Yet, he claimed to have overheard, and in fact recorded in his mind, the entire discussion on the night of August 11 when G.M. told H.L. allegedly not to "do the respirators or answer a Team 7000." When shown certain records, he admitted that the two instances that he referred to regarding the IMV valves being placed backward were not actually done by him, but rather were "found in that condition."

Staff Therapist O.A.M. then testified on behalf of his coworker, and for the Union. He observed that after H.L.'s discharge, an IMV valve was found "in a wrong direction" and that no investigation had occurred. He observed, as well, that the MA-1, other than the valve, had been found in a disconnected condition with the alarm turned off, etc., and that no charges have been filed, no investigation commenced.

Ms. R.B., another Respiratory Therapist, testified that there are "numerous occasions" when the IMV valve is improperly positioned, that the patient will "react agitatedly" to such a situation, and that "nine out of ten times the valve is backwards because someone hits it, or someone brushes up against it." Her "opinion," in hearsay testimony, continued with an assertion that a patient would last "less than 15 minutes" if the valve were improperly set up. She had been present in the conference with Dr. I. L.C., the Medical Director of the Respiratory Department, and she testified that he had said that a patient would last "less than ten minutes." She maintained that no Respiratory Therapist has ever improperly positioned the IMV valve and that it "always is found in an improper condition because of extraneous circumstances."

She observed, under cross-examination, that she had never set the valve backwards herself, but if it had happened the patient would become agitated and thrash around, the respirator alarm would go off, and the bellows would not work. She would then, she said, "take the patient off the machine and would recheck everything, while I or someone else was ambuing the patient;" nor would she leave the patient.

Agreeing that the patient would receive "some air" if the IMV valve was set in backwards, she insisted that in her opinion Mr. F.C. would not have lasted more than 15 minutes. Agreeing that the IMV weans the patient away from a total reliance on the machine in that he breathes a little and the machine helps a little, she observed that the amount of air the patient receives depends upon his condition and age. She agreed that there is inservice training on how to place the valves properly and that there are four or five different manufactured valves used on the premises. She also agreed that even if she did not hear the alarm, and that if it was "off," she would be alerted if the bellows were not operating.

At the end of this massive case, after the ten days of testimony, the Union maintains that there has been "no just cause" demonstrated for the discharge of its member. It insists that the offer to have the grievant transferred to the day shift to maintain his job was not made in good faith because the Hospital knew he could not accept that offer, and it says that greater supervision could be had on the 4–12 shift than on the day shift, even though there are a greater number of Supervisors on the day shift as well as additional physicians and nursing staff. Furthermore, it maintains that even if the offer were made in good faith, it reflects a belief by the Hospital that the events did not provide grounds for discharge.

Although there has been no tracing of an improper valve connection to any Respiratory Therapist, it [the Union] maintains that IMV valves are found in an incorrect position at times, and insists that this cannot constitute a dischargeable offense, even if H.L. had committed the error. The failure to work the "lobster shift" and the failure allegedly to do the cylinder rounds are, it says, "mere makeweights." It asserts, citing Article XIII, Section 2, of the Collective Bargaining Agreement, that the grievant properly could refuse to be transferred to another shift and this is what the grievant did with a right to do so. Terming its member a "dedicated employee," it urges that he be reinstated with full back pay.

The Hospital, for its part, says a "just result" is required, that this is a "patient care case," and that the central issue is whether the grievant did indeed place the valve incorrectly. It maintains that he did so based upon the record as a whole. If, in fact, the incident occurred, it contends there is no choice but to sustain the discharge and that the opportunity to work on the day shift was offered the grievant only because of the situation of the new Director who was eager to avoid a confrontation which had blemished and truncated the career of his predecessor and of other supervisors. This Director and his new Supervisors were eager to avoid the "guerrilla warfare" which they claimed had occurred before, and thus they had leaned over backward in an attempt to adjust and settle this "most serious and inexcusable violation."

A careful analysis of the mass of testimony adduced over the many days of hearing convinces [the arbitrator] beyond doubt that in fact the credible evidence establishes that the grievant had indeed placed the IMV valve backwards; that when this occurred and the patient was thrashing around and struggling for air, his reactions were virtually incomprehensible, insisting that the machine was not at fault and that the patient should be sedated.

The testimony of the two nurses and of Dr. J.W. are, in the circumstances, especially in view of the conflicting, contradictory, and inconsistent and virtually incredible testimony of the grievant, sufficient to convince [the arbitrator] that the infraction had indeed occurred as averred by the Hospital.

Quite apart from the "final warning" which had heretofore been issued, but especially because of the valve incident herein, the concomitant failure to record the cylinder rounds, and indeed on the record to actually perform the rounds, and the subsequent failure to work the overtime after having agreed to do so, the Hospital's determination is completely supported by "just cause."

The Hospital's attempt to achieve and preserve a "living-together relationship" and to avoid the "guerrilla warfare" of the past led it to offer the grievant an opportunity to hold on to his job by transferring to the day shift where he would be closely supervised. This offer, given the circumstances which impelled it, cannot on this record be used now, after the grievant's adamant refusals to accept it, to annul and void a discharge which is warranted and supported by just cause.

I have given unusually deep thought to the problems inherent in this case and had suggested to the parties several times during the multiple hearing days that a settlement be entered into. Regrettably, this has not occurred, and accordingly adjudication is required.

On the basis of the record as a whole and an evaluation of credibility, I am constrained to find that the Hospital's case has been amply proven and that just cause exists for the discharge of H.L. Accordingly, the Union's grievance on his behalf must be and is denied.

Analysis of the Case

Arbitration cases are time consuming and costly; the case of Mr. H.L. is a prime example. Beginning with his termination in August, it did not end until the arbitrator's award in January three years later. The union and management presented their evidence in ten hearing sessions. Discharge arbitration cases must be presented exhaustively. It is a well-known fact that arbitrators consider discharge as the capital punishment of labor relations.

Keeping in mind the broad generalization as to arbitrators' perception of discharges, such cases must be backed by clearly exhibited evidence of just cause. Among the most difficult types of discharge arbitrations are those involving allegations of incompetence or poor work performance. To ensure support of management's position in such cases, extensive documentation must be presented displaying the following:

1. management's establishment and communication to all employees of definition and levels of acceptable job performance
2. management's evaluation of employee performance measured against these standards
3. communication of performance evaluation to the employee being evaluated
4. evidence that the employee understands the shortcomings and what is required to effect behavior/performance modification
5. evidence of periodic counseling or instruction to employee in the correct methods and procedures of job performance
6. progressive disciplining for continued poor performance

The extent it is necessary to document and progressively discipline for poor performance is, of course, directly related to the nature and degree of incompetence. Cases of gross negligence may require very little documentation and time-consuming progressive discipline. Further, the nature of documentation and administration of progressive discipline will vary, depending upon the type of employer.

The critical nature of poor performance in health care facilities is universally accepted. It is only the proof—evidence by documentation—that is in question. The issue in such cases is patient welfare. Although arbitrators are impressed with the life-and-death nature of work in health care facilities, they still require a standard of proof that goes well beyond subjective evaluation, even by experts.

The case of H.L. clearly is one of gross negligence. We have seen how his performance and attitude toward F.C. could easily have resulted in the patient's death had Dr. J.W. and the nursing staff not intervened. Did H.L's attitude change after this incident with patient F.C.? To the contrary. In the wake of this serious misconduct, he did not perform the necessary function of checking cylinders and failed to work overtime after having agreed to do so.

Attitude is critical to the effective performance of assigned duties, and in the case of H.L. a different, more constructive attitude could very well have worked to his benefit. The arbitrator refers to his testimony as "conflicting, contradictory and inconsistent and virtually incredible." The arbitrator finds that in view of the patient's distress, H.L.'s reactions were "virtually incomprehensible."

Certain actions on the grievant's part might have mitigated this situation: admitting to his mistake, working overtime, performing his cylinder rounds, not attempting to cover his tracks. But such was not the case. Finally, if he had accepted management's attempt to compromise, prior to the discharge, by working the day shift so he could receive closer supervision, the discharge would have been replaced by a constructive warning and an opportunity to remedy past deficiencies.

It is well established that arbitrators universally are affected by employee recognition of incompetent behavior and generally move to give them another chance to improve themselves. It is clear that H.L.'s adamant position in not accepting serious faults in his performance and, indeed, in not admitting to the obvious negligence, presented no such opportunity for the arbitrator to reduce the punishment.

Code of Professional Responsibility for Arbitrators of Labor-Management Disputes

PREAMBLE

BACKGROUND

Voluntary arbitration rests upon the mutual desire of management and labor in each collective bargaining relationship to develop procedures for dispute settlement which meet their own particular needs and obligations. No two voluntary systems, therefore, are likely to be identical in practice. Words used to describe arbitrators (Arbitrator, Umpire, Impartial Chairman, Chairman of Arbitration Board, etc.) may suggest typical approaches but actual differences within any general type of arrangement may be as great as distinctions often made among the several types.

Some arbitration and related procedures, however, are not the product of voluntary agreement. These procedures, primarily but not exclusively applicable in the public sector, sometimes utilize other third party titles (Fact Finder, Impasse Panel, Board of Inquiry, etc.). These procedures range all the way from arbitration prescribed by statute to arrangements substantially indistinguishable from voluntary procedures.

The standards of professional responsibility set forth in this Code are designed to guide the impartial third party serving in these diverse labor-management relationships.

SCOPE OF CODE

This Code is a privately developed set of standards of professional behavior. It applies to voluntary arbitration of labor-management griev-

Source: Robert Coulson, President, American Arbitration Association. *Labor Arbitration—What You Need To Know,* Second Edition, 1978.

ance disputes and of disputes concerning new or revised contract terms. Both "ad hoc" and "permanent" varieties of voluntary arbitration, private and public sector, are included. To the extent relevant in any specific case, it also applies to advisory arbitration, impasse resolution panels, arbitration prescribed by statutes, fact-finding, and other special procedures.

The word "arbitrator," as used hereinafter in the Code, is intended to apply to any impartial person, irrespective of specific title, who serves in a labor-management dispute procedure in which there is a conferred authority to decide issues or to make formal recommendations.

The Code is not designed to apply to mediation or conciliation, as distinguished from arbitration, nor to other procedures in which the third party is not authorized in advance to make decisions or recommendations. It does not apply to partisan representatives on tripartite boards. It does not apply to commercial arbitration or to other uses of arbitration outside the labor-management dispute area.

FORMAT OF CODE

Bold Face type, sometimes including explanatory material, is used to set forth general principles. *Italics* are used for amplification of general principles. Ordinary type is used primarily for illustrative or explanatory comment.

APPLICATION OF CODE

Faithful adherence by an arbitrator in this Code is basic to professional responsibility.

The National Academy of Arbitrators will expect its members to be governed in their professional conduct by this Code and stands ready, through its Committee on Ethics and Grievances, to advise its members as to the Code's interpretation. The American Arbitration Association and the Federal Mediation and Conciliation Service will apply the Code to the arbitrators on their rosters in cases handled under their respective appointment or referral procedures. Other arbitrators and administrative agencies may, of course, voluntarily adopt the Code and be governed by it.

In interpreting the Code and applying it to charges of professional misconduct, under existing or revised procedures of the National Academy of Arbitrators and of the administrative agencies, it should be recognized that while some of its standards express ethical principles basic to the arbitration profession, others rest less on ethics than on considerations of good practice. Experience has shown the difficulty of drawing rigid lines of distinction between ethics and good practice and this Code does not attempt to do so. Rather, it leaves the gravity of alleged misconduct and the extent to which ethical standards have been violated to be assessed in the light of the facts and circumstances of each particular case.

1.
ARBITRATORS' QUALIFICATIONS AND RESPONSIBILITIES TO THE PROFESSION

A. GENERAL QUALIFICATIONS

1. Essential personal qualifications of an arbitrator include honesty, integrity, impartiality and general competence in labor relations matters.

An arbitrator must demonstrate ability to exercise these personal qualities faithfully and with good judgment, both in procedural matters and in substantive decisions.

> a. Selection by mutual agreement of the parties or direct designation by an administrative agency are the effective methods of appraisal of this combination of an individual's potential and performance, rather than the fact of placement on a roster of an administrative agency or membership in a professional association of arbitrators.

2. An arbitrator must be as ready to rule for one party as for the other on each issue, either in a single case or in a group of cases. Compromise by an arbitrator for the sake of attempting to achieve personal acceptability is unprofessional.

B. QUALIFICATIONS FOR SPECIAL CASES

1. An arbitrator must decline appointment, withdraw, or request technical assistance when he or she decides that a case is beyond his or her competence.

> a. An arbitrator may be qualified generally but not for specialized assignments. Some types of incentive, work standard, job evaluation, welfare program, pension, or insurance cases may require specialized knowledge, experience or competence. Arbitration of contract terms also may require distinctive background and experience.

b. Effective appraisal by an administrative agency or by an arbitrator of the need for special qualifications requires that both parties make known the special nature of the case prior to appointment of the arbitrator.

C. RESPONSIBILITIES TO THE PROFESSION

1. An arbitrator must uphold the dignity and integrity of the office and endeavor to provide effective service to the parties.

a. To this end, an arbitrator should keep current with principles, practices and developments that are relevant to his or her own field of arbitration practice.

2. An experienced arbitrator should cooperate in the training of new arbitrators.
3. An arbitrator must not advertise or solicit arbitration assignments.

a. It is a matter of personal preference whether an arbitrator includes "Labor Arbitrator" or similar notation on letterheads, cards, or announcements. *It is inappropriate, however, to include memberships or offices held in professional societies or listings on rosters of administrative agencies.*

b. *Information provided for published biographical sketches, as well as that supplied to administrative agencies, must be accurate.* Such information may include membership in professional organizations (including reference to significant offices held), and listings on rosters of administrative agencies.

2.
RESPONSIBILITIES TO THE PARTIES

A. RECOGNITION OF DIVERSITY IN ARBITRATION ARRANGEMENTS

1. An arbitrator should conscientiously endeavor to understand and observe, to the extent consistent with professional responsibility, the significant principles governing each arbitration system in which he or she serves.

a. Recognition of special features of a particular arbitration arrangement can be essential with respect to procedural matters and may influence other aspects of the arbitration process.

2. Such understanding does not relieve an arbitrator from corollary responsibility to seek to discern and refuse to lend approval or consent to any collusive attempt by the parties to use arbitration for an improper purpose.

B. REQUIRED DISCLOSURES

1. Before accepting an appointment, an arbitrator must disclose directly or through the administrative agency involved, any current or past managerial, representational, or consultative relationship with any company or union involved in a proceeding in which he or she is being considered for appointment or has been tentatively designated to serve. Disclosure must also be made of any pertinent pecuniary interest.

a. The duty to disclosure includes membership on a Board of Directors, full-time or part-time service as a representative or advocate, consultation work for a fee, current stock or bond ownership (other than mutual fund shares or appropriate trust arrangements), or any other pertinent form of managerial, financial or immediate family interest in the company or union involved.

2. When an arbitrator is serving concurrently as an advocate for or representative of other companies or unions in labor relations matters, or has done so in recent years, he or she must disclose such activities before accepting appointment as an arbitrator.

An arbitrator must disclose such activities to an administrative agency if he or she is on that agency's active roster or seeks placement on a roster. Such disclosure then satisfies this requirement for cases handled under that agency's referral.

a. It is not necessary to disclose names of clients or other specific details. It is necessary to indicate the general nature of the labor relations advocacy or representational work involved, whether for companies or unions or both, and a reasonable approximation of the extent of such activity.

b. When an administrative agency is not involved, an arbitrator must make such disclosure directly unless he or she is certain that both parties to the case are fully aware of such activities.

3. An arbitrator must not permit personal relationships to affect decision making.

Prior to acceptance of an appointment, an arbitrator must disclose to the parties or to the administrative agency involved any close personal relationship or other circumstance, in addition to those specifically mentioned earlier in this section, which might reasonably raise a question as to the arbitrator's impartiality.

a. Arbitrators establish personal relationships with many company and union representatives, with fellow arbitrators, and with fellow members of various professional associations. There should be no attempt to be secretive about such friendships or acquaintances but disclosure is not necessary unless some feature of a particular relationship might reasonably appear to impair impartiality.

4. If the circumstances requiring disclosure are not known to the arbitrator prior to acceptance of appointment, disclosure must be made when such circumstances become known to the arbitrator.

5. The burden of disclosure rests on the arbitrator. After appropriate disclosure, the arbitrator may serve if both parties so desire. If the arbitrator believes or perceives that there is a clear conflict of interest, he or she should withdraw, irrespective of the expressed desires of the parties.

C. PRIVACY OF ARBITRATION

1. All significant aspects of an arbitration proceeding must be treated by the arbitrator as confidential unless this requirement is waived by both parties or disclosure is required or permitted by law.

a. Attendance at hearings by persons not representing the parties or invited by either or both of them should be permitted only when the parties agree or when an applicable law requires or permits. Occasionally, special circumstances may require that an arbitrator rule on such matters as attendance and degree of participation of counsel selected by grievant.

b. *Discussion of a case at any time by an arbitrator with persons not involved directly should be limited to situations where advance approval or consent of both parties is obtained or where the identity of the parties and details of the case are sufficiently obscured to eliminate any realistic probability of identification.*

A commonly recognized exception is discussion of a problem with a fellow arbitrator. *Any such discussion does not relieve the arbitrator who is acting in the case from sole responsibility for the decision and the discussion must be considered as confidential.*

Discussion of aspects of a case in a classroom without prior specific approval of the parties is not a violation provided the arbitrator is satisfied that there is no breach of essential confidentiality.

c. *It is a violation of professional responsibility for an arbitrator to make public an award without the consent of the parties.*

An arbitrator may request but not press the parties for consent to publish an opinion. Such a request should normally not be made until after the award has been issued to the parties.

d. It is not improper for an arbitrator to donate arbitration files to a library of a college, university or similar institution without prior consent of all the parties involved. When the circumstances permit, there should be deleted from such donations any cases concerning which one or both of the parties have expressed a desire for privacy. As an additional safeguard, an arbitrator may also decide to withhold recent cases or indicate to the donee a time interval before such cases can be made generally available.

e. *Applicable laws, regulations, or practices of the parties may permit or even require exceptions to the above-noted principles of privacy.*

D. PERSONAL RELATIONSHIPS WITH THE PARTIES

1. An arbitrator must make every reasonable effort to conform to arrangements required by an administrative agency or mutually desired by the parties regarding communications and personal relationships with the parties.

a. *Only an "arm's-length" relationship may be acceptable to the parties in some arbitration arrangements or may be required by the rules of an administrative agency. The arbitrator should then have no contact of consequence with representatives of either party while handling a case without the other party's presence or consent.*

b. *In other situations, both parties may want communications and personal relationships to be less formal. It is then appropriate for the arbitrator to respond accordingly.*

E. JURISDICTION

1. An arbitrator must observe faithfully both the limitations and inclusions of the jurisdiction conferred by an agreement or other submission under which he or she serves.

2. A direct settlement by the parties of some or all issues in a case, at any stage of the proceedings, must be accepted by the arbitrator as relieving him or her of further jurisdiction over such issues.

F. MEDIATION BY AN ARBITRATOR

1. When the parties wish at the outset to give an arbitrator authority both to mediate and to decide or submit recommendations regarding residual issues, if any, they should so advise the arbitrator prior to appointment. If the appointment is accepted, the arbitrator must perform a mediation role consistent with the circumstances of the case.

a. Direct appointments, also, may require a dual role as mediator and arbitrator of residual issues. This is most likely to occur in some public sector cases.

2. When a request to mediate is first made after appointment, the arbitrator may either accept or decline a mediation role.

a. *Once arbitration has been invoked, either party normally has a right to insist that the process be continued to decision.*

b. *If one party requests that the arbitrator mediate and the other party objects, the arbitrator should decline the request.*

c. *An arbitrator is not precluded from making a suggestion that he or she mediate. To avoid the possibility of improper pressure, the arbitrator should not so suggest unless it can be discerned that both parties are likely to be receptive. In any event, the arbitrator's suggestion should not be pursued unless both parties readily agree.*

G. RELIANCE BY AN ARBITRATOR ON OTHER ARBITRATION AWARDS OR ON INDEPENDENT RESEARCH

1. An arbitrator must assume full personal responsibility for the decision in each case decided.

>   a. *The extent, if any, to which an arbitrator properly may rely on precedent, on guidance of other awards, or on independent research is dependent primarily on the policies of the parties on these matters, as expressed in the contract, or other agreement, or at the hearing.*
>
>   b. When the mutual desires of the parties are not known or when the parties express differing opinions or policies, the arbitrator may exercise discretion as to these matters, consistent with acceptance of full personal responsibility for the award.

H. USE OF ASSISTANTS

1. An arbitrator must not delegate any decision-making function to another person without consent of the parties.

>   a. *Without prior consent of the parties, an arbitrator may use the services of an assistant for research, clerical duties, or preliminary drafting under the direction of the arbitrator, which does not involve the delegation of any decision-making function.*
>
>   b. *If an arbitrator is unable, because of time limitations or other reasons, to handle all decision-making aspects of a case, it is not a violation of professional responsibility to suggest to the parties an allocation of responsibility between the arbitrator and an assistant or associate. The arbitrator must not exert pressure on the parties to accept such a suggestion.*

I. CONSENT AWARDS

1. Prior to issuance of an award, the parties may jointly request the arbitrator to include in the award certain agreements between them, con-

cerning some or all of the issues. If the arbitrator believes that a suggested award is proper, fair, sound, and lawful, it is consistent with professional responsibility to adopt it.

a. *Before complying with such a request, an arbitrator must be certain that he or she understands the suggested settlement adequately in order to be able to appraise its terms. If it appears that pertinent facts or circumstances may not have been disclosed, the arbitrator should take the initiative to assure that all significant aspects of the case are fully understood. To this end, the arbitrator may request additional specific information and may question witnesses at a hearing.*

J. AVOIDANCE OF DELAY

1. It is a basic professional responsibility of an arbitrator to plan his or her work schedule so that present and future commitments will be fulfilled in a timely manner.

a. *When planning is upset for reasons beyond the control of the arbitrator, he or she, nevertheless, should exert every reasonable effort to fulfill all commitments. If this is not possible, prompt notice at the arbitrator's initiative should be given to all parties affected. Such notices should include reasonably accurate estimates of any additional time required. To the extent possible, priority should be given to cases in process so that other parties may make alternative arbitration arrangements.*

2. An arbitrator must cooperate with the parties and with any administrative agency involved in avoiding delays.

a. *An arbitrator on the active roster of an administrative agency must take the initiative in advising the agency of any scheduling difficulties that he or she can foresee.*

b. *Requests for services, whether received directly or through an administrative agency, should be declined if the arbitrator is unable to schedule a hearing as soon as the parties wish. If the parties, nevertheless, jointly desire to obtain the services of the arbitrator and the arbitrator agrees, arrangements should be made by agreement that the arbitrator confidently expects to fulfill.*

c. *An arbitrator may properly seek to persuade the parties to alter or eliminate arbitration procedures or tactics that cause unnecessary delay.*

3. Once the case record has been closed, an arbitrator must adhere to the time limits for an award, as stipulated in the labor agreement or as provided by regulation of an administrative agency or as otherwise agreed.

a. *If an appropriate award cannot be rendered within the required time, it is incumbent on the arbitrator to seek an extension of time from the parties.*

b. If the parties have agreed upon abnormally short time limits for an award after a case is closed, the arbitrator should be so advised by the parties or by the administrative agency involved, prior to acceptance of appointment.

K. FEES AND EXPENSES

1. An arbitrator occupies a position of trust in respect to the parties and the administrative agencies. In charging for services and expenses, the arbitrator must be governed by the same high standards of honor and integrity that apply to all other phases of his or her work.

An arbitrator must endeavor to keep total charges for services and expenses reasonable and consistent with the nature of the case or cases decided.

Prior to appointment, the parties should be aware of or be able readily to determine all significant aspects of an arbitrator's basis for charges for fees and expenses.

a. *Services Not Primarily Chargeable on a Per Diem Basis*

By agreement with the parties, the financial aspects of many "permanent" arbitration assignments, of some interest disputes, and of some "ad hoc" grievance assignments do not include a per diem fee for services as a primary part of the total understanding. *In such situations, the arbitrator must adhere faithfully to all agreed-upon arrangements governing fees and expenses.*

b. *Per Diem Basis for Charges for Services*

(1) *When an arbitrator's charges for services are determined primarily by a stipulated per diem fee, the arbitrator should*

establish in advance his or her basis for application of such per diem fee and for determination of reimbursable expenses.

Practices established by an arbitrator should include the basis for charges, if any, for:

(a) Hearing time, including the application of the stipulated basic per diem hearing fee to hearing days of varying lengths;
(b) study time;
(c) necessary travel time when not included in charges for hearing time;
(d) postponement or cancellation of hearings by the parties and the circumstances in which such charges will normally be assessed or waived;
(e) office overhead expenses (secretarial, telephone, postage, etc.);
(f) the work of paid assistants and associates.

(2) *Each arbitrator should be guided by the following general principles:*

(a) *Per diem charges for a hearing should not be in excess of actual time spent or allocated for the hearing.*
(b) *Per diem charges for study time should not be in excess of actual time spent.*
(c) *Any fixed ratio of study days to hearing days, not agreed to specifically by the parties, is inconsistent with the per diem method of charges for services.*
(d) *Charges for expenses must not be in excess of actual expenses normally reimbursable and incurred in connection with the case or cases involved.*
(e) *When time or expense are involved for two or more sets of parties on the same day or trip, such time or expense charges should be appropriately prorated.*
(f) *An arbitrator may stipulate in advance a minimum charge for a hearing without violation of (a) or (e) above.*

(3) *An arbitrator on the active roster of an administrative agency must file with the agency his or her individual basis for determination of fees and expenses if the agency so requires. Thereafter, it is the responsibility of each such arbitrator to advise the agency promptly of any change in any basis for charges.*

Such filing may be in the form of answers to a questionnaire devised by an agency or by any other method adopted by or approved by an agency.

Having supplied an administrative agency with the information noted above, an arbitrator's professional responsibility of disclosure under this Code with respect to fees and expenses has been satisfied for cases referred by that agency.

(4) If an administrative agency promulgates specific standards with respect to any of these matters which are in addition to or more restrictive than an individual arbitrator's standards, an arbitrator on its active roster must observe the agency standards for cases handled under the auspices of that agency, or decline to serve.

(5) When an arbitrator is contacted directly by the parties for a case or cases, the arbitrator has a professional responsibility to respond to questions by submitting his or her basis for charges for fees and expenses.

(6) When it is known to the arbitrator that one or both of the parties cannot afford normal charges, it is consistent with professional responsibility to charge lesser amounts to both parties or to one of the parties if the other party is made aware of the difference and agrees.

(7) If an arbitrator concludes that the total of charges derived from his or her normal basis of calculation is not compatible with the case decided, it is consistent with professional responsibility to charge lesser amounts to both parties.

2. An arbitrator must maintain adequate records to support charges for service and expenses and must make an accounting to the parties or to an involved administrative agency on request.

3.
RESPONSIBILITIES TO ADMINISTRATIVE AGENCIES

A. GENERAL RESPONSIBILITIES

1. An arbitrator must be candid, accurate and fully responsive to an administrative policy concerning his or her qualifications, availability, and other pertinent matters.

2. An arbitrator must observe policies and rules of an administrative agency in cases referred by that agency.

3. An arbitrator must not seek to influence an administrative agency by any improper means, including gifts or other inducements to agency personnel.

   a. It is not improper for a person seeking placement on a roster to request references from individuals having knowledge of the applicant's experience and qualifications.

   b. Arbitrators should recognize that the primary responsibility of an administrative agency is to serve the parties.

4.
PREHEARING CONDUCT

1. All prehearing matters must be handled in a manner that fosters complete impartiality by the arbitrator.

   a. The primary purpose of prehearing discussions involving the arbitrator is to obtain agreement on procedural matters so that the hearing can proceed without unnecessary obstacles. If differences of opinion should arise during such discussions and, particularly, if such differences appear to impinge on substantive matters, the circumstances will suggest whether the matter can be resolved informally or may require a prehearing conference or, more rarely, a formal preliminary hearing. When an administrative agency handles some or all aspects of the arrangements prior to a hearing, the arbitrator will become involved only if differences of some substance arise.

   b. *Copies of any prehearing correspondence between the arbitrator and either party must be made available to both parties.*

5.
HEARING CONDUCT

A. GENERAL PRINCIPLES

1. An arbitrator must provide a fair and adequate hearing which assures that both parties have sufficient opportunity to present their respective evidence and argument.

a. *Within the limits of this responsibility, an arbitrator should conform to the various types of hearing procedures desired by the parties.*

b. An arbitrator may: encourage stipulations of fact; restate the substance of issues or arguments to promote or verify understanding; question the parties' representatives or witnesses; when necessary or advisable, to obtain additional pertinent information; and request that the parties submit additional evidence, either at the hearing or by subsequent filing.

c. *An arbitrator should not intrude into a party's presentation so as to prevent that party from putting forward its case fairly and adequately.*

B. TRANSCRIPTS OR RECORDINGS

1. Mutual agreement of the parties as to use or nonuse of a transcript must be respected by the arbitrator.

a. *A transcript is the official record of a hearing only when both parties agree to a transcript or an applicable law or regulation so provides.*

b. An arbitrator may seek to persuade the parties to avoid use of a transcript, or to use a transcript if the nature of the case appears to require one. *However, if an arbitrator intends to make his or her appointment to a case contingent on mutual agreement to a transcript, that requirement must be made known to both parties prior to appointment.*

c. If the parties do not agree to a transcript, an arbitrator may permit one party to take a transcript at its own cost. The arbitrator may also make appropriate arrangements under which the other party may have access to a copy, if a copy is provided to the arbitrator.

d. Without prior approval, an arbitrator may seek to use his or her own tape recorder to supplement note taking. The arbitrator should not insist on such a tape recording if either or both parties object.

C. EX PARTE HEARINGS

1. In determining whether to conduct an ex parte hearing, an arbitrator must consider relevant legal, contractual, and other pertinent circumstances.

2. An arbitrator must be certain, before proceeding ex parte, that the party refusing or failing to attend the hearing has been given adequate notice of the time, place, and purposes of the hearing.

D. PLANT VISITS

1. An arbitrator should comply with a request of any party that he or she visit a work area pertinent to the dispute prior to, during, or after a hearing. An arbitrator may also initiate such a request.

   a. *Procedures for such visits should be agreed to by the parties in consultation with the arbitrator.*

E. BENCH DECISIONS OR EXPEDITED AWARDS

1. When an arbitrator understands, prior to acceptance of appointment, that a bench decision is expected at the conclusion of the hearing, the arbitrator must comply with the understanding unless both parties agree otherwise.

   a. *If notice of the parties' desire for a bench decision is not given prior to the arbitrator's acceptance of the case, issuance of such a bench decision is discretionary.*

   b. *When only one party makes the request and the other objects, the arbitrator should not render a bench decision except under most unusual circumstances.*

2. When an arbitrator understands, prior to acceptance of appointment, that a concise written award is expected within a stated time period after the hearing, the arbitrator must comply with the understanding unless both parties agree otherwise.

6.
POST HEARING CONDUCT

A. POST HEARING BRIEFS AND SUBMISSIONS

1. An arbitrator must comply with mutual agreements in respect to the filing or nonfiling of post hearing briefs or submissions.

> a. An arbitrator, in his or her discretion, may either suggest the filing of post hearing briefs or other submissions or suggest that none be filed.
>
> b. When the parties disagree as to the need for briefs, an arbitrator may permit filing but may determine a reasonable time limitation.

2. An arbitrator must not consider a post hearing brief or submission that has not been provided to the other party.

B. DISCLOSURE OF TERMS OF AWARD

1. An arbitrator must not disclose a prospective award to either party prior to its simultaneous issuance to both parties or explore possible alternative awards unilaterally with one party, unless both parties so agree.

> a. Partisan members of tripartite boards may know prospective terms of an award in advance of its issuance. Similar situations may exist in other less formal arrangements mutually agreed to by the parties. In any such situation, the arbitrator should determine and observe the mutually desired degree of confidentiality.

C. AWARDS AND OPINIONS

1. The award should be definite, certain, and as concise as possible.

> a. When an opinion is required, factors to be considered by an arbitrator include: desirability of brevity, consistent with the nature of the case and any expressed desires of the parties; need to use a style and form that is understandable to responsible representatives of the parties, to the grievant and supervisors, and to others in the collective bargaining relationship; necessity of meeting the significant issues; forthrightness to an extent not harmful to the relationship of the parties; and avoidance of gratuitous advice or disclosure not essential to disposition of the issues.

D. CLARIFICATION OR INTERPRETATION OF AWARDS

1. No clarification or interpretation of an award is permissible without the consent of both parties.

2. Under agreements which permit or require clarification or interpretation of an award, an arbitrator must afford both parties an opportunity to be heard.

E. ENFORCEMENT OF AWARD

1. The arbitrator's responsibility does not extend to the enforcement of an award.

2. In view of the professional and confidential nature of the arbitration relationship, an arbitrator should not voluntarily participate in legal enforcement proceedings.

The United States Arbitration Act

Title 9, U.S. Code §§ 1-14, first enacted February 12, 1925 (43 Stat. 883), codified July 30, 1947 (61 Stat. 669), and amended September 3, 1954 (68 Stat. 1233); Chapter 2 added July 31, 1970 (84 Stat. 692).

CHAPTER 1.—GENERAL PROVISIONS

CHAPTER 1.—GENERAL PROVISIONS

§ 1. "Maritime Transactions" and "Commerce" Defined; Exceptions to Operation of Title

"Maritime Transactions," as herein defined, means charter parties, bills of lading of water carriers, agreements relating to wharfage, supplies furnished vessels or repairs of vessels, collisions, or any other matters in foreign commerce which, if the subject of controversy, would be embraced within admiralty jurisdiction; "commerce," as herein defined, means commerce among the several States or with foreign nations, or in any Territory of the United States or in the District of Columbia, or between any such Territory and another, or between any such Territory and any State or foreign nation, or between the District of Columbia and any State or Territory or foreign nation, but nothing herein contained shall apply to contracts of employment of seamen, railroad employees, or any other class of workers engaged in foreign or interstate commerce.

§ 2. Validity, Irrevocability, and Enforcement of Agreement to Arbitrate

A written provision in any maritime transaction or a contract evidencing a transaction involving commerce to settle by arbitration a controversy thereafter arising out of such contract or transaction, or the refusal to perform the whole or any part thereof, of an agreement in writing to submit to arbitration an existing controversy arising out of such contract, transaction, or refusal, shall be valid, irrevocable, and enforceable, save upon such grounds as exist at law or in equity for the revocation of any contract.

§ 3. Stay of Proceedings Where Issue Therein Referable to Arbitration

If any suit or proceeding be brought in any of the courts of the United States upon any issue referable to arbitration under an agreement in writing for such arbitration, the court in which such suit is pending, upon being satisfied that the issue involved in such suit or proceeding is referable to arbitration under such an agreement, shall on application of one of the parties stay the trial of the action until such arbitration has been had in accordance with the terms of the agreement, providing the applicant for the stay is not in default in proceeding with such arbitration.

§ 4. Failure To Arbitrate under Agreement; Petition to United States Court Having Jurisdiction for Order to Compel Arbitration; Notice and Service Thereof; Hearing and Determination

A party aggrieved by the alleged failure, neglect, or refusal of another to arbitrate under a written agreement for arbitration may petition any United States district court which, save for such agreement, would have jurisdiction under Title 28, in a civil action or in admiralty of the subject matter of a suit arising out of the controversy between the parties, for an order directing that such arbitration proceed in the manner provided for in such agreement. Five days' notice in writing of such application shall be served upon the party in default. Service thereof shall be made in the manner provided by the Federal Rules of Civil Procedure. The court shall hear the parties, and upon being satisfied that the making of the agreement for arbitration or the failure to comply therewith is not in issue, the court shall make an order directing the parties to proceed to arbitration in accordance with the terms of the agreement. The hearing and proceedings, under such agreement, shall be within the district in which the petition for an order directing such arbitration is filed. If the making of the arbitration agreement or the failure, neglect, or refusal to perform the same be in issue, the court shall proceed summarily to the trial thereof. If no jury trial be demanded by the party alleged to be in default, or if the matter in dispute is within admiralty jurisdiction, the court shall hear and determine such issue. Where such an issue is raised, the party alleged to be in default may, except in cases of admiralty, on or before the return day of the notice of application, demand a jury trial of such issue, and upon such demand the court shall make an order referring the issue or issues to a jury in the manner provided by the Federal Rules of Civil Procedure, or may specially call a jury for that purpose. If the jury finds that an agreement for arbitration was made in writing and that there is a default in proceeding thereunder, the court shall make an order summarily directing the parties to proceed with the arbitration in accordance with the terms thereof.

§ 5. Appointment of Arbitrators or Umpire

If in the agreement provision be made for a method of naming or appointing an arbitrator or arbitrators or an umpire, such method shall be followed; but if no method be provided therein, or if a method be provided and any party thereto shall fail to avail himself of such method, or if for any other reason there shall be a lapse in the naming of an arbitrator or arbitrators or umpire, or in filling a vacancy, then upon the application of either party to the controversy the court shall designate and appoint an arbitrator or arbitrators or umpire, as the case may require, who shall act under the said agreement with the same force and effect as if he or they had been specifically named therein; and unless otherwise provided in the agreement the arbitration shall be by a single arbitrator.

§ 6. Application Heard as Motion

Any application to the court hereunder shall be made and heard in the manner provided by law for the making and hearing of motions, except as otherwise herein expressly provided.

§ 7. Witnesses before Arbitrators; Fees; Compelling Attendance

The arbitrators selected either as prescribed in this title or otherwise, or a majority of them, may summon in writing any person to attend before them or any of them as a witness and in a proper case to bring with him or them any book, record, document, or paper which may be deemed material as evidence in the case. The fees for such attendance shall be the same as the fees of witnesses before masters of the United States courts. Said summons shall issue in the name of the arbitrator or arbitrators, or a majority of them, and shall be directed to the said person and shall be served in the same manner as subpoenas to appear and testify before the court; if any person or persons so summoned to testify shall refuse or neglect to obey said summons, upon petition the United States court in and for the district in which such arbitrators, or a majority of them, are sitting may compel the attendance of such person or persons before said arbitrator or arbitrators, or punish said person or persons for contempt in the same manner provided on February 12, 1925, for securing the attendance of witnesses or their punishment for neglect or refusal to attend in the courts of the United States.

§ 8. Proceedings Begun by Libel in Admiralty and Seizure of Vessel or Property

If the basis of jurisdiction be a cause of action otherwise justiciable in admiralty, then, notwithstanding anything herein to the contrary the party claiming to be aggrieved may begin his proceeding hereunder by libel and seizure of the vessel or other property of the other party according to the usual course of admiralty proceedings, and the court shall then have jurisdiction to direct the parties to proceed with the arbitration and shall retain jurisdiction to enter its decree upon the award.

§ 9. Award of Arbitrators; Confirmation; Jurisdiction; Procedure

If the parties in their agreement have agreed that a judgment of the court shall be entered upon the award made pursuant to the arbitration, and shall specify the court, then at any time within one year after the award is made any party to the arbitration may apply to the court so specified for an order confirming the award, and thereupon the court must grant such an order unless the award is vacated, modified, or corrected as prescribed in sections 10 and 11 of this title. If no court is specified in the agreement of the parties, then such application may be made to the United States court in and for the district within which such award was made. Notice of the application shall be served upon the adverse party, and thereupon the court shall have jurisdiction of such party as though he had appeared generally in the proceeding. If the adverse party is a resident of the district within which the award was made, such service shall be made upon the adverse party or his attorney as prescribed by law for service of notice to motion in an action in the same court. If the adverse party shall be a nonresident, then the notice of the application shall be served by the marshal of any district within which the adverse party may be found in like manner as other process of the court.

§ 10. Same; Vacation; Grounds; Rehearing

In either of the following cases the United States court in and for the district wherein the award was made may make an order vacating the award upon the application of any party to the arbitration—

(a) Where the award was procured by corruption, fraud, or undue means.
(b) Where there was evident partiality or corruption in the arbitrators, or either of them.
(c) Where the arbitrators were guilty of misconduct in refusing to postpone the hearing, upon sufficient cause shown, or in refusing to hear evidence pertinent and material to the controversy; or of any other misbehavior by which the rights of any party have been prejudiced.
(d) Where the arbitrators exceeded their powers, or so imperfectly executed them that a mutual, final, and definite award upon the subject matter submitted was not made.
(e) Where an award is vacated and the time within which the agreement required the award to be made has not expired the court may, in its discretion, direct a rehearing by the arbitrators.

§ 11. Same; Modification or Correction; Grounds; Order

In either of the following cases the United States court in and for the district wherein the award was made may make an order modifying or correcting the award upon the application of any party to the arbitration—

(a) Where there was an evident material miscalculation of figures or an evident material mistake in the description of any person, thing, or property referred to in the award.
(b) Where the arbitrators have awarded upon a matter not submitted to them, unless it is a matter not affecting the merits of the decision upon the matter submitted.
(c) Where the award is imperfect in matter of form not affecting the merits of the controversy.

The order may modify and correct the award, so as to effect the intent thereof and promote justice between the parties.

§ 12. Notice of Motions to Vacate or Modify; Service; Stay of Proceedings

Notice of a motion to vacate, modify, or correct an award must be served upon the adverse party or his attorney within three months after the award is filed or delivered. If the adverse party is a resident of the district within which the award was made, such service shall be made upon the adverse party or his attorney as prescribed by law for service of notice of motion in an action in the same court. If the adverse party shall be a nonresident then the notice of the application shall be served by the marshal of any district within which the adverse party may be found in like manner as other process of the court. For the purposes of the motion any judge who might make an order to stay the proceedings in an action brought in the same court may make an order, to be served with the notice of motion, staying the proceedings of the adverse party to enforce the award.

§ 13. Papers Filed with Order on Motions; Judgment; Docketing; Force and Effect; Enforcement

The party moving for an order confirming, modifying, or correcting an award shall, at the time such order is filed with the clerk for the entry of judgment thereon, also file the following papers with the clerk:

(a) The agreement; the selection or appointment, if any, of an additional arbitrator or umpire; and each written extension of the time, if any, within which to make the award.
(b) The award.
(c) Each notice, affidavit, or other paper used upon an application to confirm, modify, or correct the award, and a copy of each order of the court upon such an application.

The judgment shall be docketed as if it was rendered in an action.

The judgment so entered shall have the same force and effect, in all respects, as, and be subject to all the provisions of law relating to, a judgment in an action; and it may be enforced as if it had been rendered in an action in the court in which it is entered.

§ 14. Contracts Not Affected

This title shall not apply to contracts made prior to January 1, 1926.

Appendix C

Labor Arbitration: Procedures and Techniques

INTRODUCTION

Voluntary arbitration of controversies arising out of or relating to the terms of collective bargaining agreements is accepted almost unanimously by labor and management. But despite widespread use of this procedure, and possibly due to the rapidity of its growth, it often happens that parties mistake arbitration for other methods of dispute settlement, such as mediation and compromise. It is also confused with fact-finding and a variation called advisory arbitration.

Arbitration is a tool of industrial relations. Like other tools, it has limitations as well as uses. In the hands of an expert, it produces good results, but when abused, or made to do things for which it was never intended, the outcome may be disappointing. That is why all participants in the process—union officials, employers, personnel executives, attorneys, and the arbitrators themselves—have an equal stake in orderly, efficient, and constructive arbitration procedures.

Arbitration—A Judicial Proceeding

Arbitration is the reference of a dispute, by voluntary agreement of the parties, to an impartial person for determination on the basis of evidence and arguments presented by such parties, who agree in advance to accept the decision of the arbitrator as final and binding.

Thus, the arbitration process begins where other methods of dispute settlement leave off; in referring a matter to arbitration parties are pre-

Source: Labor Arbitration: Procedures and Techniques (New York: American Arbitration Association, 1981).

sumed to have explored every avenue of negotiation and compromise. As a last resort, they call upon an impartial person for a *judicial* decision and agree to abide by the result.

TWO FIELDS OF ARBITRATION

In general, labor-management arbitration is divided into two fields: contract-negotiation disputes, sometimes called arbitration of *interests;* and contract-interpretation disputes, sometimes called arbitration of *rights.* The latter is much more prevalent.

Contract-Negotiation Disputes

All authorities agree that it is best for unions and companies to establish terms and conditions of employment by direct negotiation and bargaining. This is the way the overwhelming majority of the 140,000 collective bargaining agreements in the United States are concluded. There are occasions, however, when parties are unable to agree on contract terms. In such cases, rather than risk a deadlock which might interfere with production, they sometimes refer disputed items to arbitration, putting the agreed-upon matters into effect immediately. Such situations come about not only when new contracts must be negotiated but also at wage-reopening dates. Some contracts provide in advance for arbitration of such wage-reopening disputes. But in any case, parties who want to arbitrate differences over contract terms may avail themselves of arbitration machinery by executing a *submission agreement* (see Glossary of Terms [of this Appendix]). In recent years the number of disputes arbitrated over new or renewed contracts has diminished.

Contract-Interpretation Disputes

Contract-interpretation disputes, usually called *grievances,* constitute the overwhelming majority of matters brought to arbitration. Before reference to arbitration, such controversies usually go through several steps of the *grievance procedure* set forth in contracts, during which each side tries to convince the other that its interpretation and application of the contract to the given situation is the correct one. It is also during the grievance procedure that compromises are attempted. Failing settlement during these negotiation steps, well over 90 percent of all collective bargaining contracts provide for binding arbitration. When time is critical, parties sometimes mutually agree to bypass earlier steps and bring a controversy directly to arbitration.

The following pages will deal primarily with the procedures for arbitrating grievances, since they constitute the bulk of arbitration practice, although many of the principles and standards developed may also be applied to arbitration of contract terms.

THE AGREEMENT TO ARBITRATE

Labor-management disputes are brought to arbitration in one of two ways; either by a *submission agreement* that describes an *existing* controversy which *both* parties want settled by an impartial person, or by a *demand for arbitration* filed by *either* party to a contract, provided that contract has an arbitration clause.

Of the two forms that the agreement to arbitrate may take, the arbitration clause is by far the most common. Surveys indicate that approximately 95 percent of the collective bargaining contracts in effect contain dispute clauses. The specific forms these clauses take, however, are varied. Often, companies and unions have found their history of bargaining and their collective bargaining relationship to be such as to justify a general agreement to arbitrate, with few limitations or restrictions. (See "A Good Arbitration Clause in Fifty Words" [below] for an example of such a clause.) On the other hand, there may be situations in which parties prefer to limit arbitration to specified types of grievances. In either case, the construction of the arbitration clause is of utmost importance to both parties, for it represents a voluntary and binding agreement to settle differences in arbitration rather than in any other way.

Advantage of the Arbitration Clause

The advantage of a future dispute arbitration clause is that it leaves nothing to chance. When a controversy arises, the parties may be in no mood to agree and it is sometimes difficult to get *both* parties to submit to the procedures of arbitration. But when they are subject to a clause, arbitration may be initiated without delay by either party.

The agreement to arbitrate, if it does not refer to established rules and procedures, may not by itself answer all questions. Among the problems that remain are:

How shall arbitrators be appointed?

When and where shall hearings take place? And who will make these decisions if the parties cannot agree?

Shall the arbitration board consist of one or three neutral arbitrators?

If a tripartite board is preferred (see Glossary of Terms), what shall the remedy be if the two party-appointed arbitrators cannot agree upon an impartial member of the board?

Who may represent the parties? Shall witnesses be sworn?

How shall requests for adjournments be handled? May briefs be filed?

How are hearings closed and under what conditions may they be reopened?

When will the award be rendered? To whom delivered?

How much should the arbitrator be paid?

All these, and many other procedural questions, are important for prompt and effective arbitration. It would obviously be impossible for parties to anticipate them all and spell out the answers in the collective bargaining agreement. An effective, though simple, solution is found in an arbitration clause which, by referring to established rules such as those of the American Arbitration Association, at once answers the basic WHAT, HOW, WHEN, WHERE, and WHO of arbitration.

Other Questions To Be Answered

Parties may also want other questions answered. They may want to be sure that certain steps precede arbitration or they may want to spell out which types of issues are arbitrable, and which are to be excluded from the arbitration process. In that case, they may vary the language of the arbitration clause to suit their needs.

> **But in any case, reference to the Voluntary Labor Arbitration Rules of the American Arbitration Association provides a quick answer to most questions and a remedy for the failure of either party to perform certain acts, called "conditions precedent," without which arbitration might be frustrated.**

A GOOD ARBITRATION CLAUSE IN FIFTY WORDS

Any dispute, claim or grievance arising out of or relating to the interpretation or the application of this agreement shall be sub-

mitted to arbitration under the Voluntary Labor Arbitration Rules of the American Arbitration Association. The parties further agree to accept the arbitrator's award as final and binding upon them.

This clause, or any other clause referring to established rules of the American Arbitration Association, answers the questions below:

WHAT—
——is to be arbitrated?
——are the duties and obligations of each party?

HOW—
——is arbitration initiated?
——are arbitrators appointed and vacancies filled?
——are time and place for hearings fixed?
——are hearings opened? Closed? Reopened?
——are costs controlled?

WHEN—
——are arbitrators appointed?
——must hearings begin?
——must the award be rendered?

WHERE—
——are notice, documents and correspondence to be sent?
——shall hearings be held?
——is the award to be delivered?

WHO—
——administers the arbitration?
——keeps the records and makes technical preparations?
——gives notice of hearings and other matters?
——appoints the arbitrators if the parties cannot agree?
——fills vacancies on arbitration boards when necessary?
——grants adjournments?

THE ARBITRATION PROCESS BEGINS

By Submission Agreement

Either party to the controversy may file a submission agreement with an office of the Association, provided it is signed by *both* parties. A submission agreement must include a brief statement of the matter in dispute and of the relief sought. A typical submission agreement, containing adequate phrasing, is shown [later in this Appendix]. The Association will communicate with the parties and the arbitrator, if already named by the parties, and arrange a suitable time and place for hearings. If an arbitrator has not been named in the submission agreement, one will be selected in accordance with AAA rules, described [later in this Appendix under "AAA's System for Selecting the Arbitrator"].

By Demand for Arbitration

Where parties have an arbitration clause in the contract, the procedures of the contract should be followed. Either party may initiate arbitration by serving notice on the other party, with a copy of the Demand forwarded to the Association. Special care should be taken to make certain that notice of intention to arbitrate is given in a manner and within the time limits described in the collective bargaining agreement. It is usual for contracts to require that notice of arbitration be given within a certain period of time after the final step of grievance procedure. Failure to observe these time limits may result in loss of the right to arbitrate that controversy.

The Demand for Arbitration should include a brief statement of the issue to be arbitrated and the relief sought, and it should be signed by the complaining party. Since the arbitrator's authority will be limited to resolving only such disputes as are authorized by the arbitration clause and to answer, within the framework of the contract, only those questions already raised, care should be exercised to avoid introduction of "new" issues which have not gone through the grievance procedure and which have not been considered before. The statement of the issue and of the relief sought in the Demand for Arbitration is usually the one set forth in the written statement of the grievance, on the basis of which grievance machinery was invoked. A typical Demand for Arbitration form, properly executed, is shown [later in this Appendix].

Checklist for Initiating Arbitration

1. Names and addresses of *both* parties involved in the Submission or the Demand for Arbitration.
2. Date of the collective bargaining agreement and the full text of the arbitration clause.
3. The issue to be arbitrated, specifically and concisely stated, with an indication of the relief sought.
4. Dates involved in the grievance, where appropriate.

5. Names of employees involved, if any, together with their positions or job classifications, where necessary.
6. The signature of the union or company official authorized to file a Demand for Arbitration or Submission.

On receiving the Demand for Arbitration, the Association, in accordance with its Rules, will invite the "responding" party to file an Answering Statement within seven days. If no answer is filed within this time, it is assumed that the claim is denied.

The Demand and the reply are read by the arbitrator at the beginning of the hearing. These two documents guide the arbitrator in receiving and giving weight to testimony, and they form the framework within which an award will be made. The statement of claim and the reply should therefore indicate precisely what the arbitrator is asked to decide. Parties should not argue their claims in the Demand or Answering Statement, but merely state the controversy as clearly as possible.

HOW THE ARBITRATOR IS SELECTED

The American Arbitration Association maintains a National Panel of Arbitrators whose members, after having been nominated (usually by prominent citizens of their communities), have been selected for their experience, competence and impartiality. The candidate for enrollment in the Panel is asked to submit a statement of professional qualifications and references as to acceptability by *both* labor and management. These data are verified by a special AAA Committee on Panels which makes the decision on the prospective arbitrator's eligibility. Once accepted as a member of the National Panel of Arbitrators, the individual's name is sent out on lists from which parties may select arbitrators in particular cases; it is also from this Panel that the Association makes administrative appointments.

In their agreement to arbitrate, parties may provide for any method of selecting an arbitrator. Methods currently in use vary widely; unions and companies are advised to consider the system they adopt carefully, as the speed and efficiency of arbitration may be affected.

AAA's System for Selecting the Arbitrator

Unless parties have indicated another method, the American Arbitration Association invokes the following simple and effective system.

1. On receiving the Demand for Arbitration or Submission Agreement, the tribunal administrator (a staff member of the Association) acknowledges receipt thereof and sends *each* party a copy of a specially prepared list of proposed arbitrators. In drawing up this list, the administrator is guided by the statement of the nature of the dispute. Basic information about each arbitrator is appended to the list. *(A facsimile of a list of arbitrators is shown [at the end of this Appendix].)*
2. Parties are allowed seven days to study the list, cross off any names objected to, and number the remaining names in the order of preference. Where parties want more information about a proposed arbitrator, such information is gladly given on request.
3. Where parties are unable to find a mutual choice on a list, the Association will submit additional lists, at the request of both parties.
4. If, despite all efforts to arrive at a mutual choice, parties cannot agree upon an arbitrator, the Association will make an administrative appointment, but in no case will an arbitrator whose name was crossed out by either party be so appointed.

Collective bargaining agreements sometimes provide for tripartite boards of arbitration (see Glossary) without setting time limits for appointment of the party-appointed arbitrators. In that case, the American Arbitration Association system, as indicated in the four steps above, will be applied so as to give force and effect to the wishes of the parties. Thus, unless parties have indicated otherwise, each side is given seven days within which to name its arbitrator.

Wishes of Parties Observed

By the same token, where the collective bargaining agreement provides for selection of the impartial member of the board of arbitration "by the American Arbitration Association," the lists will be sent to the parties, in accordance with steps 1 through 4, above. On the other hand, where parties prefer the two party-appointed arbitrators to choose the third, lists will be sent to the arbitrators directly, with the same time limits in effect.

Many states require that arbitrators take an oath to faithfully hear and examine the matters in controversy and render a just award to the best of their understanding. In the absence of such laws, AAA Rules provide for the oath, unless waived by the parties.

At all times, arbitrators are expected to observe the standards which that oath and the Code of Professional Responsibility impose. In signing an AAA Acceptance of Appointment form, they are required to certify that they have no interest, personal or otherwise, in the outcome.

PREPARING FOR THE ARBITRATION HEARING

By the time a case reaches arbitration, parties have generally spent many weeks, if not months, in discussing the grievance. In these discussions, they have become familiar with all the complications of the matter. The problem then remains of communicating this understanding of the facts to the arbitrator who, as a rule, knows very little detail about the dispute until the hearing begins. Effective presentation of these facts and arguments should begin with thorough *preparation* for arbitration. The following steps are suggested [for each party]:

1. Study the original statement of the grievance and review its history through every step of the grievance machinery.
2. Examine carefully the initiating paper (Submission or Demand) to help determine the arbitrator's role. It might be found, for instance, that while the original grievance contains many elements, the arbitrator, under the contract, is restricted to resolving only certain aspects.
3. Review the collective bargaining agreement from beginning to end. Often, clauses which at first glance seem to be unrelated to the grievance will be found to have some bearing on it.
4. Assemble all documents and papers you will need at the hearing. Where feasible, make photostatic copies for the arbitrator and the other party. If some of the documents you need are in the possession of the other party, ask in advance that they be brought to the arbitration. Under some arbitration laws, the arbitrator has authority to subpoena documents and witnesses if they cannot be made available in any other way.
5. If you think it will be necessary for the arbitrator to visit the plant or job site for on-the-spot investigation, make plans in advance. The arbitrator should be accompanied by representatives of *both* parties, and it may be helpful for the tribunal administrator to be present.

6. Interview all witnesses. Make certain they understand the whole case and particularly the importance of their own testimony within it.
7. Make a written summary of what each witness will testify to. This will be useful as a checklist at the hearing, to make certain nothing is overlooked.
8. Study the case from the other side's point of view. Be prepared to answer the opposing evidence and arguments.
9. Discuss your outline of the case with others in your organization. A fresh viewpoint will often disclose weak spots or previously overlooked details.
10. Read as many articles and published awards as you can on the general subject matter in dispute. While awards by other arbitrators for other parties have no binding precedent value, they may help clarify the thinking of parties and arbitrators alike. The American Arbitration Association reports labor arbitration awards released by parties in three monthly publications, *Summary of Labor Arbitration Awards, Arbitration in the Schools,* and *Labor Arbitration in Government.*

THE ARBITRATION HEARING

The date for the hearing is fixed by the arbitrator after discussion with the tribunal administrator, who has consulted the parties on this question. As on all other administrative matters, the function of the tribunal administrator is to handle details and arrangements in advance when either party wants a stenographic record of hearings.

After introduction of the arbitrator and swearing-in ceremonies, the customary order of proceedings is as follows:

1. Opening statement by the initiating party, followed by a similar statement by the other side.
2. Presentation of evidence, witnesses and arguments by the initiating party.
3. Cross-examination by the other party.
4. Presentation of evidence, witnesses and arguments by the defending party.
5. Cross-examination by the initiating party.
6. Summation by both parties, usually following the same order as in the opening statement.

This is the *customary* order. The order may be varied, however, on the arbitrator's initiative or at the request of a party. In any case, the order in which the facts are presented does not imply that the "burden of proof" is more on one side than the other, for *both* parties must try to convince the arbitrator of the justice of their positions.

HOW TO PRESENT A CASE IN ARBITRATION

1. *The Opening Statement*. The opening statement should be prepared with utmost care, because it lays the groundwork for the testimony of witnesses and helps the arbitrator understand the relevance of oral and written evidence. The statement, although brief, should clearly identify the issue, indicate what is to be proved, and specify the relief sought.

The question of the appropriate remedy, if the arbitrator should find that a violation of the agreement did in fact take place, deserves careful attention at the outset. A request for relief should be specific. This does not necessarily mean that if back pay is demanded, for instance, it is essential for the complaining party to have computed an exact dollars-and-cents amount. But it *does* mean that the arbitrator's authority to grant appropriate relief under the contract should not be in doubt.

Because of the importance of the opening statement, some parties prefer to present it to the arbitrator in writing, with a copy given to the other side. They believe that it may be advantageous to make the initial statement a matter of permanent record. It is recommended, however, that the opening statement be made orally even when it is prepared in written form, for an oral presentation adds emphasis and gives persuasive force to one's position.

While opening statements are being made, parties are frequently able to stipulate facts about the contract and the circumstances that gave rise to the grievance. Giving the arbitrator all the uncontested facts early in the hearing saves time throughout, thereby reducing costs.

2. *Presenting Documents*. Documentary evidence is often an essential part of a labor arbitration case. Most important is the collective bargaining agreement itself, or the sections that have some bearing on the grievance. Documentary evidence may also include such material as records of settled grievances, jointly signed memoranda of understanding, correspondence, official minutes of contract negotiation meetings, personnel records, medical reports, and wage data. Every piece of documentary evidence should be properly identified, with its authenticity established. This material should be physically presented to the arbitrator (with a copy made available to the other side), but an oral explanation of the significance of each document

should not be omitted. In many instances, key words, phrases, and sections of written documents may be underlined or otherwise marked to focus the arbitrator's attention on the essential features of the case. Properly presented, documentary evidence can be most persuasive; it merits more than casual handling.

3. *Examining Witnesses.* Each party should depend on the *direct examination* of its own witnesses for presentation of facts. After having been identified and qualified as an authority on the facts to which he or she will testify, a witness should be allowed to proceed largely without interruption. Although leading questions may be permitted in arbitration, testimony is more effective when the witness relates facts in his or her own language and from his or her own knowledge. This does not mean, however, that questions from counsel may not be useful in emphasizing points already made or in returning a witness to the main line of testimony.

4. *Cross-Examining Witnesses.* Every witness is subject to cross-examination. Among the purposes of such cross-examination are: disclosure of facts the witnesses may not have related in direct testimony; correction of misstatements; placing of facts in their true perspective; reconciling apparent contradictions; and attacking the reliability and credibility of witnesses. In planning cross-examination, the objective to be achieved should be kept in mind. Each witness may therefore be approached in a different manner, and there may be occasions when cross-examination will be waived.

5. *Maintaining the Right Tone.* The atmosphere of the hearing often reflects the relationship between the parties. While the chief purpose of the arbitration hearing is the determination of the particular grievance, a collateral purpose of improving that relationship may also be achieved by skillful and friendly conduct of the parties. Thus, a better general understanding between the parties may be a byproduct of the arbitration. To this end, the parties should enter the hearing room with the intention of conducting themselves in an objective and dignified manner. The arbitration hearing should be informal enough for effective communication, but without loss of the basic sense of order that is essential in every forum of adjudication.

The hearing is no place for emotional outbursts, long speeches with only vague relevancy to the issue, for bitter, caustic remarks, or personal invective. Apart from their long-run adverse effect on the basic relationship between the parties, such immoderate tactics are unlikely to impress or persuade an arbitrator. Similarly, overtechnical and overlegalistic approaches are not helpful.

A party has every right to object to evidence it considers irrelevant, as the arbitrator should not be burdened with a mass of material that has little or no bearing on the issue. But objections made merely for the sake of objecting often have an adverse effect, and they may give the arbitrator the impression that one simply fears to have the other side heard.

6. *The Summary.* Before the arbitrator closes the hearing, both sides will be given equal time for a closing statement. This is the occasion to summarize the factual situation and emphasize again the issue and the decision the arbitrator is asked to make.

As arbitration is a somewhat informal proceeding, arguments may be permitted to some extent during all phases of the hearing. There may be times, however, when the arbitrator will require parties to concentrate on presenting evidence and put off all arguments until the summary. In either event, all arguments should be stated fully.

Finally, as this will be the last chance to convince the arbitrator, the summary is the time to refute all arguments of the other side.

7. *Post-Hearing Procedure.* After both sides have had equal opportunity to present all their evidence, the arbitrator declares the hearing closed. Under AAA rules, the arbitrator has 30 days from that time within which to render an award, unless the collective bargaining agreement requires some other time limit. If parties want to file written post-hearing briefs, transcripts of records or other data, time limits are set and hearings remain open until those documents are received. As usual, exchange of post-hearing material takes place through the tribunal administrator; *the parties do not communicate directly with the arbitrator except when both sides are present.* The Association will see that both briefs are transmitted to the arbitrator and that an interchange takes place between the parties at the same time.

8. *How To Reopen Hearings.* When parties jointly agree to add certain data after a hearing is closed, they may arrange to do so by written stipulation filed with the Association. The arbitrator will then accept the new material and take it under advisement.

In the event new evidence is discovered, or when a situation arises that appears to require explanation, parties should not attempt to communicate directly with the arbitrator; they should request the arbitrator, *through the Association,* to reopen proceedings and conduct an additional hearing or arrange for presentation of evidence through other means. Hearings may also be reopened if the arbitrator deems it necessary.

Under the procedure of the American Arbitration Association, all contact between the parties and the arbitrator must be channeled through the Association. This eliminates the possibility of suspicion that one side may have offered arguments or evidence that the other had no opportunity to rebut.

Common Errors in Arbitration

1. Using arbitration and arbitration costs as a harassing technique.
2. Overemphasis of the grievance by the union or exaggeration of an employee's fault by management.
3. Reliance on a minimum of facts and a maximum of arguments.
4. Concealing essential facts; distorting the truth.
5. Holding back books, records, and other supporting documents.
6. Tying up proceedings with legal technicalities.
7. Introducing witnesses who have not been properly instructed on demeanor and on the place of their testimony in the entire case.
8. Withholding full cooperation from the arbitrator.
9. Disregarding the ordinary rules of courtesy and decorum.
10. Becoming involved in arguments with the other side. The time to try to convince the other party is before arbitration, during grievance processing. At the arbitration hearing, all efforts should be concentrated on convincing the arbitrator.

THE AWARD

The award is the decision of the arbitrator upon the matters submitted under the arbitration agreement. Its purpose is to dispose of the controversy finally and conclusively.

The award must be made within the limits of the arbitration agreement, must rule on each claim submitted, and must be definite and final. It may be accompanied by an opinion discussing the evidence and setting forth the reasoning of the arbitrator.

The power of the arbitrator ends with the making of the award. An award may not be changed by the arbitrator, once it is made, *unless the parties mutually agree to reopen the proceeding and to restore the power of the arbitrator.*

When the parties do agree to request the arbitrator to reopen a proceeding in order to obtain clarification or interpretation of a disputed ruling, the agreement to reopen must be in writing and must set forth precisely the question submitted. Such agreement is filed with the Association, which then proceeds to make the necessary arrangements with the arbitrator.

Note: Under certain state laws either party is entitled to request clarification or modification of the award within twenty days. In such instances arrangements should be made through the tribunal administrator of the Association.

Awards by Tripartite Boards

The occasional use of tripartite boards of arbitration sometimes creates special problems. Sometimes under law and sometimes under contracts, the award must be supported by at least a majority. The difficulty is that the two party-appointed arbitrators may regard themselves as advocates of their sides, rather than impartial adjudicators, which may make it difficult for the impartial arbitrator to get the support of one of the others for a majority award. Parties often resolve this difficulty by empowering the third arbitrator to render a decision without the concurrence of the others. This may be done either in the arbitration clause, or in the event of deadlock, by later stipulation of the parties.

> *When this is done, the third arbitrator is in a better position to rule on the issues without having to compromise for the sake of a majority award.*

THE COSTS OF ARBITRATION

The following items involving costs should receive consideration in any arbitration proceeding. *First,* the preparation and presentation of the case; *second,* the stenographic record of the testimony (if desired); *third,* the arbitrator's fee; and *fourth,* the administrative expense.

1. The *first* expense is clearly within the control of each party. It includes the time and expenses of participants, the investigation of facts, and the preparation of exhibits. Briefs, if desired, constitute another substantial cost. In complex cases parties sometimes require the help of outside experts such as time-study engineers or economists. But this added expense is seldom necessary in the average grievance arbitration.

2. The *second* item of expense, the stenographic record, is a much debated item. As a general rule, arbitrators take their own notes and do not need stenographic records. In complicated cases, stenographic records are frequently found helpful not only by arbitrators, but also by parties in

preparation of written briefs. When a party wants a stenographic record, the Association arranges to have a court reporter present at hearings. The party or parties ordering a record will be billed directly by the stenographer. It is therefore up to them to give appropriate instructions with regard to copies and billing.

3. The *third* item of expense is the fee of the arbitrator. The charges made by an arbitrator usually range from $200 up per day of hearing and per day used in the preparation of the award. It is the Association's policy and practice to have the rate of compensation agreed upon or known in advance. Along with the fee there may be the arbitrator's travel, hotel, and incidental costs.

4. The *fourth* item of expense is the fee of $75 which each party pays to the Association. For this sum AAA performs all the administrative work in connection with the selection of the arbitrator and the scheduling of hearings. The basic administrative fee also pays for the first hearing. An additional $50 is charged to each party for every subsequent hearing if it is clerked by an AAA staff member or if it takes place in a room furnished by the Association.

CONCLUSION

Arbitration is the most practical means ever devised for resolving disputes that unions and companies are unable to settle by direct negotiation. It is the application to industrial relations of the American democratic concept of "due process."

But the significance of arbitration is not only in its immediate advantages. The atmosphere of dispute settlement may have a profound effect upon the way labor and management get along in their day-to-day relations. That is why arbitration is more than a useful tool for coping with existing problems; it is also a moral force, encouraging a spirit of cooperation that often makes it possible for companies and unions to resolve difficulties without having to go to arbitration at all.

THE AMERICAN ARBITRATION ASSOCIATION

The American Arbitration Association is a private, not-for-profit organization founded in 1926 to foster the study of arbitration, to perfect the techniques of this method of dispute settlement under law and to administer arbitration in accordance with the agreement of parties. Membership rolls include companies, labor unions, trade associations, civic groups, foundations, and organizations of all kinds as well as individuals who believe in arbitration.

The Association is today the most important single center of information, education, and research on arbitration. To bring about the widest possible understanding, hundreds of educational programs are presented every year at universities and law schools and organizations of every description.

AAA's educational program includes publication of three monthly labor arbitration award reporting services, a quarterly magazine, a quarterly arbitration law reporting service, a quarterly news bulletin for members, specialized pamphlets, [such as the one from which this Appendix was taken,] covering every field of arbitration, and outlines for teaching labor-management arbitration and arbitration law courses. Among educational materials produced by the Association are ten labor arbitration films, each dealing with a typical grievance, and all illustrating procedures for resolving disputes under the Voluntary Labor Arbitration Rules of the American Arbitration Association.

Glossary of Terms

Arbitration: Arbitration is the reference of a dispute by voluntary agreement of the parties to an impartial person for determination on the basis of evidence and arguments presented by such parties, who agree in advance to accept the decision of the arbitrator as final and binding. Arbitration, therefore, is a judicial proceeding and different in nature from mediation, conciliation, negotiation and fact finding.

Arbitration Clause: An arbitration clause is a provision in a contract requiring that disputes arising out of or in relation to the collective bargaining agreement be finally determined by arbitration.

Grievance Procedure: The grievance procedure of a union contract is an orderly way to resolve disputes by successive steps, usually beginning with negotiations between union stewards and foremen and ending with meetings between top union and company officials.

Submission Agreement: A submission agreement is a jointly signed document stating the nature of the dispute and affirming the parties' intention to arbitrate and to abide by the award.

Demand for Arbitration: A demand for arbitration is a formal request made by one party to the other for arbitration of a particular dispute under the arbitration clause of a contract.

Answering Statement: An answering statement is the respondent's reply to a demand for arbitration.

Arbitration Hearing: This is the formal meeting at which each party presents its exhibits, witnesses, and arguments to the arbitrator.

Tripartite Board: This is a board consisting of a representative of each party and an impartial arbitrator.

Award: An award is the decision that the arbitrator renders after taking testimony and hearing arguments from both sides. The award is usually accompanied by an opinion explaining how the conclusions of the arbitrator were reached.

Exhibit C-1 Demand for Arbitration

American Arbitration Association

VOLUNTARY LABOR ARBITRATION RULES
DEMAND FOR ARBITRATION

DATE:

TO: (Name) _____
(of party upon whom the Demand is made)

(Street Address) _____

(City and State) _____(Zip Code) _____

(Telephone) _____

The undersigned, a party to an arbitration agreement contained in a written contract

dated _____, providing for arbitration,

hereby demands arbitration thereunder.
(attach arbitration clause or quote hereunder)

NATURE OF DISPUTE:

REMEDY SOUGHT:

HEARING LOCALE REQUESTED: _____

You are hereby notified that copies of our arbitration agreement and of this Demand are being filed with the
American Arbitration Association at its _____Regional Office, with the
request that it commence the administration of the arbitration.

Name of Claimant_____

Signed____ _____

Title_____

Address_____

City and State_____Zip Code _____

Telephone_____

Name of Attorney_____

Address_____

City and State_____Zip Code _____

Telephone_____

To institute proceedings, please send three copies of this Demand with the administrative fee, as provided in
Section 43 of the Rules, to the AAA. Send original of Demand to Respondent.

FORM L2 AAA

Exhibit C-2 Submission to Arbitration

American Arbitration Association

SUBMISSION TO ARBITRATION

Date:

The named Parties hereby submit the following dispute to arbitration under the VOLUNTARY LABOR ARBITRATION RULES of the American Arbitration Association:

We agree that we will abide by and perform any Award rendered hereunder and that a judgment may be entered upon the Award.

Employer_____

Signed by_____Title_____

Address_____

Union_____Local_____

Signed by_____Title_____

Address_____

PLEASE FILE TWO COPIES

FORM L1-AAA-10M-3-73

Exhibit C-3 List for Selection of Arbitrator

AMERICAN ARBITRATION ASSOCIATION

Case Number: Date List Submitted:

LIST FOR SELECTION OF ARBITRATOR

After striking the name of any unacceptable arbitrator, please indicate your order of preference by number. We will try to appoint a mutually acceptable arbitrator who can hear your case promptly. Leave as many names as possible.

Jane Doe

Richard Roe

A. B. Adam

C. D. Black

E. F. Gross

G. H. Denver

Walter Hamilton

Harold D. Perkins

Julia D. Sorenson

Party _____

By _____ Title _____

NOTE: Biographical information is attached. Unless your response is received by the Association by _____, all names submitted may be deemed acceptable. If a mutual selection cannot be made from this list, and if both parties do not request a further list, the Association may appoint an arbitrator.

The AAA's Award Bank includes published and unpublished awards of many of the arbitrators listed. Parties can write to the AAA's Publication Department for an arbitrator's recent awards. Copies will be provided at 30 cents per page.

Form 14-AAA

Twenty Supervisory Principles in Labor Relations Grievance Handling

PRINCIPLE 1:

What Is a Grievance?

Any person in a position to deal with grievances must understand clearly just what they are. The following points will help clarify what constitutes a grievance:

1. Anything about the job that irritates an employee or tends to make working conditions unsatisfactory may be a grievance.
2. A grievance may exist even though no verbal or written complaint is presented. Such silent or unuttered grievances may be as destructive of good will as the one that is aired.
3. Even though the complaint may be imaginary, or based on lack of knowledge of the facts, it is a grievance nonetheless until properly cleared up.
4. A worker who merely thinks a grievance exists may be just as discontented as though there were a just complaint, and the same careful handling is necessary.
5. A grievance may be trivial or important, affecting an individual or a group, caused by fellow workers or by management, financial or nonfinancial, imaginary or real—but it is a grievance in any case and requires fair, open-minded, patient, considerate treatment.

PRINCIPLE 2:

Keep Your Door Open

Any person in a position to receive complaints and handle grievances must keep the door open—must always exhibit a willingness to hear and consider complaints:

1. Nothing aggravates a grievance more than the feeling that a superior is hostile to the idea of listening to complaints.
2. Unless a worker has a safety valve—knows where to go to express a grievance fully—any complaint that employee holds will be magnified out of all proportion.
3. Make it known by word and action that you welcome the presentation of a complaint rather than have one of your people nurse a grievance in disgruntled silence.
4. Encourage workers, by your treatment of them, to make their complaints to you, who may be able to do something about them, rather than to fellow workers who probably can do nothing to correct them.
5. It is not enough to say you welcome frank and honest grievances; you must prove by the interest you show in correcting complaints that you are sincere in your open-door policy.

PRINCIPLE 3:

Put the Worker at Ease

When one of your people comes to you with a grievance, do everything you can to make it possible for that individual to state a case. Take these tips:

1. Do not let the worker with a grievance see a chip on your shoulder. Getting excited because the employee may be angry only tends to arouse the person more and makes the situation more difficult.
2. Put the grievant at ease immediately by taking a friendly attitude that rids the situation of any feeling of hostility.
3. Do, say, or show nothing in any way that you resent the worker's approach or feel that the employee is butting into your affairs.
4. Let the worker know that you appreciate this straightforwardness in bringing the grievance to you rather than bottling it up or stirring up trouble by grumbling to others about it.
5. Put the worker at ease with assurances that the individual has a perfect right to express problems frankly to you by your making clear that you are ready and willing to take all the time necessary to discuss the complaint and by manifesting a readiness to give open-minded consideration to what the grievant has to say.

PRINCIPLE 4:

Listen with Sincere Interest

The sincerity with which you listen to a grievance and the interest you show in what the worker has to say are of utmost importance in achieving a meeting of the minds. Consider these points:

1. Don't merely say to a worker, "Go ahead and tell your story—I'm listening." Your attitude and words must reflect a sincere interest in the story.
2. Don't try to rush the worker in order to get it over with because that will indicate you are not interested.
3. Listen without interrupting except to indicate by questions that you are sincerely interested in getting the worker's whole viewpoint.
4. Evidence of a lack of interest in the complaint will convince the employee that you won't give the case full consideration.
5. Even though a grievance may seem trivial, its importance to the worker is such that no competent supervisor who listens to it can afford to show anything less than a deep and sincere interest in all the facts, assertions, and opinions involved.

PRINCIPLE 5:

Discuss—Don't Argue

In dealing with a worker with a complaint, the supervisor must keep the situation on a discussion basis. No one wins in an argument. Calm discussion is best because:

1. An argument only tends to convince each party that it is right and the other side is wrong.
2. An argument raises emotional temperatures until each participant is more interested in winning than in getting at the true facts and settling the differences on the basis of reason.
3. The grievant in an argument fights more stubbornly because of a feeling of being the underdog.
4. Allowing yourself to be drawn into an argument causes loss of poise, dignity, and self-respect and is likely to put the grievance on a personal basis rather than on the basis of facts.

5. Calm discussion permits settlement by reason rather than by emotion, threat, or resort to show of authority; no settlement on such grounds is likely to be lasting or mutually satisfactory.

PRINCIPLE 6:

Get the Story Straight

Intelligent handling of a grievance is impossible until the supervisor gets the story absolutely straight. Go at it this way:

1. Ask the worker to state the complaint in clear and complete detail, from beginning to end.
2. Next, by a series of questions, get the employee to explain the case fully a second time.
3. Having the story repeated has the effect of lowering the employee's temperature because each time the person gets it off the chest, the grievance tends to come down closer to its true and reasonable proportions. Discrepancies, if any, show up. The supervisor obtains a clearer impression of the straight facts.
4. Patient use of ample time to get the story straight gives the supervisor an opportunity to do some clear thinking. The supervisor then is in a position to deal justly with the grievance.

PRINCIPLE 7:

Get All the Facts

In adjusting a grievance fairly and intelligently, all the facts must be mutually understood by both parties. Decisions based on half facts cannot be mutually satisfactory. Consider these points:

1. Unless all the facts come out, the supervisor may become the victim of a bluffer.
2. To get all the facts, consult not only the complainant but all others whose observation, experience, and knowledge of the situation may contribute to a thorough understanding.
3. When it is evident that the supervisor is seeking all the facts, any temptation for the grievant to misrepresent the true situation will be removed.

4. In seeking all the facts, proceed tactfully with the stated purpose of arriving at a fair decision rather than with an attitude of suspicion and apparent disbelief in the grievant's statements.
5. While promptness in handling a grievance is important, an attempted quick settlement should not interfere with taking sufficient time to get all the facts. Start action on, and consideration of, the grievance promptly but take the time to get all the information required for an intelligent decision.

PRINCIPLE 8:

Consider the Worker's Viewpoint

A thorough application and understanding of the complainant's viewpoint is essential. Consider these points:

1. When presented with a grievance, consider, first, all the possible reasons why the worker might feel aggrieved, and, second, all possible reasons why that viewpoint might be a mistaken one.
2. If a supervisor starts to think of defenses against a complaint before listening and completely understanding the worker's viewpoint, it will be practically impossible to thoroughly understand the grievance.
3. While listening to a grievance, keep asking yourself, "How would I feel about this situation if I were in that worker's shoes?"
4. A sincere interest in getting the worker's viewpoint will convince the person of your desire to be fair, which is the first essential in any equitable and harmonious settlement of a difference between people.
5. Be honest with yourself and with the worker in giving proper weight to the other's viewpoint and the reasons why the person feels that way.

PRINCIPLE 9:

Save the Face of the Complainer

Tactfully find a way for the complainer to save face. This applies particularly in situations in which the employee has based a grievance on misinformation, or imaginary causes, or has overstated the demands. Consider these points:

1. No person who has brought up a grievance likes to back down, admit to being wrong, or go off half-cocked. Neither does a worker like to appear to be dumb for having brought up the complaint.
2. To help the complainer save face and willingly accept a reasonable adjustment, make it as easy as possible for the worker to retract or decrease the demand.
3. Make it easy for the complainer by some such statement as, "Of course, I can see how you would get that viewpoint, based on the facts at your disposal," or, "I probably would feel the same way if I only had part of the information."
4. Make it a point to discuss grievances in private so there is no temptation for the complainer stubbornly to maintain an unreasonable position rather than back down in the presence of others.

PRINCIPLE 10:

Avoid Snap Judgments

Snap judgment in dealing with a grievant involves the dangers of making a mistake and of creating the impression that your mind is made up before you've heard the evidence. Avoid snap judgments for the following reasons:

1. Snap judgments are unfair to both supervisor and complainer because it is too easy to make an error, and a mistake will result in damage to you both.
2. Snap judgments are too-obvious evidence of a closed mind or of a careless, indifferent attitude toward the worker's problem.
3. Even though the decision based on snap judgment happens to be correct, the aggrieved worker will feel that the complaint did not receive full consideration.
4. A decision favorable to the complainer, if based on a snap judgment, may boomerang or set a precedent that can cause far more trouble, embarrassment, and bad feeling in the future.
5. Mistakes resulting from snap judgment undermine a supervisor's prestige and reputation for fair dealing.

PRINCIPLE 11:

Weigh the Consequences of Settlement

In settling a grievance, forethought must be given to the possible consequences of the action. Here are factors to weigh:

1. Even though the decision may be correct, it may generate opposition and antagonism that may cancel out the advantages of the settlement.
2. Conditions may justify settlement on compromise terms rather than on a strictly correct basis because the latter may lead to unfavorable consequences later.
3. Weigh the benefits of a settlement the employer receives against what you may have to yield in order to reach that agreement.
4. The settlement you propose may be logical but you must analyze whether it is psychological—that is, how will it strike the worker's feelings, self-interests, or prejudices?
5. Always consider how a settlement may affect the future cooperative working relationship with the aggrieved employee and the future attitudes of other workers.

PRINCIPLE 12:

Be Willing To Admit Mistakes

Some of the greatest errors in the handling of grievances are made because persons listening to and adjusting complaints are unwilling to admit their own mistakes. Here are some guideposts:

1. Frankly admitting a mistake can never injure your prestige as much as covering up an error or refusing to admit you made one.
2. Even though an employee with a grievance that resulted from a mistake you made may not call your attention to the error very tactfully, don't try to defend your actions or decisions simply because you won't admit to having been wrong.
3. The supervisor's readiness to admit a mistake encourages the grievant to do so, too. Nobody likes a person who is never wrong.
4. A grievant will deeply resent your covering up a mistake and is sure to consider it an injustice.
5. A supervisor's refusal to admit a mistake usually leads an aggrieved worker to increase the demands, even to the point of unreasonableness, because the employee is embittered by the obvious unfairness of a superior who is not big enough to be honest.

PRINCIPLE 13:

Take Prompt Action

The promptness with which a grievance is acted on is an important factor in determining worker satisfaction or dissatisfaction. These points are relevant:

1. A delay in giving a favorable decision will give the worker the impression that the action was taken grudgingly or unwillingly, which will cause the grievant to feel less appreciation for the supportive step.
2. Other matters of seemingly greater importance may push a grievance to the back burner, but nothing is more important to a worker than prompt action on a complaint.
3. Delays indicate a lack of interest in the worker's problem and breed a feeling of resentment.
4. Avoid any temptation to delay deciding on a grievance. Take no more time than is actually necessary to get all the facts and to verify them.
5. For the employer to get maximum benefit from settling a grievance, the decision must be made promptly and with justice for all concerned.

PRINCIPLE 14:

Don't Pass the Buck

Buck passing in handling grievances creates more embarrassing problems than it cures. Consider, for example:

1. To pass the buck when presented with a grievance will create the feeling that you are giving the worker a runaround.
2. Your making the excuse that "It's over my head," or, "I haven't got the authority" only increases the worker's feeling of futility and desperation.
3. To pass the buck by saying, "I'd do it but it's against hospital policy" creates the impression that you agree with the worker (whether you do or don't) and gives the person a feeling of being right, whether or not that is correct.
4. If you don't have the authority to settle the grievance, don't pass the buck or put the worker to further inconvenience. State frankly that you lack the authority but that you will get a decision from the person who does.

PRINCIPLE 15:

How To Say 'No'

Not all who come with grievances are justified in their complaints or their requests. To some, the answer must be, "No." But there is a right way and a wrong way to say, "No." Follow these suggestions:

1. Don't be afraid to say, "No," if that is the right answer. To pussyfoot or straddle only makes more trouble in the end.
2. Don't pass the buck by telling a grievant that you personally would like to say, "Yes," but that your superior doesn't see it that way.
3. By your attitude, make the person with a grievance realize that if the request were justifiable and properly grantable, you would be more pleased to say "Yes," than "No."
4. Don't say "No" abruptly without clear evidence that you are giving the request thoughtful, fair, and complete consideration.
5. If you do have to say "No," present all the reasons for your answer in a patient, considerate, and sympathetic manner.

PRINCIPLE 16:

Acting on Imaginary Grievances

Grievances based on imaginary causes can be just as irritating to workers as those attributable to real and justifiable reasons. Follow these suggestions:

1. Even though you know the complaint is groundless, handle it with the same consideration and sincerity as you do a real grievance.
2. In dealing with an imaginery grievance, make every effort to establish a clear understanding of the real facts.
3. Consider the fact that the imaginary grievance is based on conditions the worker believes do exist and don't jump to the conclusion that the person is all wet.
4. Be willing to let the discussion ramble. Don't try to pin it down to the narrow limits of the question at issue. This will give the aggrieved an opportunity to adjust emotionally to the necessity of accepting a negative decision.
5. Be sure to leave the way open for further discussion in case the worker claims later to have found further evidence to substantiate the complaint.

PRINCIPLE 17:

Don't Let It Happen Twice

If a word to the wise is sufficient, the same grievance should not be permitted to arise twice. Repetition should be prevented because:

1. Allowing the same aggravating conditions to recur causes the worker to lose respect for the supervisor's ability to run the job. It makes the boss appear weak and inefficient.
2. Repetition of the same grievance greatly increases the worker's indignation.
3. A recurrence indicates a careless, indifferent attitude toward a worker's welfare and a lack of honesty and sincerity, particularly after settling the first one.
4. The worker may understand there may be some excuse for a new grievance but may rightfully feel that there is no reason for a repetition.
5. The settlement of each grievance should serve as a warning to a supervisor to examine all conditions surrounding an employee's job to eliminate possible irritations before they become sores.

PRINCIPLE 18:

Use Authority Judiciously

The supervisor is in a position of authority over the person with a grievance and should use this power judiciously. These principles apply:

1. Set out at once to remove, as far as possible, any feeling that that authority will be used to force a settlement.
2. Establish negotiations on a discussion basis in which facts, rather than the supervisor's authority, will determine the decision.
3. Even though you have the authority to issue a ruling without discussion, remember that an arbitrary decision may be received rebelliously while the same settlement reached through free discussion may be accepted favorably.
4. Don't use your authority in such a way as to repress free expression by grievants. Talk right across the board in a democratic way, avoiding any feeling of difference in rank.
5. Authority, when wielded as a club, begets disrespect, antagonism, and opposition; used judiciously and temperately, it heightens respect and cooperation.

PRINCIPLE 19:

Don't Let Small Grievances Grow

The time to adjust grievances most effectively is when they still are small:

1. Never put off until tomorrow the adjusting of a small grievance that could be settled today because by tomorrow it may be too big for you to handle effectively.
2. Labor troubles almost invariably have their beginnings in small grievances that are fed and fattened by indifference and neglect by the supervisors and department heads who are in direct charge of the employees and of their working conditions.

PRINCIPLE 20:

Learning from Grievances

Every grievance handled should be regarded as a lesson from which something worthwhile can be learned. Consider these principles:

1. Handling a grievance gives you an opportunity to size up the worker—to judge character, attitude, loyalty, honesty, fairness, and prejudices—and learn how best to handle that person in the future.
2. Experience in dealing with one grievance can suggest where to look for other possible complaints and remove their causes before they arise.
3. If a worker takes a grievance over your head without first discussing it with you, keep cool and ask yourself what there is about your own personality and methods that discouraged the employee from coming to you initially.
4. If the employee does not receive your settlement favorably, study your own tactics to see if you have said or done anything to prejudice the individual against the terms of the decision. That way you can learn to make corrections in your methods for future situations.
5. Watch the effect of every move you make so you can learn how to deal effectively with people and can understand what methods and attitudes win them to your point of view.

Index

About the Authors

NORMAN METZGER is vice president of The Mount Sinai Medical Center in New York City, responsible for labor relations. He is a director of the League of Voluntary Hospitals and Homes of New York City, and was president of the League from 1967–1972, and from 1981–1982. He is a professor with tenure in the Department of Health Care Management, Mount Sinai School of Medicine, and a professor in the Graduate Program in Health Care Administration, Baruch College, City University of New York, as well as a professor in the Graduate Program in Health Services Administration at the New School for Social Research in New York City.

Metzger's experience in labor relations and personnel administration spans 30 years in both the health services sector and in industry. He is the author or coauthor of eight books as well as of close to 100 articles in health care journals. He is a four-time recipient of the American Society for Hospital Personnel Administration's Literature Award.

JOSEPH M. FERENTINO is director of labor relations at The Mount Sinai Medical Center in New York City, where he is responsible for multiunion contract negotiation and employee relations. He is regional board member for the American Society of Hospital Personnel Administration, representing the professional interests of member personnel/labor relations administrators in New York, New Jersey, and Pennsylvania. He is past president (1980–1981) of the Association of Hospital Personnel Administrators of Greater New York, for which he served as program coordinator from 1978 to 1980.

Ferentino, a practitioner in the field of health care labor relations for more than 10 years, has lectured at various New York City colleges and at hospitals throughout the state in addition to conducting educational programs for the Association of Hospital Personnel Administrators of Greater New York and the United Hospital Fund. He is responsible for the development of a comprehensive labor relations seminar that is part of The Mount Sinai Medical Center supervisory educational program.

About the Contributors

HERBERT L. MARX, Jr., is engaged in the practice of arbitration and dispute resolution. Among the permanent arbitration panels on which he serves are the League of Voluntary Hospitals and Homes of New York-District 1199, National Union of Hospital and Health Care Employees; National Railroad Adjustment Board; Board of Education of the City of New York-United Federation of Teachers, AFT; and the U.S. Postal Service-Postal Unions. He is an adjunct lecturer at Pace University Graduate School of Business and an adjunct faculty member of the Institute of Management and Labor Relations at Rutgers. Marx is the editor of 13 volumes in the H.W. Wilson Company *Reference Shelf Series,* including *American Labor Unions, American Labor Today,* and *Collective Bargaining for Public Employees,* and has contributed articles to numerous professional and general publications. He is a member of the National Academy of Arbitrators, Society for Professionals in Dispute Resolution, and former president of the New York Chapter, Industrial Relations Research Association.

ALLAN H. WEITZMAN is a partner in the law firm of Proskauer Rose Goetz & Mendelsohn, New York City, with offices throughout the United States as well as in London. This firm specializes in labor relations law, exclusively for management. Weitzman negotiates collective bargaining agreements, arbitrates contract disputes, and represents employers before the National Labor Relations Board and various administrative agencies. He has served clients in various fields, including national television networks, health care institutions, the maritime industry, retail establishments, commercial and savings banks, education, etc. He was adjunct professor (1976–1981) teaching two courses in labor relations law and legislation at the Cornell University School of Industrial and Labor Relations. He received his Doctor of Law, with Distinction, in 1973 from the Cornell Law School.

THIS VOLUME MAY CIRCULATE FOR 2 WEEKS

Renewals May Be Made In Person Or By Phone:

6605